TEACHING GOODNESS

TEACHING GOODNESS

Engaging the Moral and Academic Promise of Young Children

JOAN F. GOODMAN

University of Pennsylvania

USHA BALAMORE

The Episcopal Academy, Merion, Pennsylvania

Boston   New York   San Francisco

Mexico City   Montreal   Toronto   London   Madrid   Munich   Paris

Hong Kong   Singapore   Tokyo   Cape Town   Sydney

Series Editor: *Traci Mueller*
Editorial Assistant: *Erica Tromblay*
Marketing Manager: *Elizabeth Fogarty*
Editorial-Production Service: *Omegatype Typography, Inc.*
Manufacturing Buyer: *JoAnne Sweeney*
Composition and Prepress Buyer: *Linda Cox*
Cover Administrator: *Kristina Mose-Libon*
Electronic Composition: *Omegatype Typography, Inc.*

For related titles and support materials, visit our online catalog at www.ablongman.com.

Between the time Website information is gathered and published, some sites may have closed. Also, the transcription of URLs can result in typographical errors. The publisher would appreciate notification where these errors occur so that they may be corrected in subsequent editions.

Library of Congress Cataloging-in-Publication Data

Goodman, Joan F.
  Teaching goodness : engaging the moral and academic promise of young children / Joan F. Goodmann, Usha Balamore.
    p.   cm.
  ISBN 0-205-34823-8
  1. Moral education (Early childhood)—United States—Case studies.   2. Project Method in teaching—Case studies.   I. Balamore, Usha.   II. Title.

LB1139.35.M67 G66 2003
370.11'4—dc21

2002028350

Printed in the United States of America
10 9 8 7 6 5 4 3 2 1   07 06 05 04 03 02

We are grateful to Michael J. Caduto and LUNABLU® for permission to reprint the lyrics that appear on pages 20 and 101 of this book, from the musical recording *All One Earth: Songs for the Generations*, © 1994. All Rights Reserved. For more information, contact LUNABLU®, P.O. Box 1052, Norwich, VT 05055, USA, telephone/fax: (802) 649-1815.

In gratitude to the teachers we know and love best

M. R. Bawa Muhaiyaddeen
your love and integrity
taught me how to teach
and live.
—U. B.

Jonathan F. Goodman
for what you do
and who you are.
—J. F. G.

CONTENTS

Foreword   xi

Acknowledgments   xiii

About the Authors   xv

Introduction   1

ASPIRATIONAL   3
INTEGRATED   5
COLLABORATIVE   6

CHAPTER ONE

Setting Up, Getting Started   12

THE PHYSICAL SETTING   12
THE THEME   14
THE YEAR OF THE HERO   14
THE YEAR OF THE PRINCESS   20
THE YEAR OF THE BEAR   25
COMMENTARY   31

CHAPTER TWO

Hercules and Heroes   35

WHAT MAKES A HERO? EARLY APPROXIMATIONS   35
INCLUDING PARENTS   37
INSINUATING THE ACADEMIC: READING AND WRITING   38
BECOMING A HERO: HALLOWEEN   40
EXPANDING NOTIONS OF THE HEROIC: STORIES   44
EXPANDING NOTIONS OF THE HEROIC: SOUP KITCHEN WORKERS   46
EXPANDING NOTIONS OF THE HEROIC: LOCAL HEROES   46
A MUSEUM VISIT AND OUR EXHIBIT   47

HERO TRAINING PROGRAM   57

OUR LETTER TO HERCULES   62

WRITING THE PLAY   63

HEROES OF INDIA   67

COMMENTARY   68

CHAPTER THREE
The Princess and Good Qualities   71

BUILDING THE PRINCESS'S CASTLE   71

PREPARING FOR THE PRINCESS   74

THE PRINCESS VISITS   76

THE KINDNESS BOX   78

VISITING A CASTLE   79

ANOTHER CASTLE   81

MY HOUSE   81

ENLARGING OUR CONCEPT OF HOME   83

HOUSES AROUND THE WORLD   83

THE HOMELESS   85

WHAT IF WE COULD DESIGN OUR OWN STREET OF HOUSES   86

EXPERIMENTING WITH HOUSES   87

MYSTERY ISLAND   89

HALLOWEEN COSTUMES   90

KING TAIJO AND THE SWORD OF GOOD QUALITIES   91

APPRECIATING NATURE   94

CRYSTALS   95

SHELLS   95

"EGGSPERIMENTING" WITH EGGS   96

THE ABC OF FLOWERS   97

LOVING MOTHER EARTH   98

RECYCLING SHIRTS   99

DISINTEGRATION   100

MICHAEL CADUTO   100

NATURE, ART, AND IDIOMS   101

NATURE'S MYSTERIES   103

CLOSING ACTIVITIES   105

COMMENTARY   106

CHAPTER FOUR

The Bear and Respect and Responsibility   109

BEING A FRIEND   110

DEFINING RESPECT: POLITENESS   110

DEFINING RESPECT: RESPECTING YOURSELF   111

AN ETIQUETTE BOOK ABOUT RESPECT   112

DEFINING RESPECT: MAGAZINE ILLUSTRATIONS   114

MONET MAGIC   115

ISAAC BEAR IS AN ARTIST   118

THE ABC OF ARTISTS   119

INTEGRATING THEMES AND ACADEMIC SKILLS   120

MINING NATURAL RESOURCES   121

SEASONAL EVENTS   122

THE MASTER ARTIST   126

WHAT IF . . . ?   129

RESPECT TRAINING PROGRAM   130

RESPECT AWARD CEREMONY   132

RESPONSIBILITY   134

RESPONSIBILITY AT SCHOOL   134

TRUST AND RESPONSIBILITY TO THE GROUP   135

PRACTICING RESPONSIBILITY AT HOME   137

PRACTICING RESPONSIBILITY IN OUR PLAY   137

"BECOMING" A FAMOUS ARTIST   137

MARY CASSATT   140

EVALUATING THE ART SHOW   142

CONCLUDING ACTIVITIES: RESPECT AND RESPONSIBILITY STORIES   143

CLOSING LETTERS   146

THE LAST DAY   148

COMMENTARY   150

CHAPTER FIVE

Commonwealth Foundations: Setting the Tone   152

ENGAGEMENT   153

COMMONWEALTH   158

REFLECTION   163

CHAPTER SIX

**Commonwealth Foundations:
Maintaining the Tone   171**

ENGAGEMENT   171

COMMONWEALTH   182

REFLECTION   189

CHAPTER SEVEN

**Commonwealth Foundations:
Restoring the Tone   193**

RE-ENGAGEMENT: INDIVIDUALIZING INSTRUCTION   193

COMMONWEALTH   195

REFLECTION   200

CHAPTER EIGHT

Questions and Answers   203

FOREWORD

Teaching Goodness is a profoundly important book that will make many people—parents as well as teachers—reevaluate their methods of teaching the young child. Only too often we bewail the lack of certain values in modern youth—honesty, respect, kindness, tolerance, self-control, and so on. Dr. Balamore has developed teaching methods that can change this sorry state of affairs.

My own expertise in early childhood learning comes from years of studying chimpanzees—the great apes whose behavior is uncannily similar to our own. Our study has followed individuals for more than forty years and has revealed the importance of early childhood experience. Infants with affectionate and supportive mothers, brothers, and sisters have a much better chance of developing relaxed relationships as adults and enjoying a better position in their community. When chimpanzees, whose behavior is dictated far more than ours by species-specific genetic heritage, can be influenced by early experience and training, the influence of early experience on human infants is likely to be even greater. That is why the kind of learning experiences described in this book are so very important.

A great deal of human behavior is shaped by the culture into which we are born. And so often our cultures have led us into patterns of violence and hatred, patterns that become even more terrifying as weapons of mass destruction fall into the hands of repressive dictatorships and religious fanatics. We humans, in the past hundred years, have also developed patterns of consumption that are selfish and environmentally unsustainable. We have developed weapons capable of bringing about our own destruction, along with the destruction of life on earth as we know it. There is a terrible inequity in the distribution of wealth around the world: the "haves" have too much while some of the "have-nots" live in abject, crippling poverty. Many of them do not survive.

Providing children with the moral strength to control the powers that science and technology have granted us and to stand firm against material greed and human cruelty is one of the greatest challenges that we face today. Dr. Balamore is a gifted and inspired educator who has, over a thirty-year teaching career, developed insights into ways of meeting this challenge. *Teaching Goodness* provides not only the theoretical background for her unique teaching methods but also vivid descriptions of the ways in which these methods have succeeded. Human children (like chimpanzee children) have tendencies to express themselves and resolve conflicts with anger and violence. Children can also be compassionate, caring, and altruistic. And humans have a far greater capacity than chimpanzees to control any genetic tendencies for aggression and socially destructive behavior. Dr. Balamore has developed methods that nurture and reinforce the inherent good in children while helping them control negative traits, so that under her guidance, children gradually learn goodness.

This book, with its imaginative hands-on approach to teaching children (the methods can be adapted to different social environments), offers teachers and parents tools that will help children to develop strong moral values of fair play, honesty, and understanding and to suppress selfishness, intolerance, and aggressive competition. This kind of teaching is, I believe, essential as we strive for a world in which humans can live in harmony with nature and with each other. A world in which citizens around the globe understand that happiness lies in good personal relationships, in helping others, and enjoying health in a clean environment rather than in wealth and the amount of material "stuff" with which we surround ourselves—a world based on love and respect rather than power and greed. A world with more goodness.

Jane Goodall

ACKNOWLEDGMENTS

This is a book about tapping the generosity of children, but it could not have been written without the generosity of many grown-ups. We thank:

- The Episcopal Academy in Merion, PA, Usha's home for the last twelve years, for not just permitting but encouraging her to pursue her teaching aspirations. Head of School James Crawford and former Head of Lower School Josephine Walker shared her vision, believed in her innovative methods, and protected her from bureaucratic demands, allowing her to do what she loved most: teach!
- Ishaq Deis, a companion teacher for all of those twelve years, for being a model of artistic excellence, musical inspiration, literary enthusiasm, and gentle kindness—not to mention the best soccer pal a child could wish for. His imagination, creativity, and love for nature not only supported but deeply enriched the teaching. His art adds beauty to this book.
- Members of the sabbatical committee—the Head of School, board members, faculty, and parents—and the Head of Lower School, Jacqueline Hamilton, for granting Usha a year's sabbatical to write this book.
- The families, each and every one of them, for contributing wholeheartedly to every classroom endeavor. Whether it was a simple cooking activity or a trip to the moon, they always showed up to lend a hand.
- Mark Rohland, for his meticulous review of the first two chapters, providing us with precious insights.
- David Federman and Howard Lesnick, neither of them classroom teachers, for reading with red pencils in hand, every word of every page, giving us valuable suggestions and, more importantly, their friendship and encouragement.
- Diane and Davis Barnett, ever present in their children's lives, for joyously photographing our classroom antics.
- Linda Lew, for providing computer instruction with unmatched patience and grace.
- Howard Posner, for generously providing much needed help with photographs and computers at the final hour.
- Sally Green, for conceiving the embryo from which this book grew and developed.
- Jonathan Granoff, Jim Schardt, Pat Federman, and Susan and Jerry Cannon, for standing by to listen during times of enthusiasm and times of discouragement, countering our flagging spirits with their determination that this book must be completed.
- Cynthia Stern, for capturing classroom adventures on videotape for twelve years and for giving up time to spend day after day and night after night with the manuscript. She lovingly scrutinized multiple drafts to make sure that

errors were eliminated—everything from a hyphenated word to a thought miscast was of importance to her. It was a labor of shared belief and friendship.

- Frank Goodman, for 42 years of contentious conversational companionship without which there would be no books or bookwriting aspirations.
- Ximena Ahl, Veena Loftus, Dale Philips, and Andrea McGuinness, four mothers who carefully read the first drafts of each chapter to provide important feedback from a parent's perspective. I will always cherish our shared discussions, fun, laughter, hospitality, and love.
- The reviewers of this book: Renee Casbergue, University of New Orleans; Linda Schertz, University of North Texas; Thomas Worley, Armstrong Atlantic State University.

We are truly grateful to you all for your generosity of spirit!

But most of all, we thank the many, many children who have entered our lives, talking, laughing, singing, dancing, readily sharing their inner and outer discoveries, and helping us appreciate their true potential—the promise of childhood. They have enriched our lives, led us to deeper self-reflection, and made us better human beings.

ABOUT THE AUTHORS

Joan F. Goodman is a psychologist and Professor of Education at the University of Pennsylvania, Graduate School of Education. She specializes in the areas of moral development and early childhood. Her recent publication, *The Moral Stake in Education: Contested Premises and Practices* (coauthored with Howard Lesnick, Professor of Law, University of Pennsylvania), considers how schools can facilitate the growth of morality in children while respecting the diversity of our society. Professor Goodman is also a consultant to those interested in developing (or thinking about) moral education programs.

Usha Balamore teaches kindergarten at The Episcopal Academy in Merion, Pennsylvania. She also teaches at the University of Pennsylvania, where she was the recipient of the Graduate School of Education's Excellence in Teaching award. Leaving behind a career as school psychologist and college professor, Usha decided to teach young children because of her belief that many difficult-to-remedy problems of later years can be prevented by engaging children's moral and academic potential in the early years. She has recently worked with the Global Dialogue Institute (of Temple University and Haverford College) to help create teacher-training programs for elementary school teachers in Indonesia.

Teaching Goodness

A teacher in a school should bring up the children with compassion,
love, patience, acceptance, peace, unity and exalted qualities...
She must raise children with love,
and allow their natural goodness to develop.

M.R. Bawa Muhaiyaddeen

INTRODUCTION

The collaboration that made this work possible started in 1993 when Usha agreed to teach a methods course at the University of Pennsylvania, Graduate School of Education to students embarking on careers as early childhood educators. In my role as program director I had occasion to participate with Usha in planning the course and to watch her teach the "big kids" at graduate school as well as her "little kids" in kindergarten.

It did not take long to appreciate that, inadvertently, I had stumbled on a person who, like me, believes that teaching is fundamentally a moral enterprise and its overarching mission to advance morality in children. I had come to this conviction belatedly, after twenty-five years as a practicing child psychologist and professor. For Usha the conviction grew naturally from her spiritual commitments and thirty years of teaching in India and the United States, bolstered by her doctoral studies and research in moral decision making. When we neglect the moral aspirations of children, we do them as much of a disservice as when we neglect their literacy aspirations. This was obvious to us but apparently not to others; we could find no book that explained how one might infuse morality throughout a year-long curriculum for young children. There are good books on moral education and good books on how to engage children in meaningful learning (e.g., the thematic or project approach), but it was the blend that needed explication. How, while one teaches math, reading, and social studies, does one also teach morality?

For both of us, morality is a lifelong pursuit, a continuous search. It is not encapsulated by obedience to a code, formulation of codes, a set of do's and don'ts, or absolute principles by which one is bound. It cannot be well taught if teachers are given only a set of techniques for classroom management or social skills. Books on moral education, depending on an author's outlook, suggest that to be effective in this arena, a teacher will model good behavior, set reasonable rules and ask children to follow them, reward children for exceptional accomplishments, encourage them to participate in forming classroom rules, give them occasions to work out real-life conflicts together, provide service opportunities, increase their sensitivity and empathy to others by reading stories, and help them to reflect on moral issues as they arise. All this is undeniably good advice yet, we think, insufficient. Insufficient because the pedagogy is not up to the task, which, as Usha puts it, is to help children "fall in love with goodness." This ambition strikes me as highly unusual and worthwhile. Where is the educational text that advocates, as the year's primary goal or objective, "children shall fall in love with goodness"? Perhaps "children shall be well behaved" or more likely, "they shall behave in such and such a manner," but falling in love?

For most, I suspect, there is something excessive and uncomfortably naïve about the goal "falling in love with goodness." As an educational objective it might seem a bit ambiguous and unsophisticated. But what is the source of our resistance? Psychologists, after all, write of children's natural loyalty to the good, truthful, and beautiful and their antipathy to the evil, ugly, and destructive. Small children are by nature deeply romantic, idealistic, and dreamy about the topic of good and evil. They have powerful moral aspirations: They want to free the captured prince, save the endangered animal, destroy the bad witch, care for the weak, and defend the threatened. Perhaps educators see such impulses as naïve and childish because they are so quickly blanketed by other powerful impulses: egotism, competitiveness, greed, domination, wariness, and fear of others. The objections of educators are essentially pragmatic, not ideological; they believe it unrealistic to credit children's moral ambitions. The early longings for goodness, they believe, will soon and inevitably give way to more self-serving, self-aggrandizing, and insecure impulses.

Yet, is it inevitable that children must surrender their initial aspirations or that development necessarily brings about a swift and steep decline in goodness? If there was a way to extend the primal moral proclivities of the young, even transform them into sturdy enduring characteristics, would that not constitute a worthy objective? By providing a close-up description of Usha's teaching over three different years and the underlying principles that enable the classroom to flourish, we hope the reader will come to believe that the goal—to fall in love with goodness—is not as absurd as educators might once have thought.

In many ways, Usha's project-method approach exemplifies developmentally appropriate practice; more closely, it resembles the highly regarded Reggio Emilia schools. But in its explicit and pervasive emphasis on moral growth it differs from both.

Over her many years of teaching, Usha has found ways to extend and stretch the moral sympathies of children. She has constructed a set of practices that snugly fit her goals and inspire in children a genuine love of goodness. Consistency of theory and practice, a clear sense of movement toward a fetching but never to be fully found destiny, and deep joy in the journey ground her classroom and her imaginative teaching activities. The children inspire the endeavor, and together with Usha they recapture the nobility and joy of the educational mission while becoming its eager adherents. How this is accomplished is the tale worth telling.

The challenge in telling our tale was how best to depict both the goings-on in this lively, ever-changing classroom and the underlying principles animating the practices. Without both the reader cannot sensibly elect to accept, modify, or reject any aspect of the approach. Usha herself was an obvious choice for taking on the task. But the substantial intuitiveness of her work prevents her from seeing her own pedagogy. An observer (and child psychologist) can attempt to conceptualize the teaching, but analysis cannot capture the classroom's electricity; at best it schematizes. Our choice of two voices—the teacher, Usha Balamore, concretely chronicling daily classroom activities and the

Children are naïve

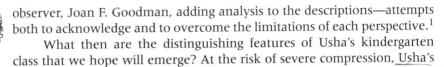 observer, Joan F. Goodman, adding analysis to the descriptions—attempts both to acknowledge and to overcome the limitations of each perspective.[1] What then are the distinguishing features of Usha's kindergarten class that we hope will emerge? At the risk of severe compression, Usha's general approach can be described as *aspirational* (that is the key), *integrated, and collaborative*. Her pedagogy assumes that young children naturally want to be, and have the capacity to become, as they put it, "gooder," and that their wants and capacities emerge only when guided by a mature adult who knows the road map but also knows that no guidance is effective unless children are endlessly free to consider and reconsider the leader's questions and their own.

ASPIRATIONAL

For Usha the goal of education is nothing less than contemplating the meaning of one's individual and common life and the tasks we should set for ourselves and others: not just contemplating, but aspiring to live by the truths we uncover. She believes that the supreme purpose of life at school is to become well informed about, and appreciative of, all global life (past as well as present, nonhuman as well as human) and to begin the process of reforming the world through compassionate caring. These aspirations, inclusive of the academic as well as the moral, are eagerly grasped and welcomed by the children.

Infiltration of the moral is everywhere apparent. It is displayed in Usha's daily dealings with children. Because she is their teacher and has much to teach, she does not shy from directiveness. Because they are their own teachers, and hers as well, she listens to them. Usha is open and generous toward children. She seeks their thoughts, experiments with their suggestions, and turns their ideas into long curriculum detours. In these ways she is highly deferential to children's initiatives. However, by directing her questions to the morally significant and by elaborating and molding the children's ideas, she leads them into thinking about an ethical community. Permeating the atmosphere and all the activities is a sense of trust—Usha's of the children, the children's of Usha and of each other. Usha regards her students as friends; she is candid with them and they with her.

Infiltration of the moral is displayed in the way Usha steers topics. When the subject is explorers, she asks, "What if the explorers came to harmonize with, not conquer, the native inhabitants?" If the topic is food preferences ("I love pizza but really hate carrots and broccoli"), she asks the class to think about the nutritional value of various foods while also considering the needs of those who lack adequate nutrition. If the topic is "great" people, Usha asks the class to consider what makes a person "great." If the topic is animals, she asks them to think about those that are endangered. If the topic is cooperation, she expands by asking how the class could be more considerate when waiting for the bus, when in an assembly,

---

[1] Drawings of the teacher and the observer (by kindergarten children) are used to indicate their individual voices in the text. However, both authors have participated in the editing of the entire work.

and when in public places. If the topic is complaining about parental failings ("Dad forgot to pack a dessert with my lunch"), she will say, "Let's stop right now and think about what you have done for your parents this week." The moral is so ingrained that Usha incorporates it into class activities without premeditation. When planning an excursion, she will deliberately create shortages so that sharing becomes mandatory; she will so structure the demands of the task that self-discipline and cooperation are necessary conditions for its completion.

Here are garden variety moral probes used by Usha:

"What might Columbus have done (what might you have done) to become friends with the Indians? . . .   OK, let's act out all your different ideas. . . . Now what worked best?"

"Megan, you were so excited today, you forgot to notice the noise and mess you made. Think back. Can you imagine anything you might have done differently? Does anyone else have a strategy that might help Megan?"

"What is the work of a school bus driver? What is hard about his work? What might you do to help him with it? Let's have lots of suggestions."

The children come up with pat, predictable answers: "We will not get out of our seats." "We will not litter the bus."

"Instead of saying what you will *not* do," Usha presses further, "Why don't you say what you *will* do to keep the bus safe and happy for everyone."

The children, beginning to absorb the message, continue: "We will stay in our seats." "We will keep the bus clean."

Usha is still not satisfied. She waits.

The children become more expansive: "I will tell the bus driver a joke." "I will bring him a snack." "I will bring him photos of my puppy to put up."

"The art teacher has been sick for a while," Usha informs the class. "How do people feel when they are sick and can't work? What can we (you, your parents, me) do to make the teacher feel better?"

The children chime in: "Send a card." "Call." "Send her one of our favorite books."

"Well, I visited her yesterday," Usha persists, "and I found that she has to lie in bed most of the day staring at a blank wall. Is there anything we could do about that?" More talk results in a class decision to make an elaborate mural—one giant card interwoven with secret messages from each of the children and a group phone call sharing their favorite song.

Because Usha's teaching is so aspirational, there is never a point of arrival; thus it is insufficient just to be good. We—the children, she herself, all of us—must continually aspire to be better, to know and do more. After a task is completed, the children come together for an evaluation. "What went well?" she asks. "How can we use what we learned? How can we do better next time?" She is completely confident that such an aspirational approach works, for in a sense the big truths of life are already slumbering within the child, needing only some gentle prodding to become a way of life. The more children become "gooder," the more they are fulfilled and content, the "gooder" they want to be.

The notion of a lifelong pursuit is central to Usha's message. As the year closes, children assess their growth by comparing who they were to who they now are. In a spirit of anticipation rather than discouragement they figure out that learning takes a lot of time but there is no hurry—look how far they have journeyed in just one year and how much time lies ahead. The emphasis is always on continuity; ends are merely beginnings. Ahead lie challenges, some of them tough, but the children have learned that mastering the long and difficult brings deeper satisfaction than quick and shallow resolutions.

INTEGRATED

Usha's teaching aspirations are filtered through year-long themes that structure her teaching. (We illustrate three of them.) Each theme has sufficient breathing and stretching capacities to absorb the year's academic and social curriculum. Integration means that subjects are not taught as separate disciplines—reading at 9:00 followed by arithmetic at 10:00 followed by copying letters at 10:30. For a week there might be no formal reading instruction, but the children, working on a play, are making posters, writing invitations, and collaboratively constructing a dictionary from words in the play.

By June these kindergarten children perceive themselves as competent scholars, and indeed they are: They write independent stories and read at preprimer or primer level. They do simple arithmetic that includes a beginning comprehension of weight, volume, measurement, and shapes as well as addition and subtraction. They understand the rudiments of scientific research and experimentation. They study the world both culturally and geographically (including topography and climatology).[2] They are advanced beyond their years in artistic appreciation and skill—including painting, sculpture, singing, acting, song- and playwriting.

As the following example of integrated teaching illustrates, to be aspirational is to be ambitious. Usha offers children as much complexity and depth of knowledge as they can handle, believing that their capacities are often seriously underestimated.

One year the children were introduced to the study of Native American culture through a life-size figure of the legendary Peacemaker from the Iroquois Nation (see Color Plate 1). The Peacemaker gave them the charge: How can you become a peacemaker at home and at school? First the children explored the concept of "peace": What does the Peacemaker mean by peace? They examined picture books, stories, biographies, myths, and songs; interviewed adults; and participated in group discussions and self-reflection. Next they were asked, "What was happening among the Native American nations that required the coming of

---

[2] Teaching of geography is enhanced by kinesthetic cues. Thus Usha will have the children put their hands on their head for the North Pole, touch their toes for the South Pole, draw a line across their belly for the Equator, touch their shoulders for Tropic of Cancer, and touch their knees for Tropic of Capricorn.

the Peacemaker? How did they live? What aspects of their lives brought them peace? What was the cause of wars between the different nations? What if their life goal had been peace, not conquest?"

The children visited a nearby Native American Center and tried on deerskin clothing, played Native American games, crushed corn the old-fashioned way (they could not believe how long it took), and spent an hour crowded into a long-house listening to songs and legends. The question of the week—"What qualities would be necessary for thirty-some inhabitants to dwell peacefully together in one longhouse?"—became more than academic as they felt the pressures of time and proximity.

Divided into six clans, the children participated in building a large model long-house. Standing under green trees, they started, in Iroquois fashion, with a prayer-ful apology for cutting down nature's bounty and promised to use all Creator-given materials wisely as they stripped tall saplings of leaves and extraneous twigs. The saplings were measured, graded by length and thickness, and gently bent and tied to form the framework of the building. Each clan undertook a different job— weaving mats for the interior, constructing ladders from twigs to reach the upper bunks, making bearskin doors and room dividers, making pots for storage and cooking, creating fields and rivers around the longhouse, and making cutouts of multigenerational people to inhabit the building. Each activity involved its share of research, math, science, geography, history, hypotheses, experimentation, and problem solving. Why are some knots better than others for fastening saplings? How high is the tallest longhouse? Does this correspond with the largest growing tree in their neighborhood? Why is it better to bake pots in a kiln rather than dry-ing them out in the sun? Did all longhouses have to be by a river or stream? Why did other Native Americans live in wigwams and tepees? Why were women, not men, chosen to be the leaders of the clan—clan mothers? (They experiment with different clan leaders and talk about leadership styles.) Would real bearskin shed as much as the fake bearskin they were using? What could they do to prevent goldfish crackers (pretend fish) from crumbling in the pretend river?

For their one-month Peace Training Program, the children identified various personal attributes that contribute to peace at school and at home. The unit con-cluded with an extravaganza of Native American songs, dances, and storytelling. At the grand Peacemaker Award Ceremony, each child was given a headdress (with the corresponding number of feathers he or she had earned) and a title that denoted their greatest personal accomplishment ("She Who Smiles" for a child who had stopped pouting, "Thunder Song" for a child who had overcome his fear of singing independently, "Friend of All Tribes" for the child who had been help-ful to all classmates).

COLLABORATIVE

Covert antagonism between teachers exercising authority and children resisting it, characteristic of many classrooms, is avoided when teacher and student are en-gaged in shared goals. Resistance and struggle occur, according to Usha, only when children are not excitedly engaged in tasks that matter to them, when they don't find the day's activities inherently interesting and worthwhile, when the curriculum is perceived as forced on them. Under such conditions the natural response is apathetic compliance or resistance, followed by rules and discipline, followed by more resistance.

In this classroom one senses that the usual "me" and "them" (often disintegrating into "me versus them") has been replaced by "us." In Usha's class one looks in vain for a set of teacher-ordained rules. "Social skills" are not isolated as objectives to be monitored but emerge through discussions about appropriate acts of compassionate and caring children. "Misbehaviors" then, are not rule violations or affronts to the teacher's authority, but temporary blips in one's own moral aspirations. Ideally, they will be corrected by the child for the child, but if not, a teacher's "correction" is merely a reminder of their common understandings, usually grasped by the child as being "for the good of all."

Leadership exists, of course, but it also is shared. Intuitively, Usha appreciates that if there is too much teacher direction, there is no child ownership—learning is shallow and evanescent; too little guidance and aspirations evaporate, and children retreat from difficult challenges. She encourages and elicits deep dialogue and sharing in class discussions. In terms of today's educational disputes, Usha's teaching is directive—she asks leading questions, offers suggestions and alternatives, creates dissonance—and it is nondirective—she invites children to pose their own questions and answers, to try out their own solutions.

Example: Directive Teaching

Child: "Peter's cubby is a real mess, Ms. Balamore. His backpack and jacket are lying on the floor, and everyone is tripping over them."

Usha: "Did you tell Peter about this?"

Child: "Yes, I did, but he isn't doing anything about it."

Usha: "Peter, do you realize that your cubby is a mess?"

Peter: "Yes! I came in late and threw all my stuff into my cubby so I wouldn't miss gym today."

Usha: "Do you know why this might be a problem for some of the other children?"

Peter: "The others have to walk around it and might trip."

Usha: "Right! What do you think you might do about it?"

Peter: "I should put my stuff away."

Usha: "That would be the responsible thing to do. Can I count on you to do this?"

Peter: "Yes!" (He leaves chanting the class jingle, "Re-spons-i-bi-li-ty, you want something done, you can count on me.")

Example: Nondirective Teaching

When children interrupt each other, as they are prone to do at the start of each year, Usha may gamely join in. Then, as the escalating noise brings complaints from the kids, Usha will assemble them together and ask (with full confidence in the answer), "Did this discussion work? Did you hear what I said? I couldn't hear what you said. Did you want me to? Can you think of a better way for us to talk together?" Or when children are doing less than a spotless clean-up, Usha will remain silent until they complete the task to *their* satisfaction and then, with the group assembled, ask her favorite questions: "Could we have done better? How?"

In the relaxed atmosphere of Usha's class, there are constant opportunities for spontaneously exposing one's own thoughts and experiences. Children feel safe and not judged. Mistakes are expected and interesting. The teacher brings up her own feelings, uncertainties, and errors. There is no question of "on-task" or "off-task" activities; all life experiences are grist for increasing sensitivity and insights into the human condition.

Enter Usha's classroom, and you may see children dancing and drumming on tables in response to the rhythm of a Brazilian drumbeat. When questioned about such "leniency" she responds, "I never worry about control. I can let them go because I know they'll be pulled back with a gentle reminder, perhaps just a look or a ring of the bell. They care about our work together, they care about me, and most of all they care about themselves and each other."

Example: Deep Sharing

Within the first month of school, as the teacher and children try to learn as much as possible about one another, parents are invited to share the origin of their child's name by writing a letter to their child. One year an anxious mother called Usha to confide that although she had told her child of his adoption, they had not yet shared the information with others. Following several conversations with Usha, Mrs. R. and her son decided that given this unexpected opportunity, they would take the plunge. They would reveal their secret, knowing that it wouldn't be easy.

After careful planning with Usha, Mrs. R. arrived in class with her son Bill, who was holding an enormous duck lamp. She began by reading aloud a carefully scripted story: For many years she knew she wanted a baby, but she didn't know how she was going to get one. Even though she had no baby yet, she dreamed of setting up the baby's room with a large duck lamp that she had seen in a store window. Her husband advised, "Baby first, duck second." So she had to wait and wait. It seemed like forever, but every time she got impatient, she repeated, "Baby first, duck second." The children, captivated, began to gently chime in, "Baby first, duck second. Baby first, duck second." Passing around Bill's earliest baby photos, Mrs. R. told the children how she adopted Bill and then purchased the beloved duck lamp that has lighted Bill's room for the last five years, six months, thirteen days, and four hours.

Usha allowed silence to engulf the room after the story ended. Bill was beaming—now at last everyone knew his special story. A child reached up spontaneously and hugged Bill's mom; others followed. Then Usha asked for questions and comments, and slowly they emerged: Is Bill your real child now? You must love him a lot! Did he like the duck lamp? Did you know if he would be a boy or a girl? What else did you get for his nursery? How come Bill looks like you? The children requested a second reading of the story, and when departing, Mrs. R. left a copy for the class library.

Usha then asked the children to draw something they had learned from the story or discussion. The duck lamp was prominent in most drawings, but some pictures depicted Bill's mother going off to the mountains to bring a baby, a crying mother giving her baby over to a smiling mother, and a baby falling from the sky into a mother's arms. After snack and playground time, Usha reassembled the children to explore more deeply the children's unvocalized fears and questions apparent in their pictures. She told them about her own volunteer experiences at an orphanage in India and the joys of adoption for both parents and children. Together they discussed the many reasons why a child may be given up for adoption and the immense love that causes a new mom and dad to adopt a baby, decorate his nursery, and welcome him home. To close the episode, children were given heart-shaped paper on which they drew moms and dads, natural and adopted, hugging their babies. On the last day of school each child received a beautiful hand-bound copy of *The Duck Lamp*, written by Mrs. R. and illustrated by Bill.

In addition to the atmosphere created by the distinguishing features of Usha's teaching—what we have called *aspirational, integrated, and collaborative*—there is an edge-of-your-seat energy created by the overall dynamic curricular structure. Most classrooms are still places. Children are quiet—or supposed to be so; the lessons are repetitive, not much difference from day to day; the ambience of the room is static, with the predictable wall adornments (tooth charts, numbers, birthdays, alphabets, weather, calendar, names of children, and rules), predictable time slots for activities, and predictable routines.

Usha's classroom is lively, its contours constantly changing. What goes on today relates to what was studied and discussed yesterday and what is being planned for tomorrow. In the course of a thematic unit on Japan the walls of the room are first covered with maps (terrain, weather, arts, agriculture, language), then hung with colorful costumes (authentic silk and child-made paper kimonos). Next, the whole room may be transformed into an elite Japanese tearoom and then into a bamboo field festooned with traditional hanging decorations celebrating the Tanabata festival. The classroom has momentum!

The only way to capture this momentum in writing is to map the evolving ideas, principles, dialogues, and activities across an entire year. Therefore this book is organized around the more salient activities of three separate years. We hope that this format will enable the reader to get a flavor of how the basic principles and practices can be applied flexibly to various thematic topics that are of interest to the children and the adults who teach them. In Chapter 1 we examine the meticulous behind-the-scenes preparations that fuel the first week of school, capture children's interests, and propel the year-long adventures. Beginnings are crucial. Setting up is not merely a matter of putting out paper, crayons, pretty pictures, and calendars; it is an opportunity to set out expectations for the forthcoming year, to use classroom walls and materials to inform and playfully engage children and parents from the very beginning. Children are hooked by the big theme of the year through letters sent home before the first day of school, dramatic mythical characters who welcome them into the classroom, and immediate immersion in inquiry.

Chapters 2, 3, and 4 describe the selection and development of three distinct themes, as well as all the detours from them, culminating with academic and dramatic extravaganzas. In planning and executing the first theme, Heroes, the children evolve from thinking that a hero is a strong, muscular, or rich celebrity to a deeper and broader understanding of the heroic. Over several months the many qualities of a hero are studied, and children select the hero they want to be. They depict their choice in a Halloween play and later in an art show. Heroes in the community are also discovered and honored. By spring it is the class's turn to get involved in herolike community activities.

The second theme revolves around a faraway princess who is searching for a class with good qualities. Will she choose us? Through interviews, stories, and biographies children study good qualities and develop a qualities-to-action training program. The princess arrives to applaud and encourage their efforts. She leaves behind a scroll of further accomplishments for the children to work toward. And so it goes throughout the year, with the princess and children corresponding, encouraging, accomplishing.

In the third theme, Mama Bear, searching the globe for a good school, wonders if she can entrust these kindergarten children to teach her son, Isaac Bear, respect and responsibility. The request opens an investigation of what is meant by these terms. What is respect in a dentist's office? What is responsibility on a visit to Grandma's for Thanksgiving? Out of their investigation the children create a manual for Isaac to follow when he returns to Mama Bear. Excited by the activities on behalf of Isaac, the children develop and participate in respect training programs both at home and at school. They evaluate their success and set future goals.

Chapters 5, 6, and 7 (Commonwealth Foundations) address the more practical nuts and bolts of the entire endeavor: how to build and maintain the sort of community—what we call a commonwealth—in which high aspirations, an integrated curriculum, and collaborative relationships flourish. What are the foundations that support a dynamic, moral classroom? How does a teacher generate, sustain, and regain momentum in this commonwealth? The technical infrastructure that upholds the teaching is examined through a longitudinal framework—first setting the tone, then maintaining the tone, and finally restoring the tone.

"We-ness," the sense of a commonwealth, is cultivated from the start. The class comes to think of themselves as a team that will stay together for a long time—through the fall, Halloween, Thanksgiving, Christmas, Hanukkah, Kwanzaa, winter vacation, New Year, and springtime. In the first weeks we-ness is encouraged through leading questions and exercises: "How are we all the same? What are our common interests? How can we help one another? How can we pool our individual strengths, our common wealth?"

From the beginning, aspirations are openly discussed, advocated, and endorsed. How will each child grow this year? How as a community will the children accomplish their joint and individual goals? Trust, a crucial foundation block of the commonwealth, is bolstered from the very first day. The class is a safe, fun-filled place. Families are included in everything. The teacher is a fully human person, vitally interested in each child. She speaks openly of risks she has taken and errors she has made, creating a context in which children can speak of theirs. Children come to realize that the journey will have its ups and downs, excitements and disappointments, all of which are subject to discussion and reflection. That's how they grow. The tone is set.

Under this ambiance, issues of control are minimal. There's nothing like shared goals to weaken the petty tensions, irritants, and power maneuvers that so often dominate the classroom. Nonetheless, children are children. Experiences from home and community carry over, influencing children's behavior in the classroom. A child can accordingly be animated, focused, restless, gloomy, or angry. Among the group there can also be fast or slow learners, attention-getters and attention-avoiders. Under the banner of "we," each child is provided with a highly individualized experience, sometimes a corrective experience, that meets particular personality features. The tone is maintained.

Finally, because the room is suffused with affection, mutual esteem, and just plain fun, the classroom climate, when disturbed, can be restored through honest dialogue, role-play, and group discussion. Usha can offer constructive criticism, knowing that the children will listen without resentment. Taking a break to reflect individually on one's course of action and unearth new solutions is a strategy available to all members of the community, one that Usha often employs for herself.

When the reader finishes the three Commonwealth Foundations chapters, certain questions about the relevance and applicability of Usha's methods may remain unanswered. Recognizing this inevitability, the final chapter of the book raises the questions most frequently asked by graduate student-teachers under Usha's tutelage: What if your school does not fully support these goals and methods? What if your children come from different backgrounds? What if you have a large class? The responses, stemming from our combined sixty years of experience with educational issues and practice, reflect our strong belief that all children will benefit from curriculum and teaching methods that are purposeful, integrated, engaging, mind-stretching, multidimensional, multisensory, and relevant to children's moral lives.

Beyond all else the book asks the interested reader to focus on the larger goal of schooling—educating children for citizenship in the world—and on new, perhaps liberating, possibilities for themselves and for children. As authors we are not advocating the universal adoption of these methods; rather, we present a documentation and analysis of successful classroom practices for the reader's consideration. These practices may be assimilated into classroom management techniques, although they are obviously so much more than that; alternatively, they may be thought of as ways to avoid "classroom management." This book is both an exploration and an invitation.

CHAPTER ONE

SETTING UP, GETTING STARTED

Imagine that you are planning for the arrival of a new baby. What exactly is entailed? Initially, you may consider the physical arrangement of the infant's room: furniture, decorations, floor covering, baby equipment, and how to make it all safe, comfortable, stimulating, and attractive to the newborn and other family members. But the baby will not remain an infant, so you factor into your planning a time dimension. The crib should convert into a bed, you decide, the diaper-changing apparatus into a dresser with shelves, and the carpeted floor into a linoleum surface. You also realize that because the baby is entering a family, the space allocated and funds expended must be proportional to what other family members receive. Finally, the preparations reflect your values, what you most care about, what you hope will attract the child's interests and attention: perhaps pictures of extended family, friends, and their children; you might prefer colorful mobiles, number and letter tapestries, books; then again maybe responsive busy-boxes, construction toys, dolls, stuffed animals, a guitar or disc player; or maybe simply empty space for the child to fill over time.

THE PHYSICAL SETTING

Arranging a classroom merits the same consideration. One wants each student to feel a rush of gladness when entering the room that first day, to sense, "Here I am safe, here I can be myself, here everyone is treated fairly, here there are lots of possibilities." That means designing a room to look attractive, colorful, and enticing, yes, but also one that is "fair," where each child finds nourishment for his or her interests and aptitudes. Finally, the physical setting will also reflect the teacher's priorities and long-term goals.

Usha's task is to construct a setting that says quietly to the observant parent and child, "Here we have high academic and moral aspirations. In this room this year we will develop a respectful, caring, lively, freedom-loving, hard-working, engaged community of learners."

With such intentions, Usha looks carefully at the student roster of the new class. Her mind races:

"There are many more boys than girls. I need to get a greater variety of masculine dress-up clothes."

"I have a child, Helena, from Mexico. How can I make her feel at home? My assistant, Mr. Ishaq Deis, can find some Mexican music. We will write the child's name in English and Spanish. We will put some pretend Mexican food on the kitchen shelves. I must find some pictures from Mexico and speak to Helena's family to fill me in on their background."

"I need intersections where boys and girls come together naturally at play time. I can place the doll corner next to the blocks and the space station next to the kitchen corner."

"The principal has notified us of a child who is very sensitive to sound. She may need a separate desk and space to work on certain projects."

Then she goes through her annual mental checklist and makes sure that:

- Pictures on the walls, books and puzzles, dolls, dress-up clothing, and musical material all represent a diversity of children (gender, color, ethnicity, culture).
- Bulletin board material arouses curiosity in different academic topics. Unlike posters of numbers and letters, they invite children to solve problems. One problem scrambles the letters in the children's names and beckons them to find their own. Another asks, "If there are twenty children in our class and eight of them are boys, how many are girls?"
- Rather than pictures of nature, the room displays the real thing. There are several bird's nests, bark from various trees, mounted insects, a plant terrarium, and an ant farm.
- A giant bulletin board is reserved to illustrate long-term goals. There are magazine pictures of children engaged in home and school activities with a caption that reads, "Which of these shows patience?" There are slots under illustrations of different classroom situations for a child to insert a *yes* or *no* card in reply to the question, "Is this child being responsible?"
- A poster contains the words of a theme song (or rhyme) specially chosen to convey the year's moral goals.
- Children's books on relevant socio-moral topics are in the book corner or special learning center. These include *Ira Sleeps Over* (about teasing a child about fear), *The Big Fat Enormous Lie* (about the burden of lying), and *The Late Bloomer* (about different rates of attaining academic readiness).
- Teachers' resource books—anthologies, poetry, short stories—and videos are readily available for use when sensitive issues arise, such as friendship, trust, divorce, religion, death, and procreation.

The setup varies each year, of course, depending on the theme, which is always portrayed by a dramatic (and very large) central exhibit. This centerpiece, with its command over the first-day activities, announces to families that the theme will carry the weight of the year's curriculum.

THE THEME

The primary criterion in selecting a thematic topic is that it will captivate the children's imagination. Topics can come from various sources: current news, summer movies, issues raised in previous years, teacher's personal interests, children's and teacher's travel, the particular ethnic configuration of the class, or the eternal fantasy figures (princes and princesses, titans and wizards, mythological animals and gods) that always fascinate. Themes that Usha has chosen include pretend trips to several countries, artists around the world, space, the Olympics, and the rainforests of the world. More important than the topic itself is whether it:

- Can hold the children's interest, stimulate their fantasy, and sustain long-term exploration.
- Has enough complexity to allow detours as the teacher follows and expands on children's personal areas of interest. For instance, when studying environmental pollution, children became interested in the lungs; that led to a month-long study of the human body.
- Allows scope for the inclusion of all subject areas. Here is what Usha's class did with the Winter Olympics theme. *Math:* Scores of every kind—speed, time, distance—were tallied and tracked. How long does it take us to run around the field? How far can each child run or jump? How far did they go? *Social studies:* Where are the Olympics? Where were they held previously? Are some places better suited for the winter Olympics? *Language arts:* Captions of events on TV were used as sight words; children wrote and illustrated their own journal of the Olympics and that became their reading text. *Moral aspirations (with drama/music/art activities):* Children learned how long individuals train for their few minutes of glory, which may or may not come to pass. A discussion on what endures—learning and good habits—promoted the idea of doing a "good qualities" Olympics. Children identified areas for training (patience, honesty, courtesy), studied flags and national anthems of different countries, designed their own Olympic flag, and concluded their program with a dramatic awards ceremony.

What follows is a description of how Usha used the first week of school, over three separate years, to introduce the children to three themes. Although the themes differ in origin and content, the reader will note many similarities: a bit of mystery, suspense, and surprise; a tug on the children's imaginations; a projection of tasks into the fairly distant future; a conditional offer of things to come (if children did their share); and strong moral and academic components.

THE YEAR OF THE HERO

 The movie hit of the summer—*Hercules*—inspired our theme. In the movie, Hercules, who attracts admiring crowds, fame, and glory for performing daring deeds on earth, is refused permission by his father to return to the kingdom of the gods.

Why? Because, his father insists, he must first become a hero; just being famous is not enough. This admonition struck a chord in me. It resonated with the point made by many moral educators that children confuse being a hero with being a celebrity, leading them to emulate the macho rather than the morally meaningful. It might be interesting to explore with children the differences between fame and heroism, applause from without and courage from within.

Heroes, I thought to myself, meet all the criteria for a theme. Furthermore, the topic affords us the chance to read biographies, myths, and legends from around the world as we set out to define the qualities of a true hero. We can compare heroes and celebrities. We can look at heroes in our families and neighborhoods. We have a preponderance of boys this year; they will love the topic! We also can look at heroines around the world and study their qualities. This will inspire the girls. As luck would have it, there is a Greek parent in the class and a Greek administrator with a rich background in archaeology. Perfect! We can begin with Hercules and see where the children's interests take us.

With our theme in place, Mr. D. and I begin to set up the classroom in preparation for the first day of school. We use cardboard boxes (which had contained our school supplies) to construct a gigantic figure of Hercules. After looking at photographs of ancient Greek carvings and pottery, Mr. D. creates a Hercules with black fibrous hair, a black mustache, and a plain white tunic rather than the red-haired, clean-shaven, cape-flying Hercules portrayed in the movie.

Next we write an illustrated letter to the children informing them of a mysterious visitor to our class who has a secret message that can be revealed only when all the children are in class together (Figure 1.1). We draw a picture of our Hercules for the letter and ask the children, with their parents' assistance, to guess the identity of this man.

The children arrive on the first day, in pairs, for a scheduled forty-five-minute visit. Accompanied by parents and obedient to the letter's instructions, they enter clutching photographs of themselves and pictures of flowers. Their eyes dart quickly around the room until they settle on the gigantic figure three times their height.

"Who is he?" they ask. "What's in the scroll?"

"It's a scroll that we cannot open until everyone is here tomorrow," I tell them. Mr. D. sits down with the children to make self-portrait cutouts for our bulletin board (to be used as part of our initial academic activities, such as graphing—how many girls, how many boys, how many with blond hair, how many with brown hair, how many like strawberry ice cream, how many prefer vanilla). After getting them started, he melts into the background and plays his guitar, offering suggestions for artistic elaboration (how to draw a checkered shirt, pleats on a skirt, or a three-dimensional bow) while observing the children's individual styles. Meanwhile, I settle down with the parents and, disregarding the usual pleasantries, ask them, "What are your hopes and fears for your child in kindergarten?" When the forty-five minutes are over, the children are reluctant to leave. "Why can't we stay longer?" they ask. "You will tell us who that big guy is tomorrow—promise?"

Alas, the next day we have an absentee, so answers to the children's guesses, questions, and hypotheses about the enormous figure are postponed another

FIGURE 1.1   The Letter: Introducing Hercules

twenty-four hours. By the third day, the children are bursting to know our visitor's identity. Seated on the floor and looking up at Hercules' tall frame, they offer their guesses:

"Zeus, the god in charge of hunger."

"Hercules, but he doesn't have a mustache or a cape."

"Jesus."

"God."

"Someone who lives in the water . . . Neptune."

"Atlas holding up the earth."

"Box-man, because he is made up of boxes."

"A man from India, because he has brown skin."[1]

We laugh together. I listen to answers. I ask for explanations. I gently encourage the quieter ones to guess, the noisier ones to wait and signal their wish to speak by raising their hands. When the guesses have been exhausted, I pull the scroll from Hercules' waistband and begin to read his letter: "Dear Children, do you know who I am?"

"Zeus, Atlas, God, Hercules," the children call out.

"I am Hercules, the son of Zeus. Have you heard about me?"

"Yes," they chorus.

"But you don't look like Hercules," some murmur.

"I lived in Ancient Greece a long, long time ago, but I heard that they made a movie about me this year. Is this true?"

"Yes, we saw it."

"Was the story real?"

"Yes," three children respond. "No," says one. Everyone looks uneasy. Even the children who said, "Yes," begin to change their minds. "Maybe . . . No . . . We don't know."

"No one in the world today has seen me, so I wonder how they drew pictures of me in the movie. Do you know how they drew my picture?"

"They probably found something that looked like him," John replies.

"Yeah, maybe they found his bones and copied him from there," Billy adds.

I hold up a miniature Hercules toy. "We have to figure out why the artist at the Walt Disney Studio decided to make Hercules look like this."

"They just made him up," the children conclude after some discussion. "But why does our Hercules look so different?" The question lingers as we continue with the letter.

"I am here in your kindergarten class to deliver this message to you. Because you cannot really see me (I am invisible), I wrote to your teachers and asked them to build a pretend me out of boxes. Here's what I want you to know about me. When I was a young man, I was quite strong, and I became famous in the world. I could kill snakes and other animals with my bare hands, and I could even hold up the sky. But when I asked my father if I could return to the kingdom of the

---

[1]Teacher–child conversations in this book are, for the most part, transcripts from video or audio recordings. All children's names have been changed.

gods, he said, 'No, Hercules, you can come here only after you become a real hero. Being famous does not make you a real hero. Being strong does not make you a real hero. Go and discover what makes a real hero.' Children, do you know what a real hero is?"

The answers emerge, some spontaneously, others with a lot of furrowing of brows and squirming of bodies.

"Saving people."

"Killing bad creatures that are killing others."

"When people are in danger and the bad guys are going to kill them, they should jump down and stab them with their swords."

"Hercules fought with a snake, and he kept cutting its head off, but other heads would grow instead."

"Heroes help people."

"Heroes should not kill people. They should really talk it over."

"Heroes are strong."

"A hero will bring people back to his house."

"When kids get captured because they see strangers who say they have candy . . . then a hero comes and kills the bad guys. So we should just say, 'No.' "

I let the discussion continue for a while. Four more children concur that a hero is one who saves people. Mr. D. writes all the suggestions on the board, and the children call out, "Did you write down what I said, Mr. D.?"

I ask, "Have you seen or known someone who is a hero?"

Now the children appear to be much more comfortable than at the beginning of the discussion, and answers pour out readily.

"Zeus, but he wasn't really strong because he got captured."

"My dad."

"Why?"

"Because he knows karate, and I do too. My cousin is a hero, because he has a blue belt in karate."

"So a hero is one who knows karate?" I interrupt.

"Yes," Billy replies immediately but then pulls back with hunched shoulders, as though reconsidering his answer.

"Dogs are heroes, because they help children get down when they are stuck somewhere. In the cartoon *All Dogs Go To Heaven*, a really big dog rescues a woman."

For the next six minutes we have an intense discussion about dogs being heroes. Children give examples about their own dogs, and we debate several issues regarding the many ways in which dogs can prevent bad things from happening.

I continue with the letter: "Can you help me become a real hero? Please think about these questions:

- Can a woman be a hero?
- Do you have to kill someone to be a hero?
- Do you have to have big muscles to be a hero?
- Do you have to kill a dragon to be a hero?
- Do you have to win a war to be a hero?

- Do you have to fight with someone to be a hero?
- Do you have to fly over a tall building to be a hero?
- Do you have to eat sunflower seeds to be a hero?
- Do you have to be very rich to be a hero?
- Do you have to be the son of a famous person to be a hero?
- Do you have to be a famous football player to be a hero?
- Do you have to be a movie star to be a hero?"

Most of the children agree that a hero has to be strong and have big muscles. The majority also agree that women can be heroes, but two of the three girls disagree. Being rich is carefully pondered; the final verdict: "It would be nice, but you don't have to be rich to be a hero." The last five questions generate a lot of laughter and chatter. Then comes the ultimate question: "Do you think YOU can be a hero?" Nine hands fly up. "Yes." Other children sit with their heads lowered.

The letter ends: "Think about these questions. Study them with your teachers and parents. Then on the sixth of December—remember that date—write me a letter and leave it on your windowsill in class. I will read it and tell you if your answers are correct. Love, Hercules."

We check the calendar and circle the sixth of December. We have three months to answer Hercules' question, "What is a real hero?"

We get right to work. I ask the children to draw pictures of heroes in action. Mr. D. brings out the books he referenced when creating our Hercules and explains the black hair and black mustache. We discuss how artists, like the children themselves, are free to depart from reality and portray things as they imagine. They scan the books on Greek architecture and art. Then they settle down and begin to draw on large sheets of paper while gentle Greek music swirls in the background. The children draw firemen, knights, dads, dogs, and people with swords saving others. Mr. D. and I walk around and talk to the children about their pictures. Meanwhile, we get a sense of their skills and individuality: two children with innovative pencil grips, another who draws minute figures in the center of the page, one ready to write on his own, the reluctant artist, the perfectionist, and the dreamer. As children complete their pictures, they dictate their hero stories, which we transcribe onto their papers. Finally, the class gathers in a circle, and each child's story is shared and admired. Mr. D. reads off the list of attributes he has compiled from their responses:

WHAT IS A HERO?
Saving people
Killing bad people
Killing snakes
Helping people
Talking things over instead of killing
Being strong
Rescuing others
Knowing karate
Dogs that help save others

The list is attached to a bulletin board. Items will be added and deleted as our search progresses over the next several weeks. The quest has begun!

THE YEAR OF THE PRINCESS

Sometimes the most creative ideas are born out of absolute need or, in truth, desperation. Another summer was coming to an end, but my summer work commitment was far from complete. I needed one more week; that left me only three of the usual eight days to set up my classroom. "I will put in extra hours each day," I tried to reassure myself. Getting the existing materials organized—bulletin boards, learning centers, and play areas—should be no problem. But what about the boxes of new material that have to be inventoried, sorted, labeled, and shelved? I pictured the giant pile of boxes that would confront me as I walked into my classroom. Suddenly, an image flashed into my mind: an enormous pyramid of neatly stacked, but still sealed, cardboard boxes, held together with a wide red ribbon, topped off with an enormous red bow. My imagination was triggered: The children could unpack the boxes, they could attempt to read the labels, they could sort the material, they could decide where to put each item, they could help write labels for containers and shelves, and we could talk about taking care of each article. Why hadn't I thought of this before? I could almost feel the children's anticipation and excitement as they opened each box, their eyes wide with delight as they unpacked new markers, paints, rulers, and Legos. Not exactly a theme yet but an exciting community-building activity.

I enter my classroom, and yes, there is a large assortment of boxes, and one especially big rectangular box. After six years of repainting and fixing our pretend kitchen appliances, we have finally ordered a new stove, counter, and sink. The pyramid is going to be huge! For two days Mr. D. and I work intensely to set up our room. This year we will have one child from Brazil (who does not speak English), two children adopted from Korea, and a child with a rich African heritage—a fortunate range allowing us to pursue the goal of respecting diversity, though diversity seems too abstract to be the theme of the year.

We create an elaborate bulletin board with a large world map (illustrated by children two years ago) and encircle it with a shiny purple ribbon. We select a song by Michael Caduto, who draws inspiration from Native American culture, because of its relevance to diversity, and we copy the following chorus onto a banner above the map:

> *Lift your hands in harmony.*
> *Make every day you live another song.*
> *Different kinds of people live around the world.*
> *It's a many colored land of rainbow hues.*
> *In the balance of the circle we're a human family,*
> *and peace is waiting for us if we choose.*
> (From *All One Earth: Songs for the Generations,* © 1994 by Michael Caduto. All Rights Reserved.)

On the first day the children will draw and cut out pictures of themselves, placing them on the purple circle—the circle of life from our song. Later we will move the pictures onto our map, attaching them to the child's country of origin. Later still we will attach pictures of parents, grandparents, aunts, and uncles to their home countries. Now we cover the low tables that run alongside the bulletin board with books about children, houses, transportation, food, shoes, and animals around the world.

After two days of preparation, exhausted, I stare at the pyramid. "Oh, no," I acknowledge, "something is wrong!" Even with a large red ribbon, those cardboard boxes will not enchant the youngsters. We need something dramatic to hook the children, to unify the curriculum components. A theme still eludes me. I consider wrapping the pyramid with colored paper and then adding the ribbon, but that would be contrary to the instruction I plan to give on recycling. Besides, it would be a tremendous waste. "Fabric! I have a large stash of it. Maybe that will work." I haul out my crates of fabric (gathered over the years from parents, friends, thrift shops, and yard sales) and start throwing long lengths of material over the boxes. The first piece of shiny aquamarine silk flies over the top and settles on the uppermost box, flowing down evenly on each side, like aqua hair on a . . . sphinx. "A sphinx," I think to myself, "I could make a sphinx." But kindergarten children will not identify with a sphinx.

Again I stare at the pyramid that rises almost to the ceiling. "Not a sphinx, but something with long hair," I muse. "Maybe a princess with flowing hair . . . and an aquamarine scarf . . . and a golden crown . . . and jewelry . . . and trailing robes." "That's it! We have a theme!" By 9:00 P.M. a spectacular princess adorns our classroom. She has streaming black hair, gleaming black eyes, a soft smile, and lots of jewelry. Never have Indian bedspreads been transformed into such exquisite royal robes; never have cardboard, hot glue, and glitter created such ornate jewelry; and never have strips of colorful fabric concealed such an abundance of classroom treasures. We now have a very dramatic figure for the kids to marvel at, but how can we link this to our moral goals? A mystery letter placed in the hand of the Princess will do the trick.

The next morning Mr. D. saunters into the classroom and stops dead, amazed at the overnight transformation of a pile of brown boxes. "The kids will go crazy over this," he gushes. "Now we're ready!"

"Not quite. We still have to write our letter to the children," I reply.

Mr. D. draws an elaborate picture of our princess, and we compose a letter about the magical princess who has arrived in our midst. It tells them that the Princess has brought a mysterious letter that can be opened only when all children are in class (Figure 1.2). The children are also told that we will be studying different lands, and so Mr. D draws a picture of the Taj Mahal for them to identify. Now our classroom is clean, organized, attractive, and mysterious. Our letter is in the mail.

On the first full day of school the children enter the class and sit facing the Princess (Figure 1.3). We sing name songs and play clapping games, getting to know each other. "But when can we open the Princess's letter?" they ask again and again. We let the anticipation build for a while, and then it is time to begin.

"What do you think her letter contains?" I ask them.

"A big letter Z for my name."

"I think there's a secret of love in there."

FIGURE 1.2   **The Letter about the Princess**

FIGURE 1.3   Discovering the Secret

"I think it's a secret about the world."

"I think the letter tells us who is going to be the Princess in the play."

I pull the letter out of the envelope and begin to read: "Dear children, I am a princess from a faraway land. I left my country because all the people became mean, impatient, and unkind. I came here hoping to find some kind, loving children. Do you think I am in the right place?"

"Yes," they all call out.

"Maybe you can tell her that you will be kind and good," I suggest.

Hannah says, "We will be kind and loving, Princess, and we'll never be mean to you, ever."

"And we always promise," adds Zack with both hands on his heart.

The promises pour forth:

"We will love you forever."

"We will not do bad things."

"We will not fight."

"Well, if I am in the right place," the letter continues, "I can tell you my secret."

"What is it?" an impatient voice pipes up.

"I brought some treasures for your classroom." There are audible gasps, and wide-eyed children chatter with excitement. "But I can give them to you only if you promise me two things." The tension in the room is tangible as children strain their ears to listen. "First, you must take good care of these treasures."

"We will! We won't fight, we won't throw them in the air, and we won't kick them around," Carl boasts.

"We'll keep them carefully in our classroom," Hannah says earnestly.

"Second, you must ask Mr. D. and Ms. B. if the class can build me a home so I may live among kind, loving people."

Carl looks very relieved, "We can do that." A long discussion follows. Everyone has suggestions:

"I have a toy castle."

"But she is so big, she'd never fit."

"We could make the whole classroom into a castle."

"We could have a drawbridge and a secret passage."

"It must have many rooms, because she is a princess. Maybe sixteen rooms."

"We'll need to make her a giant bed."

"We'll need ladders."

"Everything must be big."

"Yes, we need a large bathtub and a large toilet."

I let the discussion continue for a while and then return to the letter once more.

"I have to tell you one more thing: I am a magic princess. I can grow really big and I can get really small."

Carl puts his head in his hands, "My parents won't believe what happened to me in school today."

"Me too," Adam remarks.

"You can take me apart and put me back together. When you take me apart, you will find the treasures I have brought your class. When you find the treasures, carefully open the boxes, one at a time. But remember to take me apart gently. Put all the different parts of me in a large bag, and when my castle is built, I will reappear. But I will be much smaller. Do not break any promises. Have fun. I will see you soon. Love, Princess with a secret."

Mr. D. and I start to take the Princess apart. The children watch spellbound as we remove the crown, the face, the ornaments, and the yards and yards of fabric. "Here they are!" they call out as they catch sight of the boxes: "Oh, man, that's a lot!" We guess the number of boxes: "Twenty . . . thirty-six . . . fifty . . . a hundred." Then we count them; there are twenty-one boxes. We form a circle and open one medium-sized box. Out come stacks of paper plates and two rolls of tape.

"The Princess must have wanted us to have a party," Amelia concludes.

"And she sent us tape for building the castle," says Carl.

The next box contains two large white tubs with the word "Crayola" on the label. Some children recognize the symbol and shout, "Crayons!" "But why would crayons come in a tub?" a child asks. They try to read the label, they shake the tub, they lift the tub with one hand to find out if it is heavy, and finally Mr. D. opens the container. Powdered clay for art projects!

"I wonder, how did the Princess know that I love art," Adam comments. Mr. D. reads the label and tells them it was made in Pennsylvania but is distributed by a company in Australia.

"I come from Pennsylvania, right, Ms. B?" Zack asks and I agree.

Carl picks up the stack of paper plates. "Here, Mr. D.," he shouts. "Read this label. Maybe it will tell us which tree it was made from?"

We spend another thirty minutes unpacking three more boxes. There is a demand for every label to be read and different countries to be identified on the world map. We think of ways to figure out what is inside each box: We can weigh it, we can shake it and hear what sound it makes, we can try to peek through the corner spaces, we can smell it, we can shut our eyes and try to imagine what is inside. We decide to open a few boxes each day, and after putting away the materials we have opened and breaking for a quick snack, we plunge into our next adventure: building a castle.

Mr. D., who loves books, has borrowed twenty, on castles, from local libraries. Only two of these are children's books; the rest are large volumes on the architecture, history, and legends of castles. Over the years we have found that children always gravitate to these in-depth books; it is a rare child's book that commands the same attention. With twenty books spread out on the floor, children get to choose their own special one and peruse it in silence. They are looking for structural ideas to incorporate into our castle. I give them bright pink Post-it strips to mark the pictures they like. Then they choose one castle and draw it on paper. Mr. D. plays a tape of baroque music. I stand back watching as the children tumble into self-instruction.

THE YEAR OF THE BEAR

Mr. D.'s eighty-three-year-old mother is sick this year. She has always been interested in our classroom activities and knows about our first day strategies. She tells Mr. D. that she would like us to use a large teddy bear that someone has given her. I visit her in the hospital and realize that she is extremely ill. As I leave, I kiss her on her forehead and promise to use her bear as our introductory hook. Mr. D. stays at the hospital while I spend the first three days of the week setting up the classroom. On the fourth day I ask Mr. D. to bring the bear to my house and leave it at the front door.

Meanwhile, I remodel a meditation hut that the children built last year on our pretend trip to India. It is a cardboard refrigerator carton, whitewashed, decorated with Indian designs, and topped with a thatched roof. I place it on a tabletop at the far end of the classroom and create a garden around it. The table is covered with a green tablecloth to look like grass, and giant paper sunflowers (also from a previous year) stand tall around the house. A deer (a large stand-up Bambi retrieved from a dumpster behind a movie theater) lurks behind the house, while a wizard sits by the door saying, "Do not peek," and an owl perched atop the roof says, "Hoo lives here?" (Figure 1.4).

"I will place the bear inside the house and create a story about why he chose to live in our classroom," I think to myself. In the next two days, in some way, I will have to link this bear with our moral goals. I arrive home at 6:00 P.M. to find Mrs. D.'s bear standing by my door. It is three and a half feet tall, covered in bright blue velour, with beady black eyes, and it is ugly! Besides, it will never fit into its

FIGURE 1.4   Isaac Bear's Little House

beautiful new home in our class. I go to bed in turmoil and fall asleep with one thought in my head: A promise is a promise!

The next day I call some friends and borrow a small, appealing, furry brown bear named Isaac. I dress the ugly blue bear in a diaphanous pink dress (from our dress-up corner) to cover up as much of the blue as possible and place a tiara on her head. Sparkling earrings and a diamond necklace complete the ensemble, and we now have Princess Emma, the mama bear (named after Mr. D.'s mother), who will become a backdrop for her son Isaac. He will inherit the house and stay in our class to learn good qualities. I write a letter to the children telling them about the little house in our classroom (Figure 1.5).

I have been contemplating the pros and cons of choosing a more obvious, direct moral theme than is my usual practice. My decision is influenced in part by a school meeting at the end of last year when the teachers unanimously voted to make courtesy a primary school goal. I muse over what a one-year curriculum based on respect and responsibility might look like. The first step, I thought, was

DEAR _____
Welcome to KINDERGARTEN
We are your teachers—Ms. Balamore and Mr. Deis.
We have been setting up the classroom for many days and it looks really beautiful and inviting.

Did you know that *kindergarten* means a *GARDEN for KIDS?*
Well it does! And do you know why?
Its because Mr. Deis and I are like gardeners who will shower you with love and information and you are like beautiful flowers that are going to grow and learn and blossom.
In this *garden* you will make new friends, draw, act, sing, laugh, play, write, read, count, cook, and have many interesting adventures. You may even go on a trip to exciting places.
So get ready for Kindergarten. When you come to see us on the 9th (with your parents) please bring
1) A PHOTOGRAPH of yourself in which your face is clearly seen.
2) A LARGE PICTURE of your favorite flower that you have drawn, colored, and cut out.
3) A BIG SMILE.

When you come into our class you will meet Mr, Deis and me, and you will see a mysterious house like the one I have drawn. Someone very interesting has decided to stay in our class for the next few months.
A few weeks ago his mother wrote me a long letter to ask if I would accept her kid as an extra member of our class. After reading her letter, I agreed. I will read you her letter on the 10th, when ALL of you are here. Until then you will have to try and guess who lives in this house in our kindergarten.

Mr Deis and I are so happy you are in our class. We can't wait to see YOU.
LOVE
Miss. Balamore
Sept. 1998.

FIGURE 1.5 The Letter about the Little House

to take a close look at those words. After reviewing multiple definitions, I concluded that essentially, *respect* meant showing regard for the worth of oneself, others, and the environment. *Responsibility* meant taking care of oneself, others, and the environment. But could I integrate all subjects into this theme? I decide to go for it. I will watch the children's responses and take my lead from them.

A middle room between two kindergarten classrooms serves both as a display area for projects and artwork and as the main entrance through which parents escort children to our classroom. It is the best place to announce our curriculum. On the first bulletin board that meets the eye, I create a large sign with pictures of flowering plants and children of various races. The sign reads, "Kindergarten, a garden where children blossom." On an adjacent wall is another sign: "Children blossom with good qualities." Around this sign are ten large, colorful posters of different qualities such as kindness, cooperation, honesty, and responsibility. The stage is set!

The children come bustling in the door on our first full day of school. Yesterday, accompanied by their parents, they individually made many guesses about the inhabitant of the little house. But today is the big day! Who actually lives in that house? Who is going to stay with us all year? I ask the children to gather around the house. Stan sits far away. He looks a little worried, maybe a little nervous. They announce their guesses:

"A goblin."

"A bird."

"A wizard."

"A hamster."

Adam tells us, "I thought it was going to be Mrs. A. (our new principal), because I heard she was moving, but then in the letter you wrote 'he' and not 'she.' So I changed my mind."

We discuss the importance of paying attention to clues, and the next half hour suddenly becomes a "look for the clue" game, one that we will continue to play all year. The children make more guesses:

"A live animal."

"An owl."

"A monster."

"Would I allow a monster in this classroom?" I ask.

"No," respond the children.

"Mr. D. and I try our best to keep this classroom a safe place," I tell them, looking directly at Stan. We decide to sit really still and listen for clues. If there is a live animal, it will make a noise, but we hear nothing. The tablecloth flutters, the children are startled, and they look under the table for clues.

I pull out Emma Bear's letter as we continue to look further. We talk about the different parts of the letter: the address, the date, and the signature. "The letter was written on a computer," a child observes. I start to read, and there is a hushed silence.

> Emma Zon
> 2 c Truth Road
> Mazador
> T.B. Land. 60080
> August 1, 19—

Dear Ms. Balamore,

I wonder if you still remember me. I am Emma, the cuddly blue bear that sat in your back room eight years ago. I am the bear that every child wanted to play with during the school day. And at night, when all the children were home, I loved to walk around your class and look at the colorful artwork and dress up in all the dress-up clothes. I used to imagine that I was a doctor, a pilot, a teacher, a princess. . . .

Yes, so many years have passed, and I think of the happy days and nights I spent in your class. I remember all the good things you taught the children, and I remember how kind and loving the children were to each other and to all the toys in the classroom. Your classroom was always clean and neat—yet very *exciting*. The children were always willing to help you clean up the classroom. They always laid me down gently on a pillow or on that little yellow chair in the corner. Often, the next morning, they wondered who had moved me out of the chair and who had changed my clothes. Do you think anyone knew that I was a *special* bear?

Well, I did grow up and leave your class. Eight years have passed, and I got married to a prince in Mazador Land. I am a real princess now! I also have a wonderful son, Isaac, who is a one-year-old. Ms. Balamore, did I tell you that one year in a *special* bear's life is equal to five years in a human's life? Ask your children to figure out how old I am and how old Isaac is.

I am writing to you because it is time for Isaac to start school this year. As I visit many schools in Mazador, all I see are young cubs fighting, saying, "This is mine. That is mine." They snatch things from each other saying, "Give it to me, its mine, you can't play with it." They do not share, they are not polite, and they shout in loud voices. They also complain a lot, Ms. Balamore. You may not believe this, but they complain and brumble (a bear's grumble) about the snacks they are given at school, they brumble if they are asked to help the teachers, they brumble and growl when they are asked to put away their toys after play time, and they even brumble about washing their paws before lunch.

After visiting these schools I felt very disheartened. I sat on my soft, cozy, purple couch and thought to myself, "You are a real princess now, and Isaac will be the prince of Mazador someday. But if he is to be a prince who takes care of the people and animals in his kingdom, if he is to take care of the environment (the trees, the lakes, the rivers, the mountains, the land), and if he is to take care of himself, he must learn to have good qualities when he is young. I must find a good school for him." And that is when I thought of your classroom. I remembered how your children learned about patience, compassion, honesty, cooperation, respect, responsibility, and so many other virtues. Do you think that Isaac can stay with you, Mr. D., and your kindergarten children for a few months? Do you think your children will be kind and loving this year? Will they play nicely with Isaac? Will they teach him good qualities?

If you think they will, please write to me as soon as you can. If your answer is YES, I will bring Isaac to school on the tenth of September. I look forward to seeing you again. I will bring some palace-baked cookies for your kindergarten children.

Lots and lots of love and hugsles,

Emma

P.S. Did you know that we have computers in Mazador?

The letter was long, but the children listened attentively as they sought out clues regarding the inhabitant of the little house, voicing interesting associations:

"It has to be blue."

"Has to be a bear."

"It will probably wear a crown because it's a prince."

"Eight years ago, I wasn't even born."

"Eight years ago it was 1990, wasn't it?"

"If it was a stuffed toy, how did it walk around the classroom? Is her son a stuffed toy too?"

I interject, "Would you like to meet Emma Bear or Isaac Bear first?" We do a quick class vote, a method that we will use all year, and decide to meet Isaac first. I ask the children to shut their eyes, reflect for a minute, and think of something welcoming to say when they are introduced to Isaac. Then I carefully part the doorway curtains and lift Isaac out of his house. The children who have been sitting on the floor rise to their knees to get a good look. Stan, looking very relieved, comes closer to the group. Then each child individually greets Isaac.

"Welcome to our class. I would love to show you everything we do."

"I'm glad you're in my class."

"Isaac Bear, what are you doing here? You look so nice. I am glad you're here."

"I hope you have a good time in our class."

Next we meet Emma Bear. The girls love her jewelry and attire. A couple of the boys want to know if she opens her mouth when she speaks. And how does she walk around at night? We promise Emma Bear that we will take good care of Isaac. Mr. D. says he will teach Isaac many good songs; in fact we will begin right now. He gets his guitar and starts to teach the children our theme song for the semester. The song, "Respect Yourself and Others Too," defines several aspects of respect. The children stand up, sway their bodies and snap their fingers in tune with the music, and repeat after Mr. D:

There is something you can give to others
And others can give to you.
There is something you can give yourself,
And you'll feel so proud too.
It's not a toy or a teddy bear,
It comes from you and me,
It's a special thing everyone can feel.
Let's spell it and I think you'll see.
R—E—S—P—E—C—T
Respect for you, respect for me,
It's so important that you do
Respect yourself and others too.
It's so important that you do
Respect yourself and others too.

Mr. D. continues to sing as the children sit down at the tables to draw ways in which they will help Isaac at school. Mr. D. sings, "Respect is showing you care how someone feels, respect is listening when someone talks to you, respect is liking someone for their special ways. . . ." The children, hunched over the tables, are totally engaged. I walk around writing down dictated sentences: "I will sit next to Isaac and give him a hug." "I will help Isaac draw good design." "I will help Isaac get on the swing and push him on the swing." "I will play with Isaac and share my new blanket with him."

COMMENTARY

The most striking aspect of these beginnings is how thoroughly Usha co-opts the agenda. Her prepared environment goes well beyond collecting materials designed to tap children's natural interests. With no apologies Usha makes her soft but absolutely clear sell. From the first day children are gently and subtly induced to think about the moral dimensions of life. This is a class in which children will become attentive to one another—listening, learning, and giving. It will be a class in which they will be deliberately drawn into the world as well—from Greek heroes to Australian companies that distribute powdered clay. And it will be a class in which children accept and set high standards for the quality of their work and the range and depth of their learning. Usha also preempts some of the usual behavioral issues by anticipation. The bear letter brings up elementary courtesy such as "brumbling" about snacks and not sharing; the princess letter raises the issue of taking care of classroom materials.

What the children experience, however, is not a pressure cooker and not a demand for uniformity, but freedom, discovery, and delight. From the start Usha communicates that she will note, respect, and encourage their individuality and diversity (among themselves and others); they will be permitted to wander imaginatively and intellectually; and their curiosity and excitement will be stimulated in a never-ending and never hurried series of questions, investigations, and answers, followed by more questions.

We have here already good examples of both directive and nondirective teaching, a class that is both structured and free. Usha sets the stage by announcing the themes through a large dramatic figure who comes bearing a letter for the children—Hercules and the defining of a hero, the Princess and the search for good qualities, Emma Bear and an exploration of respect and responsibility. The letters and follow-up questions begin to convey the virtues she upholds:

"Do you have to have big muscles to be a hero? Do you have to kill a dragon to be a hero? Do you have to win a war to be a hero? Do you have to fight with someone to be a hero? Do you have to fly over a tall building to be a hero?"

"I [the Princess] left my country because all the people became mean, impatient, and unkind. I came here hoping to find some kind, loving children. Do you think I am in the right place?"

"I [Emma Bear] think of the happy days and nights I spent in your class. I remember all the good things you taught the children, and I remember how kind and loving the children were to each other and to all the toys in the classroom."

But this isn't exclusively Usha's show. She is merely the catalyst. The children are constantly invited to participate, with no preconceived expectations of what they might have to say.

"What do *you* know about heroes?"

"A hero is someone who knows karate."

"Would *you* want to be a hero?"

"Yes, then I will get a lot of money and everyone will like me."

"What will *you* teach Isaac Bear?"

"What dwelling should we build for a princess?"

"Who should we introduce first, Isaac Bear or Emma Bear? Let's have a class vote."

Usha also conveys to the children that elevated goals are not quickly attained. This is a very unhurried class. Discussions are prolonged, children are listened to. What you don't see or hear is a teacher looking at the clock and saying, "Two more comments, and then we will have to stop." In fact, there is no clock in the room! There is an understanding that the ability to probe, question, and endlessly learn is inhibited by an excessive vigilance over time constraints—"Is it time for gym yet?" "Where does the big hand have to go before I have lunch?"

Stopping obviously happens, but it occurs naturally; if a topic is not exhausted, Usha will return to it. There is a theme designed to last an entire year. There is a letter (from Hercules) received in early September but not to be answered until December sixth. (And recall that the opening of the letter was delayed for two days until everyone was present.) There are questions left dangling—"Do heroes have to be strong?"—to be answered more fully down the road.

What some might see as an extravagant indulgence—lengthy discussion and exploration—sends an important message to children: What they say and the detours they select are more important than adhering to a fixed schedule. There is virtue in patience. It takes a while, sometimes a long while, to learn, to improve, to get a matter straight. That message encourages perseverance and self-discipline.

The children also learn something of the complexity and depth of ordinary, everyday experience. Opening boxes leads to an exploration of manufacturing and geography. A Disney figure leads to an investigation of Greek mythology. A castle to be built requires the study of architecture. Education at its best is sustained, passionate inquiry. Usha takes familiar, everyday objects that have never produced a question and "problematizes" them for children. What is a box? A crayon? A scarf? What is it made of? Where does it originate? Why is it shaped just so? Could it be shaped differently? What are its uses? What else can you think of that serves the same purpose? This kind of probing, not merely memorizing facts (color, shape, number, letter), stirs the intellect and, when continuously pursued, turns children into intellectuals—hunters of knowledge, revelers in ideas.

The reach and vitality of the children's engagement that characterize Usha's classroom combined with her powerful presence resonate with the observations made long ago by the philosopher and educator Alfred North Whitehead (*The Aims of Education and Other Essays*, New York: Free Press, 1929/1967):

The environment within which the mind is working must be carefully selected. It must, of course, be chosen to suit the child's stage of growth, and must be adapted to individual needs. In a sense it is an imposition from without; but in a deeper sense it answers to the call of life within the child. In the teacher's consciousness, the child has been sent to his telescope to look at the stars; in the child's consciousness he has been given free access to the glory of the heavens. Unless, working somewhere, however obscurely, even in the dullest child, there is this transfiguration of imposed routine, the child's nature will refuse to assimilate the alien material. It must never be forgotten that education is not a process of packing articles in a trunk. . . . My point is that a block in the assimilation of ideas inevitably arises when a discipline of precision is imposed before a stage of romance has run its course in the growing mind. There is no comprehension apart from romance. . . . Without the adventure of romance, at the best you get inert knowledge, without initiative, and at the worst you get contempt of ideas—without knowledge. (Figure 1.6)

FIGURE 1.6   The Glory of the Heavens

Usha's class too is a romance, *a falling in love with goodness,* as Usha often puts it. It is a slowly emerging set of want-to-be's and don't-want-to-be's that begin to define the child's enduring sense of self. The next three chapters, elaborating each of the three themes, illustrate this emergence in some detail.

CHAPTER TWO

HERCULES AND HEROES

If feats of power and might do not make Hercules a hero, what does it take to be a real hero? The moral thrust of this theme is threefold: to help children distinguish heroes from celebrities, to undo stereotypes, and to inspire a love for virtue. But there is also a strong intellectual component to the theme. With heroes as the lens, our entire view of the world changes. Gradually, our questions are not just informational—who, what, and why—but evaluative: Was he or it good, right, fair? Stories, myths, magazines, newspaper articles, daily experiences—everything is assessed; less and less are people and events simply passed over without inspection. Is every policeman a hero? Why don't we see more policewomen? Was Robin Hood really a hero if he stole from the rich? Can a part of you be a hero but another part be "regular"? It is the beginning of philosophical speculation. Is everything as it should be? How are we to understand "should"?

During the first few weeks children demand that we read and reread Hercules' letter. This, more than any introductory letter we have ever used, has generated a lot of interest. In their search to define a hero, children scrutinize TV stories for characteristics that fit the bill and come to class each morning with fresh ideas.

WHAT MAKES A HERO?
EARLY APPROXIMATIONS

"I think I saw a hero last night. It was a man who saved two children from a river. He was so brave."

"I saw these firefighters all black and dirty, but they saved a whole family."

"These men in a helicopter saved a woman from the flood."

At this stage, "saving others" appears to be our number one criterion for being a hero.

"The firefighters were just doing their job. Does that make them heroes?" I probe.

"It's their job, but still they were brave."

"Yes, you have to be brave to go in the fire and all that stuff."

"Maybe they are just doing their job and they'll only get money if they save people."

"Do you think they get paid a lot?" I ask.

"They must." The entire group nods in agreement.

"Let's ask some firefighters these questions," I suggest, and together we compile a list.

After school I drop by a local fire station, and the two men on duty chuckle aloud as they respond to questions from five-year-olds. Making a mental note that I should have invited the firefighters into our classroom in the first place, I report my preliminary findings to the children: Most of the firefighters at this fire station did not seek the job primarily for the pay. Volunteers form a large part of their work force. The volunteers want to help, even though they know that the work is dangerous. To keep themselves safe and bring the fire victims to safety, however, they underwent a great deal of training. They learned about firefighting rules and how important it is to follow them at all times; about how to keep fit, to care for themselves and each other; and about the many complex rescue techniques and when to use which ones. The children are impressed. We read and discuss a book about firefighters.

Two new hero concepts emerge from this discussion: *intention* and *effort.* Is a firefighter who chooses the job to help others more of a hero than one who chooses it because of the money or just because his dad was also a firefighter? Is the firefighter who works hard at his training and practices the techniques he is taught more of a hero than one who just shows up for classes but doesn't put his heart into the learning?

Conditions for being a hero.

We begin to look at all professions and trades through these lenses. We look, for example, at the different reasons for choosing to be a doctor: fame, helping others, money, fancy cars, fancy homes. We look at the effort a doctor makes: many years of studying about the body, practicing, learning to read X-rays, reading about the work of others, listening to patients, being available to patients even in the middle of the night. Children talk of kind doctors and doctors that make you scared.

"Is kindness part of being a good doctor?" I ask.

"Yes!" everyone agrees.

"Can a doctor be a hero, even if he is not kind?"

"He could be a hero if he helps someone who falls on the soccer field and breaks a leg."

"He could be a hero if he helps a little child who is hurt in a tree. But if he is mean, then she could get more scared and die."

Realizing that I had begun the discussion with "he," I try to turn the conversation around. "What if it is a lady doctor?"

Females more nurturing

"Then she would be kind." No one disputes this.

I am amazed at this stereotype but continue, "So she would be a hero?"

After some hesitation they agree. The notion of women as heroes is, as yet, ephemeral. Kindness, they agree, would definitely help but is not essential to being a hero. Success seems more important than attitude. By the end of the year, after many such discussions, kindness is included as an important hero component.

INCLUDING PARENTS

Parent Night, held after the first two weeks of school, is an evening when parents hear about the teacher's educational philosophy. Parents are informed of this date early in the summer, and I send several reminders explaining the importance of the occasion. I prepare a package for each parent that contains:

- The poem "All I Really Need to Know I Learned in Kindergarten" by Robert Fulghum.
- A couple of articles that explain my methods for teaching reading, writing, and math. The readings also contain samples of children's writing stages.
- Children's current definitions of a hero, to be used for discussion and contrasted with those at the end of the semester.
- Recommended readings (with particular chapters specified):

    Teaching Children to Care by Ruth Charney
    Educating for Character by Thomas Lickona
    Why Johnny Can't Tell Right from Wrong by William Kilpatrick
    Punished by Rewards and *Beyond Discipline* by Alfie Kohn

- A list of materials that parents can collect for us (buttons, fabric, shoe boxes).
- A list of ways in which parents can participate in class activities (supervise field trips, make books on tape, volunteer to teach a special skill, read stories, introduce aspects of their cultural heritage).

The children, meanwhile, are busy preparing for Parent Night by illustrating and dictating messages for their parents to read:

Dear Mom and Dad, please see the butterfly building I built in the play area.

Dear Mom and Dad, look at the math blaster program in the computer.

Dear Mom and Dad, look at my drawings of heroes and look at my writing in my new "I Like . . ." book.

On Parent Night I emphasize that kindergarten is not merely a preparation for first grade. I want this to be a "living classroom," a classroom in which we celebrate life, where we come to understand and accept one another so that we can grow together, and most of all a place where we are willing to try anything and everything (children often refer to it as a "trying place"). But if children are to try, I explain, we must provide the criticism-free space that allows for experimentation, mistakes, and backsliding both at home and at school. Quoting from Thomas Lickona (*Educating for Character*, New York: Bantam Books, 1991), that we should try to educate for "character as well as intellect, decency as well as literacy, and virtue as well as knowledge," I describe how the hero theme will encompass the teaching of moral values as well as academic skills. Anticipating the nervousness

of parents with this unaccustomed emphasis on values and knowing of their eagerness to see the children make academic progress, I provide examples of how, in
previous years, reading, writing, math, art, and problem-solving strategies were
incorporated into a theme.

Parents then view videotapes filmed during the first two weeks of school
showing the children's initial hero discussions and their writing, math, play, and
drawing activities, as well as a special, hastily put together dramatization of the
book *The Sunflower That Went Flop* (See Color Plate 2). By bringing the parents right
into the classroom, the videotapes erase the distance between the parents' imagined construction of kindergarten and the real experience. They emerge reassured.

After parents have had time to digest and discuss the videos, I invite them to
join us on our kindergarten hero quest. It is their turn for an initial assignment. I
ask them to prepare for our Halloween celebration by helping their child select a
hero (preferably from their ancestral country). The selection should not be done
quickly. They should examine options by perusing and discussing myths, biographies, fairy tales, and other fiction. I encourage parents either to send to school—
or, better yet, come in to school and read—any inspiring book they discover. When
parents come aboard, when efforts at home and school are synchronized, children
are doubly delighted. They sense that this is indeed a living classroom, a place that
is part of, not separate from, their real life. Parent Night allows us the opportunity
to set this collaboration in motion.

Before parents leave for home, they are asked to write a note to their child
about the time they have spent in kindergarten. The notes, hidden around the
classroom, generate a great deal of excitement the next day. Parents who are unable to attend the evening meeting are invited to come in for individual meetings
over the next two weeks. Information packages and videotapes for parents are
sent home throughout the year.

INSINUATING THE ACADEMIC:
READING AND WRITING

Children enter kindergarten with varying degrees of exposure to the alphabet.
This year children range from those who can identify all consonants and consonant
sounds to children who can recognize and name only a few letters. Using a combination of techniques, we instantly plunge children into reading and writing, knowing that they will learn all the letter sounds as they proceed through the year. We
begin with journal writing and an *"I like . . ."* book. The journals are an ongoing documentation of conspicuous events in the children's lives. Two or three mornings a
week, we start the day by talking about events in our lives—visits to grandparents,
pictures we have drawn, books we have read, games we have played—and I document these on the blackboard with simple sentences, taking care to sound out the
words, to invite children's help, and to point out interesting word patterns.

> *My grandma and grandpa went to a movie.*
> *Sam found a snail in his yard.*
> *Megan saw two cardinals. She liked their red feathers.*

Then children disperse to collect the materials they will need for their journal-writing "silent workshop"—journals, pencils, erasers, crayons, and books from which to copy pictures. They first draw pictures and then attempt to write their own sentence, or if not yet able to write, they dictate a sentence, which they will later copy. Mr. D. and I walk around whispering letter sounds, encouraging children to take risks, and helping children with dictated sentences. Children learn to write by writing, and they learn to read by reading. My basic approach to the three R's is summed up by a hand-embroidered pink sign on our wall with the words GO FOR IT! (given to me ten years ago by a child).

A child says, "I think picnic begins with a "P" and ends with a "K.""

My response: "Go for it!"

"I just figured out how to spell "once"—it's "W-U-N-S.""

"Go for it!" I beam, delighted by the child's original use of phonics.

"Ms. B. I'm not sure whether to draw fifty tiles on the roof. It might take a long time."

"Go for it!" I reply. "You are the artist. If you really want to do it, you can stay in after lunch and finish."

Gradually, often in a one-on-one teaching situation, we will teach the correct sound and word patterns, and as reading develops side by side with writing, visual memory will further assist in the self-correction of spelled words. We also work at building a sight word vocabulary. In the very first week we introduce two words through flash cards—"I" and "like"—and devise several activities around them. For example, Mr. D. goes up and stands next to the two words that are placed in a pocket chart, and the class reads aloud, "I like Mr. D." Mary jumps up, "Let me stand there," and we read, "I like Mary." I hold up a box of markers, and children read, "I like markers."

Every child begins an *"I like . . ."* book, but each child works at his or her own level, with gentle but constant nudging toward the next upward step. For example, a child who knows very few letters will copy the words "I like" from the flash cards or the book cover, draw a picture of puzzles, and read me her sentence, "I like puzzles." A slightly more advanced child might write, with some help, "I like pzls," while another who independently writes "I Like Pazls," may be given the word *because* and encouraged to continue: "I Like Pazls because day r fun." As the week progresses, we discover how the stem of a sentence determines what follows. "I like to" is followed by verbs (action words) such as *run, swim, ride a bike;* "I like my" is followed by things that belong to an individual; and "I like the" is more open-ended.

The following are examples from Brian's book:[1]

I LIKE My MOM AND DAD.

I LIKE TO PLA SOKR.

I LIKE THE ZOO.

---

[1]Brian came to school with a good knowledge of letter sounds but hesitant to draw or take risks in writing and always wanting to know whether he was correct. Three years later, when we decided to write this book, Brian's mother unearthed a box containing every piece of writing he had done in kindergarten. Brian's actual writing samples are therefore most prevalent in this chapter.

Throughout the year children create a series of similar books that appear the same on the outside but are uniquely individual on the inside. Brian's *"I See. . . ."* book, for example, shows how he was inspired by Dr. Seuss's *Foot Book* as he writes:

I See BiG feeT; I See UP iN ThE AiR FeeT; I See PiG FeeT; I See housE FEET.

Derek's book, on the other hand, contains fairly safe sentences such as:

I SEE MI DOG.

I SEE A BOL.

The next book—"All About Me"—is more open-ended. Brian writes:

MY NAME is BRIAN. I WAS NAMD AFTR MY grANDFATHER. I LIKE BILDING WiTh BLOCKS. MY LitL BruThR unus [annoys] ME.

Children continue to write a lot each day. At various points during the day they write in their journals; they also dictate or write spontaneous stories, thank-you notes, birthday greetings, and notes to mom and dad. A list of common sight words grows on a word chart, and children learn that they can either sound out words, refer to the chart, or refer to various books for their writing purposes. A classroom corner is reserved for hero tales, and children create sentences or stories about heroes every week. After only three months Brian is already capable of writing a hero story:

DARBY
BY BRIAN
Once theRE WAS a Horse NAMeD DERbY WHO WAS BRAVE. But he WAS Not BRAVE SUMTIMS Becos there were MANY DRAGins URAND. But theRE WAS A Knight WHO Fot DRAGONS. WAN DARbY WAS WOCiNG HE SOL A DRAGON. DARby RAN AWAY. WAN DERby WAS BAC HOME He Went To see his FRAND. TheN WheN DARBYS FRAND TOLD him Wut TO DO DARby SID Yes. Then when DARBYS FRAND TOLD him Wot To DO DARBY WeNt TO FOLULOW The iNSCRciNS [in-structions]. DARBY BecAM brAve Becos his FRAND Hlpt him.
                                                    TheEy END

BECOMING A HERO: HALLOWEEN

As Halloween nears, the suspense builds. "Ms. B., don't you want to know who I am going to be for Halloween? I chose an awesome hero. Can't I just whisper it in your ear?"

After two months of analyzing hero stories, the children realize that heroes are made, not born, and that intention and effort as well as events and opportunities often shape their destinies. Therefore for Halloween we ask each child to examine his or her character's role in the story (or real life)—what circumstances he found himself in, what he was like, what he did—and come prepared to define two of the character's heroic qualities, expressed in deeds, and the events that shaped these qualities.

The first to arrive is Jenny the Pilgrim, smiling shyly, very demure in black and white (Figure 2.1). St. Patrick follows close behind, regal in a flowing green robe, a large golden cross, and a white bishop's miter (Figure 2.2). Henry is almost unrecognizable in a proper brown suit, his usually radiant face covered by a dark brown mustache and beard (Figure 2.3). Who is he? No one knows. His family has worked with him to find a noble hero. Borrowing a book about famous Jewish men from the library, his mother read him several biographical outlines while he hemmed and hawed, saying, "I don't think our class would call *him*

could be Hitler, Castro, Mussalini

FIGURE 2.1   Jenny the Pilgrim from England

FIGURE 2.2   St. Patrick from Ireland

great idea
b/o children
learn about
important figures

a hero." Finally, Henry selected Dr. Paul Ehrlich, who had won the Nobel Prize for discovering a cure for syphilis. "I think doctors are real heroes because they help so many people, especially when they find a new remedy," he announces, and the children, impressed by his attire, do not ask for a definition of syphilis. Whew!

Other children follow, and the classroom is soon filled with the likes of Moses (Figure 2.4), Babe Ruth (Figure 2.5), Saint George (Figure 2.6), Mr. D. as Odysseus (Figure 2.7), Pocahontas (Figure 2.8), Maria Tallchief, the first Native American ballet dancer (see Color Plate 3), and Sir Lancelot (Figure 2.9). Each child has specific reasons for choosing a character:

"I chose Maria Tallchief because she had courage. She did something no Native American had ever done before. She became a ballet dancer even though everyone said she couldn't. Everyone laughed at her when she was young, and she was very nervous when she had to go on stage, but she wore bright red and danced in the Firebird dance. She was very good."

FIGURE 2.3   Dr. Paul Ehrlich from Germany

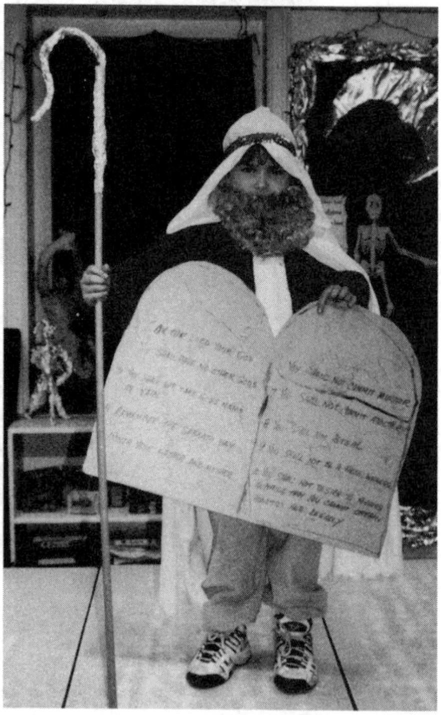

FIGURE 2.4   Moses from Israel

FIGURE 2.5   Babe Ruth from the United States

FIGURE 2.6   St. George from England

FIGURE 2.7   Odysseus from Greece

**FIGURE 2.8   Pocahontas
from Turtle Island**

**FIGURE 2.9   Sir Lancelot
from England**

"I chose Sir Lancelot because he became really kind and brave. Remember when he almost killed a guy [the children do remember because Patrick had persuaded us to watch the entire video of *Camelot*], but when he looked into the guy's face, he changed. And then, even though he was the strongest, he was no longer proud, and he became kind."

EXPANDING NOTIONS OF THE HEROIC: STORIES

Everyone who hears of our theme sends in hero stories—parents, grandparents, librarians, teachers, and friends. As each book is read, children discuss the merits of various characters. Watching hero videos at naptime affords us the added luxury of pausing and rewinding whenever necessary. We search for clues in people's expressions. We look for intention: Did he really mean to hurt his friend? Was he only pretending to be brave? Why did she look annoyed when she was doing something good? We look for effort: Is this hard for him? Has she endured distress to be helpful?

Most fairy tales support the "saving and rescuing" message, already defined by the children as essential to heroism—various princes rescue Sleeping Beauty,

Rapunzel, Cinderella, and Snow White; the woodcutter rescues Little Red Riding Hood; Lassie rescues little kids in distress. In some fables, however, we find that the ingenuity of an ordinary individual outwits the mighty opponent, as in *Hansel and Gretel* and *The Fox and the Lion*. You needn't be a prince or a firefighter to be heroic! We add cleverness to our list of heroic qualities and search legends and biographies further for other, more subtle, complex qualities.

In *King Arthur and the Knights of the Round Table,* for example, Arthur is torn between good and evil, between jealousy and love, against a backdrop of magic, evil, and witchcraft. There is much to discuss.

"Was Arthur a hero just because he pulled the sword out of the stone?"

The boys would like to believe that this is indeed the case, but Patrick, who early on has displayed an uncanny ability to perceive similarities in parallel situations, remarks, "That would be just like Hercules. When he did stuff like that, his father told him that he was not a real hero."

"When he pulled out the sword, it was only magic. Magic doesn't make you a hero."

I remind the children, "Arthur himself tells Merlin the same thing when he discovers that the sword Excalibur, used to defeat King Pellinore, is enchanted."

"But King Arthur became a hero later on when he did not kill King Pellinore."

"He forgave him instead."

"How does that make him a hero?" I ask.

"Because it is good to forgive. Like when we are playing and someone says, 'I'm sorry,' and I say, 'That's okay, you can play with us.' "

"But why was it good that King Arthur forgave King Pellinore?" I persist.

"Because killing is bad, and King Arthur did not kill the king."

"Because if he had killed the other king, that king's people would come back and kill him."

We discuss how the urge for revenge can make wars go on and on, but forgiveness can stop everything and bring peace. Earlier, we added kindness and compassion to our "What Makes a Hero" list; now we add forgiveness. However, the children are unwilling to delete the "killing bad people" component, insisting, "Sometimes you must do that."

The knights' covenant at the round table further enlarges our concept of a hero. The knights promise to be "gentle to the weak, courageous to the strong, and terrible to the wicked. They will defend the helpless who ask for their aid. They will be merciful to all men, gentle of deed, true in friendship, and faithful in love." After some discussion and deliberation we add three more attributes to our list: mercy, defending those who need help, and gentleness.

We discuss several books in this manner, often using a 0–5 rating scale to stimulate further debate. King Arthur fluctuated on our rating scale as we read different chapters, from 1 when he pulled out the sword to 5 when he forgave King Pellinore. At the end, by general consensus, he was awarded a 4 "because he had good intentions, had mostly good qualities, and was mostly brave" but was not awarded a 5 "because he had Merlin's magic to help him."

EXPANDING NOTIONS OF THE HEROIC:
SOUP KITCHEN WORKERS

These young children are still captivated by their romantic heroic notions. Despite the exposure to and discussions about firefighters, the hero as celebrity continues to have a grip on them. Largeness of the spirit remains inseparable from bigness (visibility) of the deed. A bold, courageous heroic figure makes a splash and of course gets due recognition. Reading a book about a tenderhearted man who starts a soup kitchen for the homeless opens a new door: It gives us a different perspective on heroes.

"Is this man a hero?"

"Well he's not brave or anything, but he does help people."

"I think he is a hero because he fed so many people who had no food."

"I don't know if he is a hero, because others help him cook the food."

"Once I gave money to a poor man."

"Yeah, but this man helps people every day, and he doesn't get paid or anything. He was really sad when he saw people who were hungry."

Gently steering the conversation, I question, "Who is more of a hero: someone like a soup kitchen worker who helps people every day or someone who does one famous deed?"

"I think the person who helps the most is the hero."

"It really depends on what the famous deed is."

"They could both be heroes."

"But the soup guy helps people for days and days and days."

"And never gets famous," I remark. "Do you know what such heroes are called? They are called 'unsung heroes' because no one notices how hard they work—no one 'sings their praises.' "

Our search for local soup kitchens begins. The music teacher, herself an active participant in such service, brings us a video documentary of a church soup kitchen with its accompanying song, "One of Us" by a Philadelphia musician, Eric Bazilian. (The song becomes an instant hit, and Eric Bazilian visits us later to tell of what inspires his songs.) On seeing actual footage of food being prepared and served to a vast array of weary, dejected, limping people, the children's respect for such jobs increases, and they are eager to help. However, when Mr. D. and I visit these kitchens, we decide that kindergarten children would be overwhelmed by the noise, crowdedness, and occasional offensiveness around the meal. Instead, we prepare large quantities of pumpkin bread at school and send it over to the soup kitchen. Working with the school community service program, we also enlist parents and children to cook and pack meals for home-bound patients.

EXPANDING NOTIONS OF THE HEROIC:
LOCAL HEROES

"Let's take a look at the school cafeteria kitchen," I announce one morning. "People have to work just as hard here as at the soup kitchen." Thus, as we begin

COLOR PLATE 1 ■ The Peacemaker

COLOR PLATE 2 ■ The Sunflowers That Went Flop

COLOR PLATE 3 ■ Maria Tall Chief from America

COLOR PLATE 4 ■ The Gates of Heaven

COLOR PLATE 5 ■ A Hero of Many Faces

COLOR PLATE 6 ■ **I Look Like an Indian**

COLOR PLATE 7 ■ **Beautiful in a Saree**

COLOR PLATE 8 ■ **Learning about Indian Music and Dancing**

COLOR PLATE 9 ■ **The Princess Brings Her Secret Treasures**

COLOR PLATE 10 ■ **Outer Castle Walls**

COLOR PLATE 11 ■ **Inner Castle Walls**

COLOR PLATE 12 ■ **The Finished Castle**

COLOR PLATE 13 ■ **The Real Princess**

COLOR PLATE 14 ■ **Paintings of Homes: Two-Dimensional**

COLOR PLATE 15 ▪ **Sir Lancelot and Sir William**

COLOR PLATE 16 ▪ **A Korean Castle Scene for Our Play**

COLOR PLATE 17 ▪ **Art from Beans**

COLOR PLATE 18 ▪ **The Artist and His Rhino**

heroes @ school

to look at the often unnoticed personnel in our own school community who help to make our lives better every single day, we move from the outside world to our own world. In pairs, children interview different members of the maintenance crew, the secretaries, and the library staff. Then they design and frame special thank-you plaques for their newly discovered heroes.

Dear Mr. M.,

Thank you for taking care of our yard. We never thought about your work before. If you didn't do your job, our yard would be a mess and the bushes wouldn't be so round and pretty. You are our Hero!

We will try not to litter the yard and not play soccer near the little plants.

Love,

The Kindergarten Children

A MUSEUM VISIT AND OUR EXHIBIT

From the very first day, as I watch children draw their hero pictures, I realize that their drawing skills, compared to most kindergartners entering school, are not very sophisticated. Several children still render human figures as a circle for a face, two lines sticking out of the circle for arms, and two lines below for legs. The need for formal art lessons is evident. However, just as we refrain from teaching math skills in isolation, so too with art skills. <u>The techniques must be embedded in meaning.</u>

We begin by studying the human body, which, when seen as a vital part of being a hero, becomes an object of wonder. We examine the design of the human hand, so perfect for wielding a sword, serving soup, or patting a dog. Human legs, with hinges at the knees and ankles, work perfectly to chase a thief, to climb a ladder to rescue a kitten, or to kneel down to comfort a child. Using circles, ovals, and rectangles of various sizes, we first teach children to draw human beings with heads, necks, torsos, and limbs. Once children examine their own bodies and understand the concept of joints, they are then able to draw the human body in different action modes—walking, running, dancing, and even throwing a javelin. Soon it becomes common to see children standing in front of the mirror in various poses or using a friend as a model when they draw action figures.

To further motivate and inspire the children, we bring in books about Michelangelo and Leonardo da Vinci so that children may study and copy their intricate, detailed human body sketches. An art corner filled with these books becomes an unexpected focus of interest during free-choice as children gather to copy drawings of hands, legs, and bodies.

The next logical step is a visit to an art museum, but which one? We select the Rodin Museum of Philadelphia. It is fairly close by, it is sufficiently large but not so large as to overwhelm the children, and, most crucially, Rodin's main concerns—truth and man's moral nature—coincide with our hero theme. Preparations for the museum visit proceed: We examine the differences between two- and three-dimensional art, we study various pieces of Rodin's corpus, and we even create our own sculptures. Borrowing a potter's turning wheel from the art department, Mr. D. shows children how a sculptor must plan his work from all angles, making sure that the profile, rear, and front are sculpted in the right proportions. Children are then set the task of sketching china figurines from different angles so that they may experience perspective-taking firsthand and appreciate the complexity involved in designing a sculpture.

Next, we pore over illustrated books of Rodin's work. Certain pieces catch the children's attention: *The Man with the Broken Nose, The Burghers of Calais, The Thinker,* and *The Gates of Hell.*

"I wonder what the Thinker was thinking about?"

"He looks really strong. Look at his muscles."

"Yes but he doesn't look happy."

"Those people on the gates look terrible."

"They're going to hell. That's why."

"They can't be heroes."

"They must have done something real bad."

Mr. D. points out the facial expressions and twisted body lines in various figures that convey despair and anguish. He encourages the children to pose in front of the mirror and express different emotions using both the face and the body.

Finally, two days before our museum visit, children start to work on their own sculptures. Each child sketches a hero of choice, who will then be portrayed in a three-dimensional form. To secure a base for each sculpture, Mr. D. and I collect rectangular pieces of wood from the scrap piles at local lumberyards. As material for their sculpture, children will use newspaper, tape, and aluminum foil. The foil, scrunched into a ball for a head or rolled into a cylinder for the arms, is the easiest material for children to manipulate. Later, with adult assistance, these figures will be covered with papier-mâché and painted. Surrounded by sketches, paper, scissors, tape, and foil, children set out to create heroic ballerinas, knights, soccer players, runners, angels, and children—sculptures that are over a foot tall.

Well versed in museum etiquette, the children then set off on the trip, eager to see *The Thinker* (Figure 2.10) and *The Gates of Hell.* On reaching Rodin's skillfully executed portals of the netherworld, they stand in front of the awe-inspiring structure, eyes wide, looking up from their tiny three-foot-something frames in total silence. Then the chatter and movement begin as children spontaneously contort their bodies to assume the positions of sculpted bodies or lie on the floor looking upward.

"I wanted to feel how that person felt, Ms. B."

"I wanted to look at the gates from a different perspective."

"I can't believe that Rodin could carve so many people."

"I don't think I like this, Ms. B. It makes me feel sort of scared."

As we walk around the museum, the children, to the amazement of a large tourist group, identify several of Rodin's statues and busts accurately. Then each child is given a clipboard, pencil, and eraser and is told, "Find your favorite sculpture, settle down in front of it, and sketch it." Without a murmur, these five- and

FIGURE 2.10   Thinkers—One and All

six-year-olds disperse in various directions to sketch the masterpieces Auguste Rodin created almost a century ago (Figure 2.11).

On our return from the museum, we spend the afternoon completing our sculptures. As I listen to the children's animated conversations, an idea dawns. I throw forth a question: "Would you like to create your own museum?"

"Our own museum! What does that mean?"

"You mean we can show people our sculptures?"

"But we haven't finished them."

"Would we do this in our classroom?"

"We could exhibit your drawings, paintings and sculptures," I explain.

"That would be real cool."

"What would we call it?"

"The kindergarten museum."

"The hero museum."

"The happy museum. I didn't really like *The Gates of Hell.*"

And so begins the planning for a culminating event. I call the various departments of the school and request permission to reserve two adjacent wood-paneled conference rooms for our exhibit at the end of November. In this exhibit, suitably titled "Heroes—Past, Present, and Future," each child will display four

FIGURE 2.11   Focused Artists Sketch a Rodin Masterpiece

pieces of artwork: paintings of their Halloween heroes—heroes of the past (Figure 2.12), aluminum foil sculptures along with dictated stories—heroes of the present (Figure 2.13), busts of their own faces—heroes of the future (Figure 2.14), and gold and silver box sculptures of heroes.

Making each bust takes time and patience. At recess, I work with individual children on what looks like an ancient tribal ritual. A child lies down on a table with eyes shut, her choice of music playing in the background, while I apply baby oil to her face and then cover her entire face (except eyes and nostrils) with thin, moistened strips of plaster of Paris. The entire process takes about twenty minutes, and then, as the plaster hardens, the mask, eerily identical to the child, is removed. It is later mounted on a wig mannequin (obtained from a hairdresser); painted with appropriate skin, eye, and lip colors; and topped with hair (yarn, Halloween wigs, feathers, and even a mop dyed in coffee). Hats, bows, beads, and shirt collars serve as finishing touches. Soon we have a replica of each child staring at us from a shelf along the wall. It is quite startling.

To make the box sculptures, we collect a giant pile of boxes: cereal boxes, shoe boxes, juice boxes, and tissue boxes. Using boxes for heads, necks, torsos, arms, and legs, each child assembles a human figure that is held together with hot glue and duct tape. Then yarn, strips of paper, egg cartons, fabric, paper napkins, and doilies are added as hair, armor, clothing, and helmets. The entire structure is spray-painted in gold or silver to create "box heroes." Some of these figures stand over four feet tall and are quite impressive.

FIGURE 2.12   A Hero Painting—Dr. Paul Ehrlich

A child's query, "Why did Rodin make *The Gates of Hell* instead of the *Gates of Heaven?*," is the inspiration for a cooperative art project: "What if we made *The Gates of Heaven?*"

We look for giant pieces of cardboard, create a gatelike structure, and spray-paint it a muted gold color. Each child draws, colors, and cuts out three figures of his or her choice—the tooth fairy, Mother Teresa, Princess Diana, dogs, angels, people who have done good deeds, and heroes of the past. These are then pasted all over the golden gates. Interspersed with these figures are colorfully decorated words from our ever-growing hero list: *COMPASSION, HONESTY, KINDNESS, LOVE.* In the midst of it all, Jared exclaims, "We need a Thinker on top of the Gates like Rodin had, but our Thinker will be different from Rodin's. He will look happy and look upward." He proceeds to draw a curious-looking, unidentifiable creature seated on a chair looking upward. Since the idea was his, no one challenges Jared's right to place the picture atop the gates. Another kindergarten classic is thus created (see Color Plate 4).

By the end of November our hero attribute list has changed considerably as well as grown substantially. Now included are subtler concepts such as courtesy, planning, waiting patiently for the right moment, and choosing words wisely to settle a dispute. Being a hero, we realize, requires different qualities in different

FIGURE 2.13   Exhibiting the Hero Sculpture

situations, and words such as *brave* and *courageous* alone won't suffice. I tell the children that this reminds me of Joseph Campbell's book *The Hero with a Thousand Faces*. The concept catches on, and we start to assemble yet another collaborative art project that will summarize our collective wisdom about heroes.

Mr. D. cuts out a three- by four-foot cardboard face that is deliberately neither male nor female. After inserting two white Styrofoam balls for eyes and sketching in a mouth, nose, and headgear, Mr. D. hands the face over to the children to be completed. They have planned to cover this face with a hundred or more little faces, each representing a hero quality. But do we know of a hundred qualities?

Sitting at the blackboard, I introduce children to a thesaurus. After writing the word *courage* from our hero attribute list, I look in the thesaurus and read aloud a list of similar words. Selections by the children are then written down—bold, adventurous, daring, dauntless, fearless, valiant—and very soon we do have over a hundred words.

A tray filled with one-inch squares of "multicultural" skin colored paper is placed in the middle of the floor. Children are instructed to copy a word from the

FIGURE 2.14   Does My Bust Look Like Me?

blackboard onto the bottom of the paper, draw a face that corresponds to the word, and then cross the word off the blackboard to prevent repetition. Children make at least six to eight pictures each, handing them to Mr. D. to be pasted on the cardboard face. Once the headgear is decorated with gold and silver doilies, beads, and fake gems, our "Hero of Many Faces" is complete (see Color Plate 5).

The opening of the art show will be a formal evening event. This decision grew out of a statement made by a kindergartner several years ago. When asked what an *anniversary* means, he responded matter-of-factly, "An anniversary is when your mom and dad dress up and go out, leaving you with a baby-sitter." Since then, I have tried to create opportunities every year when parents can dress up *for* their children. We send invitations requesting children, parents, and guests to dress formally. Several mothers get into the act, festooning themselves in borrowed gloves, hats, and even long gowns. The children make elaborate decorations for the walls and the entrance (Figure 2.15). A group of parents organize fancy-looking refreshments, complete with fake champagne and a pyramid of plastic wine glasses.

When all the guests are assembled, the evening opens with children and parents from past years—heroes of kindergartens past—playing a musical interlude (Figure 2.16). This is followed by three songs sung by our current heroes: the song

Dress up for exhibition?

FIGURE 2.15   Welcome to Our Museum

FIGURE 2.16   Heroes of the Past

from the soup kitchen documentary, a song about artists, and a special song the children have composed with Mr. D., containing an individual verse about each of their Halloween heroes.

(Chorus)
Heroes so brave
Heroes so bold
from a long, long time ago
Heroes so brave
Heroes so bold
from a long, long time ago

The beautiful Native American Dancer, Maria Tallchief
Entertained the people all across the land
She could leap in the air in a graceful way
As she danced the Firebird ballet

In England lived a hero who was called Saint George
His muscles were like iron but his heart was soft
A dragon caused trouble all around
Saint George he struck that dragon down

They say that Pocahontas was the daughter of a chief
She lived in America over 300 years ago
She told her father not to kill John Smith
Because she knew that life was a very special gift

Jenny was a Pilgrim girl who crossed the sea
She went to America so she could be free
On a journey so dangerous and long
She had to have courage and be strong

When do you draw the line on someone's version of a hero?

Then the school principal makes a short speech, cuts a ribbon, and opens the doors to the exhibit. Individual tables covered in black fabric (borrowed from the theater department) display the children's masterpieces. Brian stands at his table proudly explaining the contents of his display, which consist of a portrait of St. Patrick, a sculpture of Jack the Knight, a gold sculpture of a warrior made of assorted boxes, and a bust of himself. Alongside his knight sculpture is his dictated story:

JACK THE KNIGHT
BY BRIAN DOUGALL

Once Jack the knight saw that Mario was hurt. He rushed over to help him. Mario was bleeding because someone had cut him right in the chest. Jack took him to the nurse in the castle and the nurse helped him.

Then, when Mario was feeling better, he became a knight. Jack taught him how to be a knight. Then, when he became a knight, Jack said, "You should go on your own."

Mario went to another place and was happy there. So he stayed there. Jack was happy that Mario had found a place to live.

The End

Next to Brian's bust is a photograph of Brian and a mounted transcript of my interview with the young artist.

ABOUT THE ARTIST

Brian Dougall is a five-and-a-half-year-old painter and sculptor. He lives in a house with his brother Daniel, his mom, his dad, and a little brother or sister in his mom's tummy. He says he started to draw when he was one year old, but it was only scribble-scrabble. He says he kept on practicing until he got to be real good. This is his first exhibit at an art museum.

As for the future, Brian thinks that he will be very brave. He wants to become a rock star and says that his way of being a hero will be to sing songs and cheer people up when they are feeling down.

Child as hero

As the exhibit opens, the young artists stand by their artwork shaking hands and conversing with the guests who have been instructed to ask "real" questions and to treat the children as genuine artists.

Guest: What inspired you to fashion this sculpture?

Child: I was thinking about heroes, and my favorite kind of hero is a doctor, but I wanted to make a knight because knights look so cool. So I decided to make a doctor knight because you need doctors everywhere. So that's what I did.

Guest: I love the way your ballerina arches backward. How did you design this?

Child: I looked in a lot of books about ballet, and then I made her with her arms held up. But then we put too much papier-mâché stuff on her hands and it was too heavy, and the next day we saw that she was bending backward a little. But it looked good, and so we kept it like that.

Children stay at their stations for over an hour, honoring all the guidelines we have established, even waiting until the very end to taste the delicacies other guests have relished all evening. Around 8:30 P.M. the artists are taken home by their parents, tired but elated. On the weekend a local newspaper headline announces "A Heroic Effort by a Kindergarten Class." Intrigued by the children's work, a news reporter who usually covers large gallery openings had attended our celebration. The opening paragraph of her report is as follows:

It was a gala art-exhibit opening of a different sort. Sure, there were the usual trappings—fancy clothes, champagne glasses and adoring fans—but these artists were 5 and 6 years old, and they had arranged the show, called "Heroes of the Past, Present, and Future."

HERO TRAINING PROGRAM

Do we want to grow up to be real heroes? By November the answer is an unqualified and unanimous "Yes!"

"Great," I said. "You have the *intention*. Now how do we show our *effort*? Is there a way we can train for it? Are there certain qualities we can practice at school and at home?"

We list all the children's suggestions on the board and discuss their applicability and practicality. Key suggestions are:

Helping others
Being brave
Being patient
Forgiving others
Not fighting, but talking things over
Being kind
Being responsible
Listening
Becoming strong

I ask children to think of ways in which these qualities can transfer into action.
"I can help my Mom carry in the groceries."
"I can help by cleaning up my room."
"That could either be helping or responsibility," I comment.
"I'm getting stronger now. I can even take out the garbage."
"I guess I could fight a little less with my brother. But that won't be easy!"
"What quality would you be practicing then?" I question.
"Definitely patience!"
Everyone nods in agreement. Dealing with younger siblings is not always easy.
"And where does being brave fit into our training plan?"
"I have to be brave at the dentist."
"And when I get a shot."
"I know when I have to be really brave—every time I see my neighbor's dog. It's big and mean!"
"What about becoming strong?"
"I can do exercises every day."
"Yes, my Dad lifts weights, and I could try."
"We can run a lot at recess."
Out of these discussions emerge Hero Training Programs for home and school, using the same basic categories as those selected by the children. On the suggestion of a child we move "being brave" to the bonus points category. It is argued that trips to dentists and doctors are few and far between and will result in an unfair (distorted) scoring. But then we talk of inner bravery—being loyal to a friend and standing by her despite peer pressure, being honest despite the

consequences—and we begin to look for this in our own actions. "Becoming strong" is relegated as an assignment for the gym teacher, who agrees to monitor and report children's progress. Every teacher who interacts with our children is informed of our training program, and we are ready to begin. The letter sent home reads:

> On November 10th, we will begin our Hero Training Program. The qualities we (the teachers and students) have decided to develop and record are listed below. We ask that you (the parents) help us in our task. Please put this sheet on your refrigerator or bulletin board and record your child's progress until December 15th. Every time you observe an act of kindness, cooperation, patience, etc. please mark an X on the corresponding line. We ask that you spend a couple of minutes each day at bedtime to discuss and document these qualities with your child. Please have high expectations for your child and do not document behavior that is less than expected. This is also a good month (an expression of Thanksgiving) to read books about unsung heroes who help others constantly, to talk about your own professions and ways you help others, and to do family projects that help the environment or the community. We have been inspired by our study of heroes. We hope this process inspires everyone at home.

The group appreciates that this training program is a matter of individual improvement, not a competition. Therefore it is immaterial that some children will attain more points than others. The objective is clear: Each child will try to be the best hero trainee possible. We also ask children to come up with strategies that will enable them to assist each other. They decide that they will look out for each other and that they will remind each other to do the right thing by gently whispering, "Be a hero." We also ask for their assistance in reporting acts of kindness and caring that are observed in the playground, when Mr. D. and I are not present.

The children, through many discussions, have understood that one does not become a hero through a month-long training program. They also understand that each child will receive a participation award, which differs from an achievement award. Yet I feel the need to readdress several issues before the grand finale.

I begin by saying, "I am a little concerned that we may have been doing some things at home and school just to gain an X on the sheet. Let's reexamine why we decided to be heroes in the first place, and let's think of ways we can help each other long after the award ceremony is over. Let's shut our eyes and think of two things: Why did we decide to do this training program, and how will we help each other to continue in the same manner after the ceremony?"

After a few moments of silence children share their thoughts:

"We wanted to be heroes because it is good and it helps everyone. I know my mom is definitely a lot happier with me these days."

"I think being heroes is good but it is difficult."

"At first it was harder, but it isn't so bad now."

"Ms. P., the gym teacher, thinks we are doing great."

"How do you feel about yourselves?" I inquire.

"Pretty good. It's not always easy, but on the whole, pretty good."

"My dad doesn't have to yell at me so much, and that feels good."

"I like being a hero, because then when I grow up, I can be the greatest ballerina and go on stage, and I will feel so happy. I'm even practicing standing on my toes every day," announces Charlene with great gusto, and everyone smiles. Her imagination has, from the very start, been completely captivated by the training program, and the children are used to her enthusiastic comments.

"What can we do to make sure we continue our efforts after the December break?" I persist.

"We can remind each other like we do now."

"You and Mr. D. can remind us."

"You can begin another training program," I say semifacetiously.

A few children groan.

"Maybe we will be heroes by then," another adds hopefully.

"How about an oath like we saw in the Olympics," I suggest. "Do you remember how athletes from all over the world started the event by promising that they would play in the spirit of true sportsmanship, not merely to win?"

"Yeah, but what would we say?"

"I like that!" Charlene exclaims. "We could place our hands on our hearts and say, 'I promise to be a hero.' "

"And that we will always, always, try."

"That we will be good sports when we play."

Together we compose an oath, taking a vote when necessary, until everyone is satisfied. The children help Mr. D. to spell each word as he writes on the blackboard and the final version, not as elaborate as I had hoped, states:

I, _____ [child's name], promise that I will continue to try to be a hero. I will not do it to score points, but I will do it because it is the right thing to do.

Trying to create a little dissonance, I remark, "If *we* shouldn't do helpful, kind acts for the sake of scoring points, do you think *I* shouldn't bother to count up the points tomorrow?"

There is a loud protest. All except two want the points tallied up.

"I would actually like to tally the points," I tell them, "because it will give us some important information."

"It will tell us who is the best."

"Is that what we are looking for?"

"No."

"I'll give you a clue: The points will help *you*. . . ."

"I know—it will tell me what I did good at."

"And what we didn't do so good at."

"Why is that important?"

"Well, if you know you did good at something, you can be happy about it, and the other parts, you can say, 'I have to do some more of that.' "

"That's right," I affirm, "it will help you to understand what you do well and at what you must work a little harder."

Two days later, parents assemble in our classroom for the ceremony while the children wait excitedly in the small back room. A little platform (two tables) has been constructed, with three steps leading up to it. A large banner over the platform proclaims "HEROES OF THE FUTURE—WAY TO GO!" Mr. D. turns on some taped music, and the children enter in single file, bow to the audience, and take their assigned seats beside the platform. The ceremony begins with a song, adapted from a sunflower song learned earlier in the year.

Like a true hero
we follow all the guidance in our hearts
As we turn toward Truth
and follow it—with love

In sincer-ity, clar-ity, we follow
In sincer-ity, pur-ity, we follow

Like a true hero
we follow all the guidance in our hearts
As we turn toward Truth
and follow it—with love

Then, as solemn music (chosen by the children) plays in the background, each child is called forth.

"Charlene, are you ready to take the oath?"

"Yes, I am."

"Place your right hand on your heart and begin."

Although the children have memorized the oath, several of them, inspired by the occasion, use additional words for emphasis, such as "I will do this forever" or "This is the very best thing to do."

Then, reading from Individual Hero Certificates, I address Charlene's strengths and weaknesses. She listens intently; this is, after all, a personal tribute from her teachers.

"Charlene, we are delighted that you took part in the Hero Training Program. Your special strengths are that you have grown to be very responsible, especially when it is time to clean up after lunch. (Charlene nods while the other children smile, remembering how she used to leave a trail of noodles or macaroni or rice behind her every day.) You are also very unselfish and always willing to share your space and materials with others. You are definitely better at following instructions than you were when we started the training program. We hope that you will continue to focus on your work and use a calm voice at all times. Mr. D. and I are proud of your efforts, and it is with great joy that we present you with the Hero Trainee Award."

Mr. D. steps forward, places a yellow ribbon with a gold star at its end around Charlene's neck, and shakes her hand. Charlene turns toward me, and I present her with the Hero Certificate and a surprise gift: a box of Hero crayons, sent to us by a proud uncle, an executive from the Crayola Company.

For each child the message is personal. I include messages that parents have written or whispered in my ear during the training period: "Tommy has been helping a lot at home but continues to torment his baby brother." "This was a first: Dinah didn't cry at the doctor's office." "Gary has been nice to the kid next door even though he doesn't like him." With the large figure of Hercules watching over the proceedings, Mr. D. awards each child a well-deserved gold star (Figure 2.17).

Finally, with Hero stars (wooden stars from a craft store, painted gold and emblazoned with the word "HERO") gleaming on their chests, the children assemble on the platform for well-deserved applause (Figure 2.18). We invite the parents to stand up with us for a few moments of reflection as we listen to "America the Beautiful." Two children spontaneously close their eyes and place their right hands on their hearts, setting the tone for my closing statement: "Let us reflect, how we, as a community, can make the world a better place by doing what is right and good—not merely to be famous, but in the spirit of trying to be real heroes."

FIGURE 2.17   Hercules Observes the Hero Award Ceremony

FIGURE 2.18   Proud Heroes

OUR LETTER TO HERCULES

On December 6th, as requested, we compose our reply to the question posed by Hercules at the beginning of the school year. Now, three months later, the children have very definite ideas, and they gush forth as I try to write rapidly on a large piece of paper.

Dear Hercules,
    Thank you for your letter. We have been studying about heroes and heroines for the last three months. We have learned a lot. We made sculptures of heroes to remind us how to be heroes ourselves and not get in trouble at school.
    We have been working on a Hero Training Program. Our teachers and parents mark scores on a sheet for us. We have been practicing some of the qualities of a hero, such as courtesy, kindness, obedience, patience, respect, responsibility, and unselfishness.
    We think a real hero has all of these qualities and some more. Other qualities are bravery, being good, compassion, unity, politeness, and kindness. We think that

a real hero should help others at home and at school; he should save people, be kind to people, and follow instructions.

We also think that a real hero should not kill others, be mean to others, do anything bad, roughhouse, push others, be selfish, poke another's eye out, or start a fight. He should not take things that belong to others or break them; he should talk things over rather than fight. He should understand that two wrongs don't make a right. He should never steal. He should never say, "I did it because he did it."

We learned that there are a lot of heroes that nobody knows about (the unsung heroes) like policemen, firefighters, those who work in an ambulance, doctors, construction workers, workers in a soup kitchen, dentists, lifeguards, and nurses.

Now we will answer your questions.

Can a woman be a hero? YES

Do you have to kill someone to be a hero? NO

Do you have to be rich to be a hero? NO

Do you have to be famous to be a hero? NO

Do you have to be strong to be a hero? NO

Do you have to kill a dragon to be a hero? NO

Do you have to fly over a tall building to be a hero? NO

Do you have to be a football champion to be a hero? NO

Do you have to be a basketball player to be a hero? NO

We have decided that we will all try to be heroes. We hope that you never forget to be a hero. When you are in a battle, try not to stop and get killed. But better yet, never get in a battle.

We would like to wish you

A Merry Christmas

A Happy Hanukkah

and A Merry Kwaanza

Love from the Kindergarten Children

WRITING THE PLAY

On their return from vacation in January we set children the task of creating a play. In the past I have used plays from books, children's magazines, and other sources, but over the years I have grown to realize the tremendous benefits from children doing their own creating—as authors, poets, and songwriters as well as scenery painters, actors, and dancers. Children's increased levels of engagement, exuberance, commitment, and perseverance far outweigh the risk-taking that is involved. When the curtain rises, there is a delicious sense of ownership in knowing that the play is the product of their hands and heads—it is truly "their" play.

On completing the writing, which usually takes about three weeks, we sit in silent reflection, marveling at the fact that this play did not exist on the face of the earth a mere three weeks ago. It was brought into being by the creative minds of a group of kindergartners living in Philadelphia. Truly amazing!

Mounting a play is an enormously potent activity. It presents children with the opportunity to appreciate and master (at least somewhat) the range of activities that a theatrical production demands: conceiving a plot and writing a sequential story; designing invitations; creating songs; learning new skills (such as dancing); acting as, and convincingly projecting, their character; memorizing a part; rehearsing until everyone has mastered their role; understanding cues; and synchronizing with others. In addition, I have found it to be the single most powerful tool for uniting the entire class as they create, argue, cast votes, review, revise, and eventually cooperate to produce a one-hour musical. Finally, it boosts self-confidence considerably; children, even the shy ones, will regularly volunteer to perform for others.

"We can sing our play songs at the old folks home."

"We can have a special performance for our third grade buddies."

"We can create another play for the end of the year."

Assuming that one is convinced of all the advantages, what is the process for creating a play from scratch, especially with a group of excited young children? I begin by delivering my usual playwriting speech. This year, I tell them: "The only things you have to keep in mind are that this is a story about heroes and that you will continue to be your Halloween character. You are in charge of the rest. As authors, you can choose any setting, the characters can do anything you decide, you can sing any song you select, and the story can have any kind of ending you like. Each one of you has the deciding vote on what your own character can and can't do. Think about this for a minute, and let's begin. Who would like to go on stage first?" (A clear space in the middle of the room is our make-believe stage.)

Brian volunteers enthusiastically, "Me, me, I'll go first."

The group smiles and sighs, "We knew he would say that. Let him go first."

"As St. Patrick, I want you to decide where you would like to be when the play opens," I tell Brian.

"In England."

"Why in England?"

Brian studies the world map behind him, on which are located the origins of all their Halloween heroes. "I guess I traveled from France to England teaching Christianity."

"And what are you doing in England?"

"I guess I am just walking around thinking about how I have to teach people in England."

"Help me write the introduction. Where in England are you, and what kind of day is it?"

"He could be in a field, or a farm or something."

"Yes, I'd like to be walking in a field, and there could be cows or sheep or some other animals. It could be a sunny day. I wouldn't want to get wet in the rain."

"Show me how you would enter the stage and what you would say."

Mr. D. strums his guitar as Brian strolls across saying, "I wonder who I can teach Christianity to. In France I taught many people, and now I must do the same in England."

"Did the people in France listen to your teachings?" I ask.

"Not really."

Since our play will be a musical, I suggest, "Maybe you can sing a song about that."

"What, that no one will listen to?"

Jared jumps up. "We have a song about listening. We could use that."

By now the children are familiar with our method for creating new songs. We find a melody that children already know and then change the words to project the meanings we wish to convey. Mr. D. rummages among our audiotapes and finds the song "Listen" by Jack Hartman.

"Brian do you like this melody? Would you like to work with Mr. D. to create your own song?"

"Sure."

"All right, what happens after you sing the song? Who wants to go on stage next?"

King Arthur and Sir Lancelot volunteer simultaneously, and the class decides that King Arthur should enter first.

"Show me how you will enter and what the two of you will say to each other."

King Arthur walks across the stage. St. Patrick turns around and says, "Who are you and why are you here?"

"I am King Arthur, and this is my country."

"Hello, King Arthur, I am pleased to meet you. I am here to teach about Christianity."

This is how the final draft of the opening scene turned out:

SCENE 1

Narrator: Once upon a time, a long, long time ago, St. Patrick traveled from France to England teaching people about Christianity. On this warm, sunny day, he is walking along the fields, watching the sheep graze on the grass, and wondering who his new students will be.

St. Patrick: In France I taught so many people about Christianity, but they never listened. Very few people want to listen to the things I have to say. I wonder whom I can teach in England. Will anyone listen to me? (Looks at some sheep) Will you listen to me?

(He sings)

Listen, really listen
To what I have to say
Listen, really listen
There's so much I have to say

It's so nice to pray and talk to your Lord
It's better than sitting down and just being bored
But there are times when being quiet is best
And you listen, listen to your heart

(The song has two more verses.)

For the next three weeks I work on the script using children's suggestions, adding, deleting, and refining. And every morning the children wait eagerly to hear and critique what I have transcribed. This year they choose three different locations for our three-scene play: a farm in England, a redwood forest in North America, and an open arena in Greece. Each child, defining his or her part in the play, composes a song with Mr. D.'s help. Moses, in his usual loud voice, persuades the class to allow him to deliver the Ten Commandments on stage. And since he has just begun violin lessons, he decides to play the violin as he delivers each commandment. The play thus derives its title, "The Heroes and the Ten Commandments." Performance is scheduled for the middle of March, and we begin rehearsals (Figure 2.19).

The crux of the play, as it turns out, is the choice heroes have to make at various points between virtue and pleasure (depicted as two Greek columns on stage). Hercules, for example, wakes up one morning and is reluctant to follow his usual routine of exercise and meditation with Odysseus. The temptation to relax and be idle grips him. Odysseus counsels him, and together they sing (our adaptation of the Hercules song from the movie):

> *To look beyond the glory*
> *Is the hardest part*
> *For a hero's strength*
> *Is measured by his heart.*

FIGURE 2.19   Members of the Cast

Like a shooting star
I will go all the way
I will act with virtue
I won't fear anything at all
I don't care how far
I can go all the way
'Til I find the light of wisdom
Shining inside my heart.

HEROES OF INDIA

Since the beginning of the year the children, fueled by the kindergarten interna-
tional travel legends of older siblings and friends, clamor to be "taken" to India. We
could make this a detour, I thought, without losing our focus on heroes. Therefore
after the children return from spring break, we decide to spend the last two
months of school on a pretend trip investigating India. We spend three weeks
preparing for and embarking on this pretend trip, complete with passports, tickets,
luggage, security check (using a Dustbuster), a basement converted into the interior of a plane (cockpit, passenger seats, in-flight Indian snacks and Hindi movies),
pilots, and travelers checks. As we "journey" through India, we learn numbers
and rhymes in four different languages; dress in sarees, sarongs, and turbans (see
Color Plates 6 and 7); prepare and taste a variety of Indian foods; appreciate Indian
musical instruments and dances (see Color Plate 8); and learn about the qualities
valued by the culture, especially hospitality, courtesy, and respect. Throughout the
journey we maintain individual journals documenting people, places, and events.
New hero concepts emerge.

"If there are over twenty-eight languages in India, a hero would have to
learn a lot of languages."

"Gandhi was a hero, but he looks very weak and he dressed kinda weird."

"Gandhi gave people good advice. That helped many people."

"People who work in orphanages are heroes."

"Those who share their water with others in the desert are heroes."

"Those who give people a place to stay during the monsoon are heroes."

The Ramayana (the exploits of Rama), one of the two major epics of India,
captivates the children with its mythic heroes, evil antagonists, and monkey
armies. Borrowing four three-hour video segments of the story from the Indian
store, we watch spellbound as miraculous events unfold on the screen. As children
lie on Batman and Barbie blankets at naptime, I sit among them translating this
great legend from Hindi to English, interpreting events in terms of their religious
and cultural significance. For the first time I view this story, familiar from my own
childhood, through the eyes of American children. The cultural exchange goes
both ways!

Our final project takes the form of creating, writing, and illustrating an Indian heroic legend. To help with the writing, we create a wall of Indian words with

separate alphabetical lists of male and female names, places, rivers, mountains, animals, fruits, and flowers. Most of the children create their own legends, but Brian, still enamored of the Ramayana, writes his version of the story, in which the heroes turn out to be monkeys.

**MY VERSHIN OF THE RAMAYANA
BY BRIAN DOUGALL**

[underlined words are those spelled with teacher assistance.]

Rama was up with the Indian GODS and his wife was <u>captured</u> by a demon and Hanuman <u>tried</u> to help her. But there were ather demons. The monkey was hiding in a tree. When all the demons were gone the monkey <u>jumped</u> down from the tree. He said, "come with me." The woman said, "ok. He took her with him to find Rama. They finalie found him. Hanuman said, "bye-bye," He went back. It took him a long time But when he got back the demons were <u>conquering</u> the land. the monkey tried to help But he couleit do it But the arme of monkeys helpet him. They won. The peple cherd [cheered]. They took a baw [bow] they were prowd.

The End

On the very last day of school the children, seated in special "author" chairs, read their legends to the group. Then, before Mr. D. and I send them onward with hugs and endless blowing of kisses, we all hold hands in a circle and solemnly repeat our hero oath: "We, the students and teachers of kindergarten, promise that we will continue to try to be heroes. We will not do it to score points or to be famous, but we will do it because it is the right thing to do."

COMMENTARY

The extended process of determining what makes a hero again exemplifies how Usha shapes the agenda or, as she likes to think of it, shapes the quest, while fully honoring children's ideas. Believing as she does that children, given sufficient time for questions and reflection, will come to appreciate the qualities of a true hero, Usha doesn't have to lay on the message; she can let it emerge. Let's see how this plays out.

The conversation is about firefighters who save people. Usha might have concluded by saying, "Right, you've got it." She doesn't. This is not an exercise in right answers. Usha is helping the children to refine their own notions. So instead of a blanket endorsement, she interjects, "The firefighters were just doing their job. Does that make them heroes?" She then asks the children if they think the firefighters get paid a lot of money for their work. Subtly, she is getting across the point that, sure, saving lives is heroic but less so if you are commanded to do it or if a great reward is hanging in the balance.

Usha is asking these kindergarten children to consider the endlessly complex relationship of our judgments to action, motive, effort, and reward. The same theme is pursued with doctors: Can you be unkind (motive) but still a good doctor (action)? The children aren't there yet; naturally enough, they think generous deeds are accompanied by generous rewards, so yes, firefighters inevitably must be paid a lot of money for the risky actions they take. Usha might have set them straight by saying, "No, they are not paid a huge amount of money. They like to help people even though it doesn't make them rich." She doesn't. Instead, she suggests that the class get information from real firefighters. Let the children get the information from the most authentic source. Let them puzzle over the relationship of compensation to work and puzzle over fairness.

Usha is more likely to pursue a child's discovery than to give the "right" answers. A child notes that rather than killing King Pellinore, King Arthur forgave him. Usha does not respond, "Yes, to forgive is a truly heroic quality," end of discussion, but nudges the child to pursue this insight. "How does that make him a hero?" she asks. The child answers, "Because it is good to forgive. Like when we are playing and someone says, 'I'm sorry,' and I say, 'that's OK, you can play with us.' " The child's answer shows that he genuinely gets it. He is not trying to please the teacher with the right answer but is assimilating the answer into his own life. It is *his* answer for *himself,* not for her.

Again, Usha chooses to tell the class a story of a man who worked in a soup kitchen. Rather than explain *why* this man is a hero, however, she asks *if* he is one. The children themselves begin to ponder whether working "for days and days and days" without recognition might not be more admirable than a single big splash.

It is her suggestion too that, in imitation of the Olympics, the children take a hero oath. But it is up to the children to compose the oath. (They also had the freedom to reject the idea.) In the end, as it turns out, Usha is a bit disappointed with the brevity of the content. However, so be it; it is *their* oath and the chances of it taking hold are much greater than if she had written out a more elaborate one.

Just as Usha manages simultaneously to lead and follow children, so too she is able simultaneously to do group and individual work. Everyone has an "I like . . ." book, but each book is composed of different likes expressed at different levels. Usha does not have reading groups; they unduly homogenize abilities. Instead, children read by themselves and with her individually. And so it goes: Each child has an individual Hero Training Program, but everyone is committed to becoming a hero; each child sculpts an individual bust, but all share in the museum presentation; each child contributes his or her own heroic qualities to a common enormous face; each child is a different Halloween character, but all participate in a joint theatrical production.

Once more we note Usha's irreverence toward the passage of time. The children spend three months defining a hero. They could have looked it up in the dictionary and posted it in three minutes!

A field trip is not a deadline to comply with, not a "must do" on the third Friday of alternate months, but scheduled as befits the class's activities. The trip to the Rodin museum, for example, grows out of the human body studies and is taken only after children have begun to do their own drawing and sculpting. It comes after the children have become familiar with the work of Rodin, familiar enough to recognize his major works when they go to the museum. The children have become genuinely learned—more so, I imagine, than most of the other museum visitors, but then the other visitors were rushing through Philadelphia; these students took their time.

The art show too has a protracted gestation. It takes children a month to complete their self-sculpture, their box sculptures, and their hero with many faces. They spend more than a month in their Hero Training Program. Even so, Usha regrets that time—the winter break—interrupts the work.

Finally, note how ambitious Usha is for her students. Although she carefully orchestrates the development of reading, writing, and arithmetic skills, her goals are considerably higher. Because she has faith in the children's capacity and curiosity, she is more demanding, candid, and tough than many teachers of the young.

Usha's class is an introduction to world culture. She and the children plunge into the history, geography, literature, art, architecture, music, and social practices of other societies, present and past. The plunge is not a shallow splash. Study is balanced by doing. The children construct artifacts, compose paintings and songs, dress up, and prepare different foods to secure a deeper understanding of others. Parents are cautioned not to underestimate their children's sophistication.

In the protracted schedule and the insistence on high standards, Usha models and mentors her "passionate inquiry" approach to learning. Heroes of the past and present are to be approached modestly, with reverence for their character and humility before their accomplishments. The tasks they performed came from a base of great knowledge, not easily acquired. They must be studied well to be appreciated adequately.

In the Hero Training Program, points for good deeds are not distributed evenly among the children; Usha is not concerned that some will receive more than others. The children know that she values them, each fully and equally. For the most part they too recognize, and often calmly volunteer, their own and each other's shortcomings. Usha is willing to point out areas in which they have improved and areas in which they need to improve. These refined, individualized, mostly mutual judgments are, of course, a much higher form of respect than whitewashing everyone with the same unrefined, inaccurate, and not fully sincere strokes.

Usha sees no need to continuously prop up children's self-esteem. Yes, it is important and pleasurable to point out genuine improvement and success, but it is also important to point out difficulties and setbacks in order to sustain and increase accomplishments. Progress is sometimes slow and arduous, not always a gift for the asking. So children need to think about enduring effort, the work to be done after the applause stops.

They also need to think about others. Note Usha's closing statement on the occasion of the hero ceremony: "Let us reflect, how we, as a community, can make the world a better place by doing what is right and good—not merely to be famous, but in the spirit of trying to be real heroes."

CHAPTER THREE

THE PRINCESS AND
GOOD QUALITIES

The Princess (see Color Plate 9), her letter, her gifts, and the urgent need to build a castle help to jump-start the year with a bustle of excitement and activity. Her request for good qualities, meanwhile, sets the moral tone. Each day for a week we open new gifts—boxes of classroom materials that turn out to be exactly what we require.

"How did the Princess know that we needed markers, paper, and erasers?" a child asks. Another grabs for the marker box, but Carl stops her short.

"Remember, we promised to take care of her gifts and use them well," he says firmly, if a bit self-righteously, and so we set about finding logical spaces and containers to put away the materials.

"What does it mean to take care of markers and use them well?" I question.

"Say, 'thank you' to them?"

"I know—we should put the tops back on when we finish."

"Yes, my sister left the tops off her red and pink markers, and they dried up."

"We shouldn't scribble on the tables, and we shouldn't waste them."

"We shouldn't pound the markers on the paper because the tips get mushed up, and then they don't work so good."

"Does this have anything to do with the good qualities the Princess spoke about?" I probe.

"Is taking care of things a good quality?" Hannah asks.

"It certainly is, but do you know what it is called?" I ask.

"Caring about your stuff."

"Remembering."

"Not being messy."

"They are all part of responsibility," I tell them as I write the word on a Good Qualities List that we begin to compile.

BUILDING THE PRINCESS'S CASTLE

As children pore over the books Mr. D. has gathered from several libraries, we learn about the structure of castles—about turrets, gatehouses, drawbridges, moats, baileys, towers, battlements, merlons, and crenelations—and we begin to realize that castles, like homes, also need kitchens, bedrooms, and bathrooms. We look at castles around the world and discover that initially they were built of timber and earth and later of stone, with stone walls up to thirty feet thick—longer than our entire classroom! However, the purpose of our castle, to provide a place for the Princess's visit, differs from that of most castles: to ensure protection from enemy attacks. Whew! The children are relieved; our castle will not need such thick walls.

We record each new word that we unearth on our ABC chart: A for alcazars (Spanish castles); B for baileys, battlements; C for castles, crenelations, chapels; D for dungeons, donjon, dirt, defense. Before our study is completed, every child will have composed an "I like . . ." book in which they draw pictures of things they like about castles and either write or dictate a sentence. But we begin our study of castles by asking children the basic question "What is a castle?" There is an interesting evolution to their responses. At first, because their categorical knowledge is scant—they may recognize castles, they may have built sand castles, but they have not formulated the concept of a castle—the replies are self-referential:

"A castle is a thing you go into. You eat there, you sleep there, you stay there, and you play there—if they let you."

"A castle is where a prince and princess live. I would love to be a princess and live there."

"A castle is so much fun. You can catch prisoners and put them in dungeons."

A month later, with a greatly enriched knowledge base and practice in formulating generalized definitions, their answers are more informed and objective:

"A castle is a strong building used to keep away the enemies."

"A castle is a fortress for a king. It is from a Latin word that means fortress."

"A castle is a place from where the king rules and where the treasures are kept and also the weapons."

On large sheets of paper each child designs a castle for the Princess. We measure the space available for this project in the room between the two kindergarten classes, and we talk about the materials we will use in our construction. Then, from the collective designs we choose the features that we agree will be possible (not the drawbridges, moats, and dungeons so close to their hearts!)

The large, now opened "gift" boxes are an obvious choice for constructing castle walls. We talk about how the process of recycling is a way of taking care of the earth—another component of responsibility. Boxes are stacked and restacked until walls stay upright around a seven- by five-foot area. Duct tape, hot glue guns, and wooden rods inside boxes provide at least minimal stability for a fairly tottering structure. The roof, a very large piece of strong cardboard found in the science building, is hoisted on top of the walls but soon begins to sag in the middle. A child, fearful of an impending collapse, hurries into the center and supports the roof with upraised arms, giving us the idea for a pillar. A tall, rectangular box soon serves this function, and now we need only towers and battlements. We use intermittently spaced, upright shoe boxes on the roof to give the impression of battlements and I point out the ABAB pattern (shoe box, space, shoe box, space), recently explored in math, that we have thus created.

With the basic structure in place, we set about the important task of designing a crest that will represent our class's aspirations. We look at various crests, brainstorm ideas, list every idea on the blackboard, discuss the merits of each title, and finally select one through a class vote: The Secret Castle of Love. How do we portray this symbolically? Children suggest two hands folded over the heart as a representation of love and a sparkling gem behind the hands to represent the secret (Figure 3.1). With this overall motif in place, we design wallpaper for the castle. Square pieces of paper with drawings of children doing loving deeds are arranged like tiles along the outer walls, and the in-between spaces are grouted with shimmering silver and gold glitter (see Color Plate 10). The children work diligently to produce their best drawings. This is, after all, a castle for a princess. For the inner walls we draw on our math curriculum—squares, rectangles, triangles, pentagons, and hexagons—and arrange silver paper shapes, inlaid with colored shapes, in an open mosaic pattern around windows with square window panes (see Color Plate 11).

Finally, we make flags representing good qualities that will fly high over our castle. Through consultation with parents, librarians, and other adults, children come up with a variety of qualities, and we make over sixteen colorful flags. Finishing touches for the castle are provided by gold paper doilies edging the

FIGURE 3.1   A Crest for Our Castle

roof, fake jewelry embedded in the ceiling, a rug for the interior, and fake potted plants for the exterior (see Color Plate 12).

PREPARING FOR THE PRINCESS

It's time to get ready for the Princess's visit. I suspect that she will ask us about good qualities—not just names for them, as arrayed on our flags, but how they are transformed into action. The children agree. In all likelihood, that is what she will want to know. We read stories and biographies, and discuss how the characters do and do not display each quality. Then we rate all the characters on a scale of 1 to 5 for their inherent good qualities and intentions.

Now it is time to go from the fictional characters to ourselves. With parental guidance, each child chooses a virtue that he or she will focus on and practice at school and at home. When the Princess arrives, the children will be ready to demonstrate their "getting gooder" efforts for her reaction. To represent their virtue of choice, each boy designs his princely shield and each girl a conical princess crown emblazoned with artwork (Figures 3.2 and 3.3). Charity, for example, is depicted by a prince giving food and money to the poor, and honesty is depicted by a child with several thinking bubbles above her head—the untruth bubbles crossed out and the truth bubble outlined in gold.

FIGURE 3.2   All Dressed Up and Waiting

FIGURE 3.3   Lady-in-Waiting

Anticipation builds as the teachers record children's "good qualities in action" on a long scroll of paper. We believe the Princess will approve and be proud of the class efforts.

> John was brave and patient while waiting for the school nurse.
> George shared his lunch with Sarah when she left her lunch on the bus.
> Amy taught Paul how to tie his shoelaces.
> Paul reminded Amy to retrieve her jacket after gym.

Interested in this documentation we are providing, the children pay close attention. They gather around at spare moments to read the sentences written about them and to help us spell words. Parents are invited to participate in the Princess's visit. They provide food, drink, and decorations, while children prepare individual speeches, create a welcome song with Mr. D., and pull out every minuscule musical experience they have encountered.

"I can play the flute to accompany our opening song," George suggests, although his only prior experience was two futile attempts on a toy flute. So we get George a flute. The joy and delight in his twinkling eyes and the puffy cheeks, red and distended from his efforts, make up for his lack of technique (Figure 3.4). (As it turned out, George, now completing fourth grade, will play the cello with the Main Line Chamber Orchestra of Philadelphia.) Only Marco, our musically inclined

**FIGURE 3.4   The Ardent
Flute Player**

student from Brazil, appears not to be engaged in the proceedings. Noting the withdrawal, Mr. D. searches for a melody that Marco can play on a musical instrument. The rhythm of a fairly raucous African song hits its mark. Marco begins to practice on the drums with enthusiasm while others learn the words of the song. We are ready!

THE PRINCESS VISITS

On the designated day, the Princess, a remarkably talented parent I encountered three years ago and recruited for this occasion, enters our class through a winding "secret" stairway that emerges from the basement. Robed in green velvet and yellow satin, a long elegant black wig masking her normally light hair, her crown and jewelry sparkling and resplendent, she walks across the room to a throne fashioned by the children (see Color Plate 13). Trumpets (Mr. D.) blare, and violins (George's parents) play, while children, round-eyed and enchanted, gasp audibly. Each child comes forth to greet the Princess and tell her of the virtue they have chosen: kindness to animals, truth, patience, helpfulness, love (Figure 3.5). Each virtue is lis-

FIGURE 3.5   Conversing with the Princess

tened to, applauded, and often elaborated on by the Princess, who has been well briefed about the preparations for her visit. Then the Princess invites questions:

"Why did you want to leave your castle? Wasn't it wonderful there?" a child inquires.

"Where is your country?"

"What does its name mean?"

"What is the magical creature you ride on?" (referring to her letter from earlier in the week).

"My castle is wonderful," she replies. "But my people think only of the beautiful things in the castle, not the beautiful things in their hearts." Introducing Greek mythology, her speciality, the Princess continues, "This is why my country is called Malanima, the land of unkind hearts. My magical steed and close companion is a chimera, with the head of a lion, the body of a goat, and the tail of a serpent." The children are fascinated.

"What's a steed?"

"What's a chimera?"

"How could a goat have a lion's head?"

With great pride they perform the songs they have practiced. The Princess gives them a standing ovation.

"You have learned songs from many parts of the world. There is something good, something we can learn from every single country. Recently, I visited Korea."

The two children adopted from Korea cannot believe their ears. "We come from Korea," they chorus, and everyone pitches in to share their knowledge of other lands—cities, food, clothing, and especially language.

From a rose-pink document decorated with gold and silver and entitled "Good Qualities," the Princess reads aloud a list of suggestions for children of all ages. The "Good Qualities" document (actually designed by Mr. D.) is hung on the wall as a reminder of the Princess's advice. The list includes statements such as:

Be kind to the earth and accept gladly what the earth gives to you.

Be patient with your brothers and sisters.

Listen to the wisdom in your heart and the wisdom given to you by your parents.

The concept of wisdom—the inner guiding voice—is explored. "What is wisdom?" a child asks. "It's the kind of knowing that comes from deep down, like when you just *know* that though it would be fun to stuff colored tissue paper down the drain and watch the colors run, you shouldn't do it," the Princess answers. "Oh, I get it, like when I just *know* I shouldn't tell my mom and dad that I brushed my teeth when I didn't."

Then it is time for food and drink. George's parents serenade the Princess with violins while individual children walk up to the Princess, telling stories, sharing secrets, and hugging her spontaneously. But soon the Princess must depart. The children sing, "Dear Princess, you're always welcome here, 'cause you are our friend, please come again, don't stay away, come back some day!" As the lights go off, they blow her a kiss and shut their eyes. The Princess disappears down the stairs.

The carefully choreographed visit works! We have been in school for only five weeks, and already the "goodness" motif has taken hold, not just in theory, but also in action. With nothing but the gentlest of reminders, cooperation, patience, kindness, respect, high standards of work, and personal responsibility prevailed throughout the complex tasks of building the castle, throughout the preparations for the Princess's visit, and most especially during her visit, convincing me once again that an enticing curriculum can eliminate most of what we call "classroom management" issues.

THE KINDNESS BOX

A kindness box instituted before the Princess's visit now takes center stage. The colorful wooden box has beside it index cards, pencils, markers, and a list of children's names with matching photographs. Whenever a child perceives an act of kindness, she records it on an index card and drops it into the box. Recording can take the form of a drawing by the child with a corresponding message written by the teacher or a statement written by a group of children who assist each other in spelling the words correctly. The kindness box is opened once a week, messages are read, and individuals are cheered. The box not only honors various children but is a constant reminder for children to stay alert to kindness in all its multiple expressions. For example, one note reads, "Chip was very kind. He comforted Jack, who was upset because he never got to turn off the lights at naptime. Chip said,

'You can come to my house for my birthday and turn off the lights before I blow out the candles.' " Another note says, "Hannah was very kind. She crawled under the tables and picked up the spilled Cheerios."

Gradually, we seek to extend kindness to others in the school—other children, other teachers, the secretary, cafeteria personnel, janitors, and visitors. And as we notice subtler shades of kindness, we learn to thank others, especially those who have always been kind to us—mothers, fathers, grandparents, uncles, and aunts. The day before Thanksgiving we spend a special hour writing thank-you notes to parents and relatives, and for the Chinese New Year we make special gifts for parents: red notes in red envelopes, offering to do a household chore as a way of saying "Thanks!"

VISITING A CASTLE

Mr. D. finds a unique neighborhood castle that we can actually visit. Fonthill Museum is a castle with forty-four rooms, eighteen fireplaces, and over two hundred windows (Figure 3.6). It was built by Henry Mercer in 1912 with the help of only eleven men and one horse. Across a field is a tile works that was constructed to preserve the hand-made craft of designing and sculpting clay ornaments. A "real castle," designed by a single individual and covered with exquisite hand-made tiles—nothing could be better, given our fall experience.

FIGURE 3.6   Fonthill Museum

We begin preparations for the trip. The bus ride will be an hour and a half long. We ask children for strategies to keep themselves occupied and quiet on the trip. The children suggest word games, number games, drawing, coloring, and the ever-popular GameBoy. We ask each child to pack a special assortment of material they will need on the ride, with a little extra to share with a neighbor.

Then, to give them a real appreciation for tile making, we get a block of clay from the art teacher; soften it to make it pliable; roll it out; cut it into square, rectangular, and triangular tiles; and etch our favorite designs with homemade tools. We carry our tiles on trays to the art studio and wait four days until they are baked and ready for the final glaze. After estimating and making guesses about the area our tiles will cover, we lay them on the floor to check out our hypotheses. We then reflect on the incredible patience and perseverance it must take to make enough tiles to cover entire walls, ceilings, and floors in the castle. We note that it took twenty of us two hours to make our tiles. The more dramatic children in our class fall down in a pretend faint on contemplating such a prospect.

The visit to the castle is magical. The seemingly haphazard design of the castle and the random tile patterns in certain rooms look like kindergarten artwork. The winding stairways, the dark spooky corners, and the walls and columns embedded with tiles of every color captivate children and parents alike. The tile factory evokes special interest (Figure 3.7), and children ask the workers a battery of

FIGURE 3.7   Standing Next to a Kiln at the Tile Works

questions, even sitting in rapt attention to watch a twenty-minute video on tile making. A child's comment at lunch summed up the experience: "I've waited my whole life for this day!"

The next day children build their own miniature castles out of sugar cubes, glue, and toothpicks on large cardboard trays. A lot of care, concentration, and patience is required. The castles are painted with silvery-gray paint, and permanent markers are used to make mosaic tile patterns.

ANOTHER CASTLE

A short distance from Fonthill is another castlelike structure, the Mercer Museum, built by Henry Mercer in 1916. This museum houses over 50,000 antique objects from the preindustrial era and represents sixty trades. From tools used in whaling ships to sewing thimbles used in regular households, the museum oozes history. Such a place demands a detour. Everyone—children, parents, and teachers—will benefit from this experience.

To introduce children to the concept of tools, we play a game (adapted from psychologist Jerome Bruner) in which two Antarctic teams try to catch and bring back the largest number of seals. In the game, seals take the form of paper clips hidden all over the classroom, in pairs, individually, or in packs. The only instruction is "You cannot touch the paper clips with your hands." Very soon children begin to invent tools of every kind—paper scoops, pencils used like chopsticks, books used as carrying trays.

Then, to examine how tools have changed, we trace backward from the computer to electric typewriters, to manual typewriters, to ballpoint pens, to fountain pens, to dipping-ink pens, to quills. Using examples from parents', grandparents', and our own lives, we speak of the patience and care that were required to use the tools of the "olden days."

After our visit to the museum, we create our own tool museum by asking each family to unearth old, unusual tools that have been used by members of the family. We have fun guessing the identity and use of each tool. Personal stories about Henry's great-grandfather who had shod horses, Carl's great-great-grandmother who had used a butter churn, and Hannah's grandmother who had, every single Sunday, made ice cream for her children in a hand-operated ice cream machine— these form the real history of our kindergarten commonwealth.

MY HOUSE

The study of castles, especially children's amazement at the number and size of castle rooms, doorways, and windows, led to a discussion about the size and shape of their own homes. We followed up on this interest because it is in the home where the child truly "lives" and where good qualities are most likely to be developed.

Why is the door of a regular house smaller than the door of a castle? Who decides door size? Can the tallest person on the school campus enter our classroom door? What about the tall basketball players? Why do we have windows? How did they bring this wide table into our classroom? Do you have furniture in your house that is wider than your door? How does water come into the faucet? Why are most rooms square or rectangular? Children use pattern blocks and graph paper to design a floor plan with triangular rooms, octagonal rooms, and even circular rooms. With parents' help we graph the numbers of windows, doors, chimneys, chairs, cushions, and lamps in each person's house. We also count the numbers of steps to the nearest fire hydrant, neighbor's house, tree, and sidewalk.

As we talk of apartments, condominiums, rowhouses, and townhouses, the discussion centers on what makes a place a home. In class we make a list of the good qualities that help to make a house a home. Then we enlist parents' participation and even assign parent homework. We send home a large cardboard cutout house that they are to fill on one side with pictures, drawings, and photographs and on the other with a written statement, both sides depicting "What Makes Your House a Home?" We request participation and contribution from every member of the household. On three consecutive days parents arrive with their children to observe or make joint presentations of their compositions (Figure 3.8).

FIGURE 3.8   What Makes a House a Home?

A musically talented family with three young children assembled these messages on their cardboard house:

WHAT MAKES A HOUSE A HOME?

All You Need Is Love
Love Is All You Need

The love of God	Being together
Praying together	Jumping on the bed
Playing with my brother and sister	Fluffy pillows
Inviting my friends over	Cooking together
When the house is really clean	A little mess
Watching T. V. together	Good food
Playing with toys	Singing
Watching the baseball game with dad	Dancing and drumming
Lots of hugging and kissing	Growing vegetables
Reading stories	Feeling safe and warm
The Power of Prayer	The Joy of Music
Making Memories	Returning to the SOURCE

ENLARGING OUR CONCEPT OF HOME

A charming, thought-provoking book, "A House Is a House for Me" by Mary Ann Hoberman, extends our concept of "home." Verses such as "The cookie jar's home to cookies. The breadbox is home to bread. My coat is a house for my body. My hat is a house for my head"[1] send the children off on a new adventure. For two weeks they view everything through this magnifying "house" lens, compiling lists of houses at home and school: A cassette box is a home for a cassette, a frame is a house for a picture, a soccer ball is a home for air. We cover an entire wall with magazine pictures of Jello boxes, pickle jars, stables, kennels, birdcages, CD organizers, gloves, and seeds—everything is a house!

This work uncovers the literary talents of the group. I marvel at their level of abstraction—a book is a house for ideas, a computer is a house for knowledge, a flower is a house for color. Marco, whose English is improving rapidly, comes alive on this project, volunteering, "My room is a house for my bed, my bed is my house at nighttime, and my head is a home for my dreams." Later in the year we steer their literary talents toward idioms. Stay tuned!

HOUSES AROUND THE WORLD

House questions proliferate:
"I thought all houses had sloping roofs."
"I wonder why some houses are built so high above the ground?"

[1]From *A House Is a House for Me* by Mary Ann Hoberman, copyright © 1978 by Mary Ann Hoberman. Used by permission of Viking Penguin, an imprint of Penguin Putnam Books for Young Readers, a division of Penguin Putnam, Inc. All rights reserved.

"Did your house in India look like our houses, Ms. B.?"

We hang a large world map on the wall and begin to investigate why houses are built differently in different parts of the world. We focus on climate: tropical, arctic, and temperate. After understanding the rudiments of weather—rain, wind, sunshine—we locate various places on the map and hypothesize what kind of house would be appropriate for each locale.

"This place is right on the Equator, so it must be very hot."

"If someone builds a house here, they will have to build thick walls to keep out the heat."

"Maybe a thick roof also."

"Should it have windows? I can't decide."

"The windows will let in the hot air."

"But if there are no windows, the people will die."

"It can't be hot all the time, can it?"

After much open-ended brainstorming, children are primed and ready to absorb the answers; it's back to our books about houses around the world. A special favorite is "This Is My House," written and illustrated by Arthur Dorros. Each page has a picture of a home followed by a brief description: a yurt from Mongolia, a round house from Samoa, a house on stilts from New Guinea, an adobe house from Mexico. The simple yet colorful pictures are appealing to the children, and they decide to copy the pictures individually for a wall mural.

We demonstrate the specific skills involved in reproducing a picture: mapping, proportion, angles, measurement. Then, defining four distinct stages of the project—the pencil sketch, tracing the outline with black permanent marker, painting different areas of the house with watercolor, and painting the background—we draw up a four-day project plan. In this way children will work carefully on each stage without rushing to finish the entire picture. With Mr. D.'s help, children make signs for our project area that read Patience, Practice, Perseverance.

When the pictures are completed (see Color Plate 14), I steer the children toward construction of three-dimensional houses, a perfect entry into another aspect of our math curriculum: three-dimensional shapes. Soon the classroom floor is covered with cubical tissue boxes, rectangular prism shoe boxes, spherical Styrofoam balls, yarn cones, cylindrical coffee cans, and paper towel rolls, all building materials for designer homes (Figure 3.9).

When the houses are completed, we return to our good qualities theme, speculating on the specific qualities that are required in each abode.

"If you live in a house with paper walls, you have to play music quietly, or you'll disturb everyone else."

"If ten people sleep in one room, you must cooperate. Like if one person wants to turn the lights off or something."

"If you live in a tent as you travel through the desert, you must be patient sometimes, even if you are thirsty."

"If you live on a houseboat, you must have self-control or you'll tip right over."

Meanwhile, writing, reading, and drawing skills are constantly nurtured through the creation of a variety of "house" books. Following the pattern in one of our selected readers, the children make their own *Tree House* books, writing sen-

FIGURE 3.9   Building Homes: Three-Dimensional

tences such as: "Up went the scnc (skunk), up went the fish, up went the kaml (camel), up went the munkee (monkey); down came the tree house, bim-bam-bumpy." In their *More about Houses* book a child writes, "I like teepees bcos (because) they r (are) cool." And in their version of *A House Is a House for Me,* a child writes, "A lantn (lantern) is a house for lit (light), A snak skin is a house for a snak (snake)." For Valentine's Day we make special red heart-shaped books entitled *My Heart is a House for. . . .* George fills his four pages with "My heart is a house for love; My heart is a house for compachn (compassion); My heart is a house for God; My heart is a house for loving dad and mom."

We send the princess a photo journal telling her of our house adventures and of the good qualities we are studying and practicing. She replies, encouraging children's efforts, patience, and hard work. The housing detour seems to be working, so we continue with it.

THE HOMELESS

Does every creature have a home? Rabbits have burrows, pigs have sties, horses have stables, lions have dens, but what about humans? Does every human have a house?

"I've seen the homeless."

"Yes, they sleep on the streets."

"They never work."

"They sleep in boxes."

"What do they eat?"

"Why do you think they are homeless?" I ask.

"They are poor."

"They are lazy."

"They don't want to work."

Even at ages five and six the stereotypes are evident. We talk about the various reasons one might be unable to afford a home: illness, sorrow, physical handicaps, misfortune ("Like when your house gets burned down"). We sit in silence for five minutes and reflect about how it must feel to be homeless—and how we can help.

At Thanksgiving, along with the first graders, we cook a large batch of soup and bake several loaves of fancy breads for a homeless shelter. In the winter we collect warm clothes, especially caps and gloves for those who spend cold, wintry nights on the street. We write a note of thanks in our journals for the homes we have.

"I am thankful for my home and my bed and my mom who gives me food."

"I am thankful for my house which keeps me safe."

"I am thankful for my house and my dog Huffy who sleeps in my room."

WHAT IF WE COULD DESIGN OUR OWN STREET OF HOUSES

Daniel M. Pinkwater's book *The Big Orange Splot* ignites a lot of "what if . . . ?" thinking. In the book Mr. Plumbean lives on a street where every house is exactly the same until one day a bird flying overhead accidentally drops a can of orange paint on his roof and leaves behind a big orange splot. Instead of painting over the splot, Mr. Plumbean creates the colorful house of his dreams and discovers the joy of being himself.

What if we could create our dream houses on our very own street? "And wear whatever we wish, and choose our own names," the children add. Colored paper, scissors, wallpaper, gummy shapes, glue, markers, pencils, and rulers are eagerly rounded up as children go to work.

"My house is a crystal house. I love crystals. I'll wear all nature stuff, like the Native Americans."

"Mine will be a Tiger House, strong and brave, with a tiger to guard the house."

"I'll build a loving palace with heart-shaped windows. I'll wear a long pink and purple dress and call myself Princessa Francesca."

"I'll put a lot of stepping stones around my house so people won't get their feet muddy."

"I love dome roofs, and I'll make my house pink because that is a happy color."

We create an interactive mural along the main hallway wall. Children's multicolored houses with floral gardens, fountains, and rare animals line two streets, named "Explosion of Colors Street" and "Dream House Street," while a parallel street of identical black and white houses is named "Boring Street" (Figure 3.10). A

FIGURE 3.10   Kindergartners' Dream Houses

pocket chart with a large sign explains our project, provides index cards and pencils, and invites passers-by for their comments. Teachers, school visitors, first graders, parents, and work personnel continue to drop notes and messages for a whole month. The big excitement on Fridays is counting and reading the messages. In pairs children hunch over the index cards, trying to decipher each comment—They want to read!

EXPERIMENTING WITH HOUSES

The story *The Three Little Pigs* starts us off on a series of experiments with building materials—soluble and insoluble, flammable and nonflammable, absorbent and nonabsorbent. Like the wolf, we try to huff and puff, but we cannot even blow a piece of paper across the width of a table. "But a big wind can. The 'hands' of the wind can tear down a house," a child remarks. Once again, I am struck by the children's naturally poetic use of language as I direct them toward our final house question: If you could build your house with any type of material, what would you choose and why?

Surrounded by groups of assisting children, Mr. D. carefully constructs miniature houses employing various building materials: a mud hut with a thatched roof, a house of raw clay bricks, a castlelike structure of baked clay, a cement and stone house, and a wooden house. For our grand experiment, the houses are placed in three large fish tanks, with two perched on our constructed hill and others placed in low-lying areas.

Four weather conditions are tested on each house: strong wind (hose from the blower end of a vacuum cleaner directed at the house); rain (water from a watering can (Figure 3.11)); storm (a combination of wind and rain with sound and lighting effects); and snow (week-old snow collected and stored in a freezer, dropped from above). Children make predictions before each phase of the experiment and then watch with great interest as roofs fly away, low-lying houses get flooded, structures collapse, and mud and clay disintegrate.

"I knew that mud house would collapse."

"That roof needed reinforcement."

"The wood house will rot if the water gets in and there is nothing to protect the wood."

"There is no drainage for that house. That's why it flooded."

We leave the houses as they are—covered with melting snow and flooded with water—to evaluate long-term weather damage over the next two weeks. Children shut their eyes, reflect on what they have learned from the experiment, and report their understandings.

"If you are going to build with clay, you must bake it or protect it in some way, or it will wash off."

"Houses must be made strong, or they will be damaged by strong winds."

"My basement always gets flooded. We should have built our house on a hill."

FIGURE 3.11   Which House Will Survive the Rain?

"I learned that when you make a house, you must make a good plan first."

The experiments take up the entire morning, yet children continue to be focused, drawing on everything they have learned in forming their responses.

MYSTERY ISLAND

In the afternoon, after the experiments and analyses, we introduce a task that involves decision making and synthesis. In pairs children are given a map of a mystery island drawn on a large piece of paper. They are instructed: "You have a map of a mystery island. No one lives on this island. The map shows you the rivers, the lakes, the four directions—north, south, east, and west—and the different amounts of rainfall in each area. Pretend that you and your partner sail in a boat and reach this island. With the information you have, find the best place on the island to build your house. Then decide what kind of house you will build."

We discuss an example: "If I built my house along the rainy northern shore and Mr. D. built his house in the central dry area near a lake, how would our houses be different?"

"You would have a lot of rain, so you may have floods."

"It's dangerous to live by the shore. The waves could come in."

"But you could walk on the beach."

"You should build a strong house on stilts—maybe with stone and cement."

"Mr. D. will not have much rain, but he can get water from the lake."

"If it gets too dry, he can dig deep in the ground and get to the water underneath."

"He can make almost any kind of house because he will be safe in the middle of the island."

Children are given forty-five minutes to complete the activity and plan their presentation. Most pairs work effectively, but one pair, having decided where to build the house, cannot resolve their conflict about the kind of house they wish to build. With a little help they finally settle on building a twin house, with each side completely different from the other in color, design, and building materials. With long pointers in their hands they explain their decision making, interrupting, contradicting, and embellishing each other's statements (Figure 3.12).

In contrast with their morning intentions—to build efficient functional houses—practicality is often disregarded in this task in favor of imagined possibilities: a picnic by the lake, a riverside restaurant, a castle on the shore.

One pair explains: "We built our house facing east so we could watch the sunrise. We picked the area with little rainfall, but by a lake so we would have water. We did this because there is good clay by the lake and we can bake bricks. And we can swim in the lake and catch fish in the rivers."

A threesome insists: "Look at the top of our house. Do you see how it is divided in three? Those are our three bedrooms, and the circles are our three bathrooms."

"Yes, that's important."

"But we really built it here because we could go to a restaurant on the river."

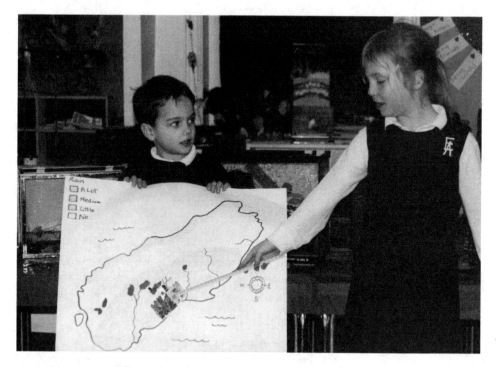

FIGURE 3.12   Building Plans for Mystery Island

Another pair remark: "We built our house in a very rainy area so we could hear the sound of rain, the sounds of fish swimming in the river, and the sound of drips on the roof. We built it by a river because we like to go canoeing and we can plant stuff all around the river."

The next day, children sum up their understandings by drawing and writing about houses. They are now able to transfer their spoken vocabulary and sentence structure into writing. This is a child's writing in December:

> I like tHe CLA HOUSE. it HAS a A FRAMe RooF. it is A StRONg HOUSE. it DiD NOD FL DOWN in tHe WiND R iN tHe RAN.

HALLOWEEN COSTUMES

Alongside our study of houses, from November to mid-December we work on creating a play about good qualities. In preparation for Halloween we asked children to select a character with a minimum of two good qualities from a legend, biography, autobiography, or real life. We informed parents of this very early in the school year and strongly encouraged them to do a lot of reading to their child prior to choosing a character. The school librarian was also recruited to help parents, and she promised to lend three take-home library books to any parent who called. On

FIGURE 3.13   Manonmani from Sri Lanka

Halloween the children came to school in costumes, told us the gist of the story, and defined the character's good qualities. Our cross-cultural characters ranged from Sir Lancelot of France, who is brave and loyal, Sir William of England (see Color Plate 15), and Princess Manonmani of Sri Lanka, who is kind and compassionate (Figure 3.13), to Anansi the spider from Africa, who is clever and persevering.

KING TAIJO AND THE SWORD OF GOOD QUALITIES

To create our play, we write each hero's name on a chart, along with the two virtues that will determine that character's role in the play. Two additional factors influence the writing of our story: the setting—the children choose Korea as the setting for the play in honor of our two Korean children—and the sword that would be used by King Arthur. A child, with his father's help, has created a mechanized papier-mâché rock that releases the sword "magically" at the right moment. The story that evolves portrays a Korean king and his son who set out to find the sword of good qualities in order to bring peace and prosperity to their country. Throughout the story various characters encounter situations that cause them to become "gooder."

Mr. D. composes songs individually with each child while I use group discussions and impromptu dramatization to construct the story with the children. Because songs, like advertising jingles, remain in one's memory for a long time, we try hard to inject inspiring themes into them. Snowy the rabbit (Figure 3.14) for example, sings (to the tune of "Keepers of the Night" by Michael Caduto):

I was frightened, Oh so frightened,
and I lived in a hole.
I was scared of the animals, the fish and the birds,
I was a very sad soul.

Then I met a wise old man,
Iron John was his name.
He told me to find my inner strength,
and now I have courage and fame.

I'm the rabbit who is brave,
the rabbit who is brave,
I jump up when you need help,
I'm the rabbit who is brave.

FIGURE 3.14   Snowy the Rabbit

The prince of Korea creates a song with his parents' help (with music from *The King and I*):

> *I've traveled around the world*
> *to find good qualities*
> *I had to go in disguise, so*
> *no one would suspect I'm a prince.*
>
> *A prince I was meant to be*
> *by working in harmony*
> *with all those who share with me*
> *the love of Truth for eternity.*
> *The result of this long journey*
> *is very plain to tell:*
> *that all of my friends in my country*
> *have faith in God as well.*
>
> *Now back to Korea I go*
> *to say, "Ana Hasayo,"*
> *which means in Korean "Hello,"*
> *and all our hearts will grow and grow!*

The performance is scheduled for mid-December, and we encounter several problems. First, it is a fair distance from our kindergarten to the performance space, and the pathways are snow-covered and slushy as we walk over for rehearsals. Second, the musical we have so joyously created is an hour long, and the children who are waiting off-stage need to be occupied. Third, we have a couple of children who do not behave responsibly in unsupervised situations. Fourth, we can schedule our practice time only in large chunks, and the children get hungry and thirsty. Fifth, we have a large number of props that need to be placed on stage and packed away every time we practice (see Color Plate 16). Sixth, I find myself getting impatient with the children, and the restlessness spreads.

Mr. D. and I take a deep breath and evaluate the situation. We have to be the first to calm down. I decide to limit my tea and coffee consumption until the performance and try to meditate for at least fifteen minutes before I come to school in the morning. Mr. D. decides to walk or bicycle to school so that he will be energetic and rejuvenated. We decide that detailed planning with the children will help us to enjoy rather than survive each day. We have a class meeting, outline all the problem areas, share our personal strategies with the children, and ask them to brainstorm group and individual solutions. As we list solutions on the blackboard, responsibility emerges as the key factor:

1. Mr. D. will go to the theater ahead of us and be responsible for setting up all the props.
2. The children will walk responsibly in assigned pairs, avoiding all mud puddles.

3. While waiting off-stage, children will create individual sketchbooks of the play. Two children offer to be in charge of distributing and collecting sketchbooks and pencils.

4. Other strategies for keeping busy include thinking of every riddle one knows, sitting still and breathing calmly, silently practicing various positions of tai chi, practicing one's song silently, and bringing something to keep hands occupied, like a Slinky, cat's cradle, or furry toy.

5. We will remind each other to do the right thing.

6. We will practice songs and spoken parts responsibly at home.

7. We will evaluate progress at the end of each rehearsal and setting new goals.

8. We will recruit one of my graduate education students to be in charge of bringing snacks and drinks from the cafeteria to the theater.

9. Recruiting school secretaries from various departments to drive us to the theater when the weather is bad.

10. Overall, everyone must try to be helpful, cooperative, and attentive.

We send this list and a copy of some songs to the Princess. We know she will be delighted by our problem-solving strategies! We design invitations and a fancy program filled with children's drawings and writings. Each child writes a sentence about his or her character:

"I am Sir Lancelot and I act like a true knight."
"I am Sir William and I am loving and kind."
"I am Anansi. I turn into a man once more."

A couple of problems continue until the day before the show, but at the "real" performance there are hardly any mishaps. The children prove to be responsible in the presence of an admiring audience of parents, relatives, and friends, but Mr. D. and I know this is just the beginning. There is more to responsibility.

APPRECIATING NATURE

The theme of good qualities is enhanced during the second semester by the children's avid interest in nature. This year in particular, recess has been a time to fill pockets with stones, bark, twigs, and weeds. Post-weekend sharing often consists of displaying newly discovered shells, bird nests, pebbles, and of course, the most prized possession: crystals. Therefore discarding our earlier plans to visit a foreign land, we wholeheartedly pursue the nature trail.

We have a class meeting to discuss what aspects of nature children would like to investigate. The choices are crystals, shells, and flowers. It is now late January, and since the whole lower school focuses on Earth Day in April, Mr. D. and I decide to weave topics such as recycling and pollution into the curriculum. Good qualities such as appreciating and taking care of the earth will thus permeate our study of nature.

CRYSTALS

What if we converted our class into a nature museum? The children love the idea! We might even invite the Princess to our museum. What fun! We start with one wall that will exhibit our findings about crystals. (Most of our wall space is covered with corkboard to provide ample space for our constantly changing displays of art, numbers, shapes, graphs, letters, and words.) We send out an appeal to parents of kindergarten to third grade students asking for shoe boxes, and we ask cafeteria personnel to collect small boxes of every kind. Open boxes facing forward are then stapled to the corkboard, to form display cases for crystals.

Crystals brought in by the children and some that are borrowed from the science department are examined, sorted, and labeled. Each crystal, held in place by a blob of Play-Doh, is displayed in a separate box, and an index card with a descriptive child-written sentence is placed inside the box. The signs read:

QUARTZ. Looks like glas. Veri pritee shinee crystals. Quit hard. [Looks like glass. Very pretty, shiny crystals. Quite hard.]

PYRITE Shins like gold. It has mny crystals. I thinc it will mak good jewlree. [Shines like gold. It has many crystals. I think it will make good jewelry.]

Xeroxed pictures of additional crystals complete our exhibit. We create an "ABC of Crystals" chart: A for alabaster, azurite; B for bauxite; C for calcite, chalcocite, cinnabar.

To incorporate math and science, we estimate and weigh crystals, we measure the volume of water each crystal displaces in a beaker, we grow crystals, we test crystals by rubbing them on porcelain, and we learn more about three-dimensional shapes. The encyclopedia tells us that the inside of a crystal is like "rooms" formed by the crystal's atoms. Amazing! We found it hard to design triangular and hexagonal rooms for human homes, but such houses abound in nature. *A crystal is a house for rooms of many unique shapes!*

Guessing games are invented as children, adopting the role of a crystal, ask: "I am bright yellow. I melt and burn with a match. Who am I?" [Sulphur] "I am shiny and bright and very valuable. People wade in the water and try to find me. Who am I?" [Gold]

Geographical skills are enriched as we try to locate mineral origins and discover several interesting facts. For example, Philadelphia, where we live, exports mostly grain and coal, but Minnesota has plenty of iron ore, manganese, limestone, and sandstone. A chart with a summary of findings completes our wall display, and we move to the next unit: shells.

SHELLS

The shell exhibit follows the same route as the crystal exhibit but is of greater interest to some children because shells house living creatures. In nature journals we document our research by writing and drawing pictures: Shells are like strong suits of armor. Shells come in all sizes and shapes. Shells are a home for oysters, crabs, turtles, and clams. Some shells have bright colors. The shell of the South Pacific giant clam is over four feet wide. If a kindergartner could take a cozy nap in such a shell, imagine the size of the clam!

New concepts emerge: A shell is also a house for a nut. Why do nuts have shells? What if we had a shell that we crept into each night? What if every living creature had a shell? Why can't we call our skin a shell? Do all seeds have shells? Several seeds are planted in glass jars, and shell changes are noted. Children also shell peanuts for snack, make peanut characters for art, and write stories about peanut people. Eggs also have shells!

"EGGSPERIMENTING" WITH EGGS

As Easter approaches, we begin an "eggsciting" new "eggsploration." First we study the life cycle of creatures that hatch out of eggs: frogs, butterflies, and chicks. Then we discover that the dinosaurs that came from eggs are now "eggstinct."

"Eggstinct, eggstinct—there are no more eggs and so they are eggstinct," a child exclaims in delight.

And so for a week children are sent on a novel egg hunt; they must find words whose beginnings resemble the sound "eggs." Each day they rush in to add words to our list: eggsactly, eggspert, eggsercise, eggsit, eggspand, eggsample, eggshibit. As a group we are eggstatic when we create long sentences with these words: "I am an eggspert with a lot of eggsperience, so I can eggsplain eggsactly what eggsercises you can do for your eggscruciating pain without getting eggshausted." We teach the children that the sound "eggs" is spelled "ex," but they like their new "egg" words, and so we let them eggsperiment. Parents join in sending us more words and sentences. Eggscuse me, but we do talk a new language these days!

In a series of science experiments we weigh raw and boiled eggs to see if there is a difference, we put them in water to see if they will float or sink, we drop them onto different surfaces from different heights, we coat them in paint and roll them across sheets of newspaper to trace their path, and we even force a boiled egg down a narrow-necked flask by creating a vacuum. We also make egg salad sandwiches for snack. Yum!

The egg finale is an experiment that starts at home. On the weekend each child must wrap a raw egg with any material he or she chooses to keep it from breaking when we drop it from the second floor fire escape of our school. Only material found in the house may be used, but no limits are set as to creativity of design or layering techniques. Parents may help with the actual construction but must encourage and use children's ideas as much as possible. We don't know what to eggspect from this eggsperiment. Some children have gone to eggstreme lengths, creating eggstravagant wrappings, even parachutes. The children are eggsuberant, eggsuding eggscitement. But will the eggs eggsplode?

Each child explains his or her reason for choosing the materials and design for this project. We document our predictions, hold our breath, and gaze upward as each encased egg is dropped from a twenty-foot height. We hear some eggs crash as they hit the table; with others we are not so sure, and we hastily tear open the wrapping to proudly hold up an intact egg or to grimace at a gooey mess. And so ends an eggstraordinary educational event.

THE ABC OF FLOWERS

A parent hands us a beautifully illustrated flower book with large, colorful pictures for each letter of the alphabet, and we design our flower wall accordingly. Each child chooses two or three flowers to illustrate. Mr. D. again reviews with children techniques for reproduction and watercolor painting. Within a couple of days we have a spectacular wall display. We continue to bring in flowers of every shape, size, and color, borrow a couple of microscopes, and set up a research station. All day long children settle down in pairs to view different parts of the flowers, discovering mites and various other microscopic creatures in the process.

The function of the flower is to make seeds—incredible! Shutting our eyes, we reflect on how this process repeats itself day after day after day, all over the world. Scientists cannot make living reproductive seeds, yet without human help, nature's cycle continues! Without seeds we would have no new plants, and without plants we would have no flowers, fruits, or vegetables. We are in awe as we sit in silence clasping single seeds in our hands. A video, "The Man Who Planted Seeds," inspires us further. It is about the life of a patient, persistent shepherd, Elzeard Bouffier, who uses his knowledge of nature to single-handedly plant and nurture a forest of thousands of trees, changing arid surroundings into a thriving oasis. The transformation brings families back to the now bountiful land, but none realize that this is the result of one man's work, pursued in peace and anonymity through two world wars. We start by planting sunflower seeds at school so the birds will have food in the fall, and then we go on a planting excursion to our principal's house.

How do we use flowers? As decorations and as symbols of deep emotion: of love and long life at weddings, of respect at funerals, of caring at hospitals, of celebration on special birthdays and anniversaries. On our next visit to the senior citizen's home near our school we decide to take flowers to express our love. We look up the national flowers of various countries: cherry blossoms for Japan, edelweiss for Austria, tulips for Holland and Turkey, and the rose for the United States. Perfumes, potpourris, and scented oils are also ways in which flowers are used. Children design several scientific experiments with varied results: Rose petals boiled in water to make rosewater turn into a strange glutinous substance when refrigerated overnight; flower petals dried for potpourri grow slightly moldy; flowers put in bottles of oil keep fairly well for a couple of months; squishing flowers to create perfume produces colorful droplets and the discovery that flower and leaf juices can be used as paint.

We conclude with an "If I were a flower" activity. Each child chooses to be a particular flower at an informal class parade. Dressed or made up as flowers, they announced in turn:

"If I were a flower, I would be a tall sunflower because I would look bright and yellow like the sun and I could give my seeds to birds, squirrels, and people."

"If I were a flower, I would be an apple blossom because I could turn into an apple and help someone."

"If I were a flower, I would be a rose. Then I would never die; my perfume would live forever."

LOVING MOTHER EARTH

A single line from a speaker at a social studies conference rings in my ear: "Young children should not be presented with material that makes them feel burdened. Do not introduce a topic as 'Save the Earth'; introduce it as 'Appreciating the Earth.' " And so we chose to celebrate the marvels of nature and appreciate what nature provides for us so that children are inspired, not threatened, to take care of the environment.

The study of houses around the world has already opened our eyes to the variety of building materials provided by nature. Now we take other components of nature—water, air, trees, animals—and evaluate their benefits. As a group we write thank you messages: Thank you, trees, for our chairs, tables, fences, decks, houses, pencils, picture frames, paper, paper plates, boxes, bookshelves, Cuisenaire rods, building blocks, playground equipment, picnic tables, oxygen, shade, fruits, and nuts. Then we list a few things we can do to honor trees:

Use paper wisely at school and home.
Protect the tender limbs of trees by not climbing on them.
Recycle paper products, especially brown paper bags.
Plant trees.
Bring cloth napkins for lunch instead of paper napkins.
Take care of furniture.
Take care of your house.
Hug trees.
Inhale the oxygen and whisper sweet messages when walking among trees.

"What if" thinking results in much reflection and personal action plans. What if everyone took care of the rivers and streams? What if no one did? What if every child took care of the playground? What if you turned off all lights in unused rooms? What if we turn on the faucets gently, using only as much water as we really need?

Terrariums constructed by my graduate students as part of their science methods seminar capture children's imagination. Can plants really grow in an enclosed environment, without further watering, for several years? We study the origin and purpose of the first terrariums. In 1932 Dr. Nathaniel Ward devised terrariums as a way to send seeds and plants from one country to another. Out of his ingenuity 20,000 tea plants were sent from Shanghai to the Himalayas, Chinese bananas were introduced in Fiji, and Brazilian rubber trees were shipped to Sri Lanka. We look closely at the world map and trace these early voyages. The first ferns and grasses survived an eight-month sea journey to Australia. Collecting an assortment of clear plastic containers, we set to work measuring soil, charcoal, and gravel before we plant seeds and grasses (Figure 3.15). How long will our terrariums last?

FIGURE 3.15   Making Terrariums

RECYCLING SHIRTS

The primary grades will celebrate recycling on a special day with each class discussing methods of recycling a particular item. Since our class signs up at the very end, the usual recyclable materials (paper, cans, plastic) are already taken, so we decide to recycle shirts. We go for broke in our brainstorming session, giving careful consideration to even the most outlandish ideas about how shirts can be reused. With shirts contributed from parents and a local thrift shop, we set to work in small groups. Shirts are cut up to make cleaning rags, collages, polishing cloths, fabric flowers, exotic turbans, and padding for doll mattresses. Colorful Hawaiian shirts, slit down the middle, are artistically hung and tied to create curtains for our castle windows. Long shirt sleeves are cut out, stuffed with remaining shirt fabric, sealed at the edges, and decorated with multicolored fabric markers to make "fish pillows." With the assistance of three children, Mr. D. devises how, using a pair of scissors, we can carefully cut a single shirt (like peeling an apple to create one long strip of apple peel), transforming it into seventy-two feet of roping that goes around the entire perimeter of the classroom (Figure 3.16). Finally, we collect and donate shirts to a homeless shelter. One long-term consequence of the project is the use of shirt rags rather than paper towels to

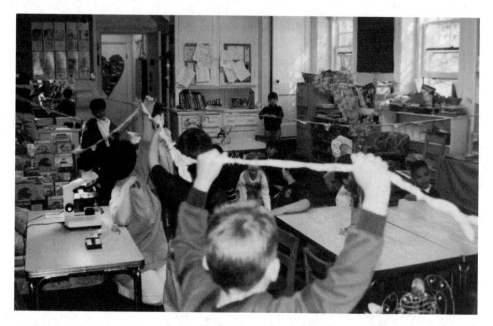

FIGURE 3.16   One Shirt = Seventy-Two Feet of Rope!

clean classroom tables after lunch—a really good idea that might have a life beyond our classroom!

DISINTEGRATION

What happens when we throw soda cans and plastic into the woods, parks, and playgrounds? Why are some materials better for nature than others? With permission from the school we dig up a patch of land behind our classroom and bury various articles: *plastic* cups, spoons, forks, soda bottles, and detergent bottles; *wooden* blocks, twigs, and bark; *paper* towels, newspaper, and magazine pages; and an assortment of stones, leaves, coconut fiber, corks, and bits of glass. The location of each object is marked with a nine-inch metal rod that rises above the soil with an identification sticker. Two and a half months later we dig up the soil to see which objects have and have not disintegrated.

MICHAEL CADUTO

Most of the songs for the nature unit come from Michael Caduto, the environmentalist, educator, and folk singer. "Keeper of the Night," a riddle song about creatures that stay awake at night, is the children's favorite.

[excerpt]
I'm a Keeper of the Night
Keeper of the Night
I get up, when the sun goes down
I'm a Keeper of the Night

In the treetops I am calling
eyes as big as the moon
my wings are whispers in the dark
your midnight is my noon [owl].

Late at night when you're lying in bed
I am up and around
the moon and the stars help me find my way
and I hardly make a sound.
From the garden I come crawling
feeding on the dead leaves
I turn garbage into gold
it sounds strange but you'd better believe [earthworm].

(From *All One Earth: Songs for the Generations* © 1994 by Michael Caduto. All Rights Reserved.)

We use this song to make our own flip-open book. Each page is folded in half with the words written on the top half and an illustration hidden under the fold. On reading each verse, readers must identify the hidden creature and then flip open the page to check if they are correct. Some children create original verses of their own, and everyone reads and rereads each other's books.

Several Caduto songs instruct and inform children about nature issues. "All Our Relations" is particularly effective in its portrayal of animals that are becoming extinct. Once children learn the songs, song sheets become favored reading material, and we place several in our silent reading corner. And then, wonder of wonders, Michael Caduto accepts the school's invitation and will visit us as part of our Earth Day celebrations! We decide to honor him by making a special gift. A group of students paint a large portrait of the singer while others design an elaborate frame with carefully chosen pieces of bark, shells, and pebbles. On the big day the children listen to Caduto in reverential awe as he speaks of his nature experiences and meditations. Finally, after singing several of their favorite songs, he turns to them and invites them to sing "Keeper of the Night" with him. What a day!

NATURE, ART, AND IDIOMS

Designing the nature frame for Caduto sparks the imagination, leading children to design individual animal pictures for the school art show. Each child draws an animal or animal head on a large piece of cardboard and uses objects from nature, instead of the usual paints and crayons, to complete the project. In preparation we collect trash bags full of bark, leaves, twigs, dried flowers, and acorns, while parents contribute various colored lentils and beans from their kitchens. For two days we don't allow the cleaning staff into the room! Hannah makes a rabbit almost entirely of white beans (see Color Plate 17), Carl uses pine needles, bark, and a few red beans to make his hedgehog, while George uses rough bark and flat white stones to make a fairly realistic rhino head. This is indeed a patience task. With tables removed to create floor space, children bend over their work in utmost concentration, pasting individual beans, leaves, and twigs, while taped bird sounds play in the background.

Meanwhile, pursuing the group's flair for language, we have introduced familiar sayings on every possible occasion.

> At Easter: Don't count your chickens before they hatch. Don't put all your eggs in the same basket.
>
> Investigating crystals: All that glitters is not gold.
>
> When studying about plants and flowers: Great oaks from little acorns grow. Small is the seed of every greatness. Money does not grow on trees.
>
> About patience and good qualities: Rome was not built in a day. We must learn to walk before we can run. Actions speak louder than words.

Children's conversations are now filled with pithy proverbs, used appropriately for the most part:

"Dave, don't cry over spilt milk. I'll help you rebuild your castle."

"Come on everyone, we must make hay while the sun shines. Let's finish our project."

"How can the homeless people live? Money does not grow on trees."

"Ms. B., I think I bit off more than I can chew. Can you help me?"

"I keep forgetting to bring my library book. But better late than for ever."

I ask children to incorporate a proverb into their animal art title. The titles read:

> This is the cat that curiosity did not kill.
> Birds of a feather may flock together, but I stand alone.

In addition, many children choose to write brief poems about their animal. For his rhino (see Color Plate 18), George writes:

THE NATURE RHINO
Rhino's are as tough as nails
Is the rhino a relative of the Dino
with tough armor skin and strong horns to win?
We must protect the rhino from becoming extinct like the Dino.

A week before the art show, a large tree in our school is struck by lightning. Mr. D. takes several enormous branches into the display area and hangs children's artwork on the branches. We add a few real flowering plants, and voila—we have an ideal setting for the nature-masterpieces (Figure 3.17).

FIGURE 3.17   The Art Show

NATURE'S MYSTERIES

Throughout our nature studies I marvel at children's creative thinking, hypotheses, and deductions. I decide to document them by creating a special end-of-year book—*Nature's Mysteries: Questions about Nature Answered by Kindergarten Children*—as a gift for parents and children. With pertinent illustrations by Mr. D., the book consists of children's spontaneous, often poetic, often scientific, often humorous replies to nature questions. The following are responses to the question "What makes today so hot?"

> "I think my dad told me how [dad was a science teacher], but I'm not sure I remember. The sun can almost reach the earth on such a hot day. When it is hot, the sun's arms reach toward the earth."

> "The sun gets hotter and hotter in the sky, and then it takes one step down toward the earth and it makes the place hot."

> "Because God wants the land to be calm and not freezing cold. He has magic . . . and because there is only one sun. God sucks it up into His arms and throws it to the other side of the earth."

"Well, for real, this could happen! There is not much clouds to cover the earth and so it is hot. That's really true."

"I think . . . Well my reason is pretty funny, but it could happen. I think God is kind, and so when it is hot it is because He has a bad fever, or maybe He just wants it to be hot today."

"Maybe every day the sun gets a little bit bigger, and today it could have gotten a little bit bigger than usual. You know the rays that come out of the sun . . . well, they could have gotten bigger."

"I think there is a cloud-eater that eats the clouds to make the sun show out more. If there was no cloud-eater, the world would get so dark, it would be just like it was before the sun got created." (Figure 3.18)

"Sometimes the clouds cover up the sun and it is not so hot. But when the clouds are not around, the rays can really reach us."

"Maybe the earth gets bigger until it can reach the sun, and God kinda stands a little away from the sun so He doesn't get burned . . . and then the sun gets even bigger and it gets very hot . . . close to the summer."

"Just like we make fire in the winter, God could make the sun hot."

"Maybe the sun is just a ball and fire covers all of it."

"I think it is like Alice said, when it is windy it is God's breath . . . and the sun is made out of fire and chemicals, and that is why it is really hot."

Brainstorming of this kind is always followed by actual investigation: researching in books and on computers and asking parents, science teachers, and other adults. We often list all the answers on the blackboard and promote both critical and creative thinking by asking two questions: "Which of these could really be the answer?" "Which of these could make a wonderful legend?"

FIGURE 3.18   The Cloud Eater

Our book, *Nature's Mysteries,* concluded with a question and response that we hoped would encourage parents to do something similar: Why do they call a class for five- to six-year-olds a kindergarten?

Ms. B: "Because it is a garden of kids, and many of the principles of gardening apply to the tending of little children. If you want a beautiful flower garden, you must first prepare the soil and get it ready to receive the seeds. In the same way, if you want a child to learn a concept, you have to prepare the child's mind to receive the new information. Asking a child a question, getting a child to think, encouraging a child to formulate an answer utilizing existing knowledge—these are the ways to till the mind and make it fertile so that new seeds of thought may take root easily, develop further, and blossom."

CLOSING ACTIVITIES

At the end of the year children work on several activities that integrate reading, writing, and math skills. They maintain a book of nature words, write individual number poems ("One, one, I see the sun. Two, two, I'm off to the zoo"), write a book about what comes in two's ("two tires on a motorcycle, two eyes, ears, and legs on a person"), and, modeled after a book we have read, write a rhyming story to be published ("Eeny Meeny Miney Bear, have you been sleeping in my hair? Eeny Meeny Miney Mouse, have you been climbing up my house?").

A special closing ceremony on the last day of school will embody all that we have learned this year. The children choose five of their favorite songs, the classroom is adorned with nature decorations, invitations are sent to the parents, and a colorful banner lists all the good qualities we have put into practice. The Princess sends an elaborate scroll, which will be opened on the big day. Our final preparation is to plan "graduation" speeches. Under a white garden arch with (imitation) climbing roses, individual children will talk about the things they have learned in kindergarten, including, if they wish, special messages for peers and teachers (Figure 3.19). Parents are asked to help with mnemonic strategies for delivering the speech. Our suggestions: a series of index cards with words, pictures, or symbols; a computer printout of the speech for easier reading; symbols drawn on the palm of the hand. The final day dawns. Each child, proud of his or her personal journey and all dressed up for the occasion, delivers a speech with great dignity. The following excerpts reveal the variety of themes that are significant to children:

"When I came to this class, I didn't know my letters, but now I can write stories. The Princess told me to be honest and kind, and I think I did that."

"I never thought I was an artist, but now I am an artist and a reader."

"I thank my teacher, and friends, and the Princess for teaching me about compassion."

"Nature art was the best thing of all. My message to teachers is keep teaching about good qualities. That is important."

"I had plenty of time to play with my friends at recess, and we had so much fun."

FIGURE 3.19   Graduation Speeches

"This year was the best of all because of the Princess. I hope she comes to see us in first grade."

"I think I am ready for first grade because I have learned so much and my writing is really good now. My message to my friends is always play fair and take care of people and nature like we did this year."

COMMENTARY

As previously, we note Usha's invitation to discuss difficult, possibly unanswerable, questions. She asks the children, "What does it mean to take care of . . . ?" "Why do you think they are homeless?" Again we see that she individualizes tasks within group assignments: Children play different instruments to greet the princess, make different types of houses, choose to be different flowers in a class parade, and select different characters for Halloween costumes.

This chapter illustrates the considerable curricular flexibility, what we have called detours from the theme. Many of the topics were not anticipated—houses, crystals, shells, flowers—but emerged from the group. As long as the thematic thrust of good qualities was maintained, Usha picked up on the children's interests and enthusiasm. It is through the detours that motivation and excitement are maintained. Teaching in this way makes it impossible to plan the entire content in advance. Skills, however, unlike content, are defined and continuously incorporated into the current topic. Usha knows what skills need to be attained and by when, and she keeps tabs on the progress of each child. Given the contemporary attention to accountability, even in kindergarten, it is important to separate as well as integrate these two aspects of the curriculum.

One notes with a certain envy the richness of these children's learning. There is little that is told; most of the learning, though it is advanced, comes from personal experience. Take the study of crystals. This difficult, complex topic has been transformed into fare fit for five-year-olds. As so often, Usha starts a new topic by asking children to *do* something (other than listen)—in this instance build a display case in which to mount crystals and spontaneously describe what they see. She asks—and perhaps only five-year-olds can answer such a question—what it would be like to *be* a crystal, to be different crystals. Then there is the growing, measuring, and weighing of them. At times Usha moves from the personal to the objective, from the idiosyncratic to the uniform. At other times she will go from the general to the personal and perhaps back again to the general. The study of houses, for instance, starts with castles. Next the children take a close look at, and make renderings of, their own homes. Then they investigate other homes, including unlikely ones (cassette box, frame, soccer ball, pickle jars, kennels, cages, gloves, etc.). Moving from the impressionistic to the realistic, they then study the actual design and material structure of houses—how to build and preserve them against the forces of nature.

Depth of learning with young children depends on recursiveness: returning to and elaborating on the same topic from different angles (and through different methods). A good example is the castle topic. First, castles are studied in all their variety, and then one is built. However, this is not the end. The class goes to visit a real castle, but first they do their own tile work. On returning, they make individual castles. So too with the tool museum: First the children make tools, then they visit the museum, then they return and create a tool museum. The order does not much matter, for each experience enlarges the children's grasp and stimulates their imaginations.

Learning is not merely the collection of information—from the teacher's mouth to the children's ears—though it includes assimilating large quantities of knowledge. Rather, there is a close encounter between the child and the to-be-learned; learning is an expansive and transformative individual experience. The study of castles does not end with a building for the Princess, valuable though that work is. The children become part of the castle; in a sense they inhabit it through their representative flags and shields. Similarly with the study of flowers: Flowers are not just studied and grown, good though that is. The children establish personal and emotional connections to flowers by learning about how they contribute to our lives and our planet, about how they cheer us when we are sad and when we are happy. Finally, they become flowers at a class parade and explain why they have made their particular selection and what their choice means to them.

Throughout all this careful teaching, there is the theme of reverence for, and humility toward, life. Recycling isn't just advocated as something we should do because the earth is to be protected; it is a serious subject of experimentation (burying plastic, wood, paper), and it is *done* (with shirts). The children become recyclers.

In Usha's class the simple and obvious are made complex and, in the realization of their complexity, more deeply valued. For example, building materials are examined in detail. It becomes apparent that materials are not interchangeable. Each has its own use and value. In my favorite experiment, the variously constructed homes are subject to various natural "disasters." The children learn in their gut how natural forces and man's resistance to them face off. Tools too are not taken for granted. They are carefully examined, their functions are clarified, and innovative tools are created (in the paper clip game). The tool maker is understood to be as valuable and interesting as the architect. The laborer becomes appreciated in a most nonacademic way when the children design and make their own clay tiles, then figure out just how many tiles they would have to prepare for a castle! The message, subtle but clear, is that princesses, kings, and queens count for no more than the patient laborer and that the magnificence of the castle depends on the simplest of the tools.

Finally, it is worth noting that all objects and experiences have a moral component to them. There is nothing preachy or prescriptive, however, in the exploration of these components. They naturally infiltrate the activities. Drawings of loving deeds are arranged along the walls of the castle; shields, crowns, and flags all represent good qualities. The study of houses is connected to the good qualities that make a house a home and to an appreciation that there are those without homes. It is not enough to deeply appreciate the beauty of flowers, the children are invited to share them with others at the senior citizen home. Gratitude is expressed for nature's bounty. And from gratitude comes naturally the desire to protect our blessings.

CHAPTER FOUR

THE BEAR AND RESPECT AND RESPONSIBILITY

A contented Emma Bear, with the Respect song echoing in her ears, bids her son Isaac farewell at the end of the first school day, entrusting him to the care of a willing group of kindergartners. The children, in various states of excitement, awe, and disbelief, accept responsibility for Isaac, promising Emma that they will "take good care of him, love him, hug him, make sure he is never lonely, and most of all, teach him about being good" (Figure 4.1). When the school bell rings, they tuck Isaac into a comfortable chair, place a blanket over his knees and a couple of good books beside him, and leave, blowing kisses and promising to be his friend.

FIGURE 4.1   I Will Hug Isaac Bear

BEING A FRIEND

"Isaac Bear has never been to school before," I announce the next morning, "but some of you have been at this school for a year, and the rest of you have been at different preschools. I want you to think of ways in which you can help Isaac today. How can you be his friend?"

"We can sit next to him."

"I can take him outside with us."

"I can tell him funny jokes."

"I'm really good at drawing. I can help him draw."

"I've been in this school the longest. I'll show him where everything is."

"I can hold him in my lap at circle time so he won't be lonely."

After listing their thoughts on the board, I suggest that we put the various friendship ideas into action all day. "Let's show Isaac Bear how it feels to be in a friendly class. Let's try all these ideas with Isaac *and* with each other."

All day long I observe little acts of kindness: Sarah draws Isaac close at naptime; Jim sits Isaac by him at lunch; Rachel and Tom dress Isaac in costumes as part of their free-choice game. At the end of the day we gather for an impromptu meeting to evaluate what Isaac might have learned about friendship. "You can also tell me what *you* learned about friendship."

"It feels good."

"I made two new friends today."

"Rachel waited for me in the girl's room."

"I think Isaac Bear felt good because we took care of him."

"He looked really cool when we dressed him up as a pirate."

"I think he liked it when I pushed him on the swing."

"Maria, I saw you playing and drawing by yourself. Was that your choice?" I inquire.

"Not really, but I only know Sarah, and she was playing with someone else."

"Did anyone notice that Maria was fairly lonely today?" I pursue.

"I sort of noticed," Anne responds, and a couple of children nod their heads.

We discuss strategies to help each other, not just Isaac, feel safe, happy, and cared for and decide to try them out the next day. Shutting our eyes for a few moments, we reflect on how it would feel if everyone in our class looked out for and befriended each other. We also decide to list our "friendship findings" each day so that we can share them with Emma Bear in our letters.

The success of this impromptu meeting determines the end-of-day activity for the rest of the school year. As the closing activity each afternoon, we gather together in a cozy corner to talk about what we learned, what worked, what did not work, what was fun, and what we could try the next day.

DEFINING RESPECT: POLITENESS

Entrusted with the task of teaching Isaac about good qualities and given my original intention to use respect and responsibility as the overall framework, the words of our theme song, "Respect Yourself and Others Too," provide a sound starting point.

I note the lyrics "It's so important that you do, respect yourself and others too" and ask, "How exactly does one respect another? What does one do?"

"You don't take others' stuff."

"You say you're sorry when you bump into them, specially if they get hurt."

"Or when you push them down, really by accident."

"I have to say I'm sorry when I burp at the table. Grandma is always telling me that."

"No, no. You should say, 'Excuse me.' "

"I have to say, 'Excuse me,' when I want to speak and my mom is talking."

At the end of this discussion we decide that politeness is a key component of respect, and we write "BEING POLITE" in large letters on our "What Is Respect?" chart.

But why should we be polite? Why be respectful to others? To answer these questions, we sit in quiet guided reflection. With the children seated cross-legged and eyes shut, I begin speaking softly and slowly, with pauses between sentences. "I want you to imagine how it would feel if everyone you meet is respectful, everyone is polite. When they meet you, they smile and say, 'Hello,' in a friendly voice. They listen attentively when you tell them about your adventures, and they thank you when you help them in any way. At meal times, everyone converses pleasantly and listens to what each one has to say. No one grabs food, and no one is rude or mean. On the playground everyone asks for turns politely, 'May I have a turn on the swing when you are done?' 'May I have the spade? I want to make a sand castle.' You create new games, play together, laugh, and have fun. In class, everyone—teachers and children—helps each other with work and with cleanup. As you walk through the school, you greet everyone you see with a happy smile. You greet Ms. M., the secretary, Mr. S. who delivers milk and cookies from the cafeteria, Mr. P. who takes care of the yard, and they smile and greet you in return. If everyone you meet is kind and polite, how would that make you feel?"

"I guess I would feel good."

"It would be easy."

"There would be no fights."

"It would be like we were in a movie or something."

"Why don't we give it a try," I suggest. "Let's try to be respectful and polite to each other in every way we can, and, who knows, it might be like a movie. We can talk about it at the end of the day."

I provide children with large sheets of paper on which they illustrate and write four ways in which they can make school a happier place for everyone.

DEFINING RESPECT: RESPECTING YOURSELF

We listen to the Respect song:

> *Respect is showing you care how someone feels*
> *Respect, respect*
> *Respect is listening when someone talks to you*
> *Respect, respect*
> *Respect is saying, "Please," and "Thank you," every day*

Respect, respect
Respect is liking someone for their special ways.

After we discuss each of these lines at length and share tons of personal experiences, both pleasant and hurtful, the words "CARING," "LISTENING," and "ACCEPTING" are added to our "What Is Respect?" chart. We then move to the latter part of the song:

Respect for yourself is eating well each day
Respect, respect—three good meals a day
Respect for yourself is sharing how you feel
Respect, respect
Respect for yourself is sleeping well each night
Respect, respect—get a good night's sleep
Respect for yourself is being proud of who you are
Respect, respect—feeling proud.

Respecting yourself is a new concept for kindergarten children, but in a couple of weeks the concept takes root, and the "Respect Yourself" list flourishes:

Eat healthy food.
Don't eat too much candy or drink too much soda.
Stay clean.
Brush your teeth well.
Wear clean clothes.
Speak the truth.
Don't allow others to tease you.
Tell people how you feel instead of crying and whining.
Use a calm voice at all times.
Play safe on the playground, and don't do anything dangerous.
Walk safely on the street.
Do the right thing.
If others tell you to do something wrong, don't do it.

The general conclusion: Respecting yourself means taking good care of yourself at all times. The children want this list, "Respecting Yourself," to be mailed to Isaac's mom, and so we do. "She'll be so happy that we are teaching Isaac all this good stuff," Rachel declares. Later, we compile and mail "Respecting Others" and "Respecting the Environment" lists.

AN ETIQUETTE BOOK ABOUT RESPECT

The school nurse and the science teacher are invited to talk to the children about taking care of their physical selves. A volunteer parent, who is a dentist, turns out to be a consummate teacher who conducts a very memorable hands-on dentistry lesson by bringing in the tools of his trade for children to handle. For two hours the children observe demonstrations, manipulate instruments and fake teeth, and listen in rapt attention. Adding brushing, rinsing, flossing, and regular dental checkups to our "care of teeth" itinerary, we settle down in the afternoon to compose a letter of thanks. Our new dentist friend has done a splendid job of convincing the children that a dentist's mission is to protect and safeguard children's teeth; they should therefore not fear a visit to the dentist.

"If a dentist's job is to help us take care of our teeth," I ponder, "what is *our* job at the dentist's office? How can we be respectful?" As I document the honest, original, and delightful responses that follow, a new idea is born: an etiquette book for Isaac. Compiling such a book will be a great culminating event, drawing together all that we learn about respect and responsibility. The following are some pages from the book:

RESPECT AT A DENTIST'S OFFICE
1. Don't scream or run in the waiting room.
2. Don't mess up the magazines.
3. Greet the dentist.
4. Be patient as a patient.
5. Do not kick when the dentist is near you.
6. If the dentist leaves, do not touch any dental tools or buttons or switches.
7. Try not to cry when the dentist works on your teeth; he is really trying to help you.
8. Don't scream at the dentist.
9. When you are done, say, "Thank you very much. Goodbye," and hug the dentist (or shake hands).

RESPECT WHEN COOKING IN A GROUP
1. Wash hands well so that no one spreads any germs.
2. Do not put your hands in the food.
3. Do not lean over the table so that everyone can watch the process.
4. Be patient and wait your turn instead of saying, "What about me?"
5. Don't play with the ingredients.
6. If you sneeze, cover your mouth and then wash your hands.
7. Cooperate. Don't push or pull the bowl when others are trying to stir the ingredients.

RESPECT AT THANKSGIVING
1. Greet relatives and friends by saying, "Hello! Happy Thanksgiving."
2. Wash your hands before the meal.
3. Be polite at the table. Say, "No, thank you," or "Yes, please." Do not grab. Say, "Please pass the. . . ." Cover your mouth when you cough or sneeze. Talk politely, not with food in your mouth.
4. Thank the people who made the food.
5. Offer to clean up after the meal.

6. If you don't like the food, don't say, "Yuck." Just leave it on the plate.
7. If others visit your home, share your toys.
8. If you visit others, be friendly and nice.
9. Be thankful for all that you have.

Every event merits a page in our etiquette book: respect for third grade buddies who visit us once a week, respect at birthday parties, respect in the car, respect on the school bus, respect at the supermarket. A charming book about a spider's tea party even inspires a couple of parents to create an elegant tea party at school so that we may teach Isaac to partake of all the delicacies like a prince—respect at a royal tea party.

DEFINING RESPECT: MAGAZINE ILLUSTRATIONS

Some of the best small-group respect discussions were elicited by the following activity. Seated amid heaps of assorted magazines, children in pairs are given the task of creating a respect poster using pictures that depict respectful actions. They are instructed to discuss each picture of choice with their partner before cutting it out. After they explain their final pile of pictures to either Mr. D. or me, their selections are pasted onto colored posterboard with brief captions. Pictures enable children to look for facial expression and body language that denote the intention behind the action. For example, when James and Andrew find an illustration of a man carrying a baby in an infant carrier while a woman strolls by his side, they discuss the merits of the observed action as follows:

"I think the man is being respectful because he is helping his wife. She takes care of the child all day, and so he comes home and says, 'Honey, I'm home. I'll take care of the child.' "

"I don't think so. Look at his face. He doesn't look happy."

"He must be tired after work."

"No. I think his wife told him that it was his turn, and he doesn't like that."

"I'm not sure."

"Just look at his face."

"O.K. Let's look at another picture."

Mr. D. and I walk around and intervene when necessary, as in the case of a child who has pulled out several pictures of beautiful women from cosmetic advertisements.

"Can you tell me why you chose these pictures for your respect poster?"

"Because they are pretty."

"They certainly are pretty, but does that mean that they are respectful?"

"Yes. I think so."

"Do you know someone in real life who is like that?"

"Yes, my mom."

"But aren't there pretty people who are not respectful?"

"Yes, I know two ladies who are quite pretty but not always nice."

"So if someone is pretty, we can't always tell if they are respectful or not."

"Right."

"Then let's look again at the pictures you've chosen. Look at what each lady is doing and decide which ones you will use in the respect poster."

(Child selects one of four original pictures.) "This woman is helping her child."

"And is helping a way to show respect?"

"Yes!"

The finished posters that cover the entire length of our wall are remarkable in their variety of depicted actions. A sampling of these is as follows: RESPECT IS—Saying, "Good morning" or "Good afternoon" to someone (picture of President Clinton saluting a guard); getting married and sharing your life with someone; showing someone you care how they feel; helping someone get to work, get to school, or just get around; teamwork; resting together peacefully (picture of four racoons cuddled together); taking care of the earth; helping a friend prepare for a canoe ride; exercising and staying in good health; taking turns while playing; eating right (picture of two elephants eating grass); giving people your best smile; dressing neatly every day; dancing beautifully together (from a Viagra advertisement!); swimming together without fighting; being very gentle to a cat. In just a few weeks our concept of respect has enlarged considerably!

MONET MAGIC

One rainy afternoon in October the children watch a naptime video, *Linnea*, which portrays a young girl's adventures as she discovers Monet's art and travels to Giverny to see the gardens that inspired his work. The children are intrigued and insist on watching the entire video in one sitting, frequently requesting to review portions of the tape where Monet's splotches of paint turn into water lilies and lily pads as Linnea walks away from the paintings.

Seizing on the children's interest, Mr. D and I get several Monet books and posters from local libraries and spread them on the tables before the children arrive the next day. Burying themselves in the books, they ask a million questions.

"How come there are so many books about Monet?"

"Did he paint only gardens?"

"Did he ever not smudge paint, but paint 'regular'?"

"His paintings are kind of weird, aren't they? They're like my little sister's paintings."

I observe one child holding up a large Monet print while two others scrutinize the painting from up close and then pull away to view it from afar. For some reason Monet's mystical appeal prevails even in our kindergarten. We decide to make Monet our curriculum for one week.

Monet—Social Studies

We locate Paris, Normandy, and the Rouen Cathedral on a map, we study the climate of France to understand Monet's many paintings of wheat stacks and gardens in changing seasons and weather conditions, we examine the place of Impressionism in art history, and we look at the evolution of paints and art supplies. (Monet was one of the earliest artists to paint outdoors because of the availability of paint in tubes.)

Monet—Math

To develop time and length concepts, we explore several questions: If Monet lived from 1840 to 1926, how old was he when he died? Were your parents, grandparents, or great-grandparents alive when he was? Did any of them live where he lived? If Monet painted pictures that were over forty feet long, do we know how long that is? The children measure forty-feet on a football field and then try to figure out how many children it will take to cover the forty-foot line.

Monet—Science

We study the effect of sun and wind on open containers of water color, acrylic, and oil paints compared to closed containers (tubes) of the same. We also experiment with mixing several colors to produce new colors and look through Vaseline-smeared lenses to get a "perspective" on Impressionism.

Monet—Vocabulary

Impressionism, water lilies, poplars, cathedrals, pigment, canvas, Giverny—each word, instituted as our "password" for the day, soon becomes a part of everyday kindergarten conversations. A password, chosen at morning circle, must be recalled every time a child wishes to leave the room. Children are encouraged to develop personal recall strategies, which vary from repeating a word over and over again to association (sounds like *popular* but is *poplar*) to creating a symbol (a pig on a pavement for pigment). The more creative children integrate the password into sentences that inform us of their need to leave the classroom.

"I'm as thirsty as the ducks on the pond at Giverny," Amy proclaims.

"I have to pee and it rhymes with Giverny," James announces with a delighted chuckle.

Monet—Respect

If Monet painted passionately even after he was eighty years old, if he followed his inner conviction despite all criticism, does this denote respect? Do his paintings reveal a respect for nature? We ask children, parents, and high school art teachers to help us answer these questions.

Monet—Art

In our attempt to see impressions, we walk in the playground, scrunching our eyes to view blurry outlines of trees and bushes. We try our hand at smudging paint to create impressions of the sky, soccer fields, and school buildings. Then each child selects and replicates one of Monet's Impressionist paintings in crayon and in paint.

Monet—Finale

"No one can paint a picture forty feet long!" Never one to let such a remark go uncontested, I tell the children, "Monet certainly painted several pictures that were over forty feet long. Besides, even here, in downtown Philadelphia, we have mural artists who paint enormous pictures. When people are inspired and determined, they can do amazing things. Instead of saying, 'No one can do this,' why don't we try to make the largest possible picture in our classroom!"

Stripping everything off a wall that runs almost the entire length of our classroom, we clear a space that is eighteen feet wide and seven feet high. Mr. D. and I cover the entire area with pale blue paper while the children make sketches of the picture they would like to paint in this space. An amazing ninety percent of the class want to paint Monet's bridge with water lilies below. So Mr. D., instructed by the children, who direct his every move, sketches the bare outline of a bridge, the skyline, and a boat with Monet seated in it.

For the next three days, with half of our classroom covered in dropcloths, jars of brilliant colored paint, paintbrushes, smocks, rags, paper towels, and assorted sponges, the children set about creating a Monet mural. Attired in smocks (Dad's shirt worn backward) and straw hats (like Monet), groups of children, perched on table-scaffolding or kneeling on the floor, use sponges and paint to create impressionistic water lilies, weeping willows, and ripples of water (Figure 4.2). While Mr. D. and I supervise small groups of children at the mural, three other groups work diligently at trust tables (see Chapter 5), helping each other with math, writing, and construction activities. The music of Debussy (provided by the music teacher) wafts through the air, providing the flavor of Monet's era as children steadily add finishing touches to their mural. Finally, the painting is completed, and as we roll up the dropcloth, now covered in paint spills, we joke about the new art technique we have created: the drip technique. But despite the many drips that result from painting on a vertical surface, the finished painting, viewed from a distance, makes us proud (see Color Plate 19). It looks like Monet's paintings, and it is impressionistic. Our classroom is transformed by this enormous masterpiece. Parents, teachers, relatives, and friends come to admire and applaud the children's efforts. The children are delighted by their own prowess, the attention, and the praise, but most important, they have discovered that it is possible to do the impossible!

FIGURE 4.2   We Can Paint Like Monet

ISAAC BEAR IS AN ARTIST

Lest the children feel that Isaac Bear has been left out of the art process, I decide to have him write a note to the children. The morning after we complete the mural, the children, much to their amazement, find a beautiful Impressionist painting of a single water lily and a note that reads:

Dear Children,

    The last few days have been very exciting. I have learned a lot about Monet. My favorite painting is *The Garden (Irises)* because I love the spectacular shades of purple. I have also learned a lot from watching you paint your MAGNIFICENT painting. You have been patient, cooperative, and very artistic. I was so inspired by your work that I decided to paint my own picture. Here it is. I am so happy to be in this class. Continue with the good work.

              Love, Isaac

"Isaac Bear is a really good artist."

"He writes so well."

"He likes being in a class."

Thus begins a new line of communication between Isaac and the kids, each acknowledging and applauding the other's attempts to "get gooder." The letters start to flow on a regular basis, as Isaac, perched on his high chair, perceives every small act of respect and kindness (and communicates with those I may have missed noting during the day).

Dear James,
    I noticed how you stayed back at recess to clean up the class. You even picked up two pieces of gooey bread that would have been mushed into the carpet if someone stepped on it.
    Love, Isaac

Dear Amy,
    How thoughtful of you to help Russ pick up the thumbtacks he spilled. I was worried that they would hurt someone at circle time.
    Love, Isaac

Dear Margo,
    I realized that you did not like the story about the crocodile. But you tried very hard to sit still and not play with Amy's hair. That was respectful!
    Love, Isaac

The notes from Issac continue all year, and children respond to Isaac with notes of their own, often including photographs, pictures they have drawn, flowers from their gardens, and even special candy treats.

THE ABC OF ARTISTS

The Open Court Reading Series, with its assortment of flip-around cards, has been my established method of introducing the various sound–symbol connections of the alphabet. The story that runs through the cards is appealing to young children, and the interest it generates causes them to come bounding in each week demanding to know, "What happens to Millie next?" The first letter in the story, the letter M, is introduced as Millie licks an ice-cream cone, saying, "Mmm." The reading specialist, who drops in to see our Monet mural, remarks, "I see that you have studied Monet in conjunction with the letter M. Are you going to study an artist for each letter of the alphabet?" I look across at Mr. D., who shrugs his shoulders as if to say, "Why not? We've done crazier things before."

My mind races: "Will we find an artist for every letter? Do we know of any artists whose names begin with a Q, Y, or Z? And what about respect and responsibility?" But the idea of studying an artist for each letter is too intriguing. My thoughts continue, "We can all learn so much. Look how much we have accomplished with just one week of Monet." So brushing aside my doubts and knowing that Mr. D. and I will have to do a lot of research, I ask the children, "Would you like to study an artist for each letter of the alphabet?" The answer, a resounding "YES!" seals our fate. Looking back at the year, would I make the same decision again, despite the increased workload? Absolutely!

INTEGRATING THEMES AND ACADEMIC SKILLS

How do we integrate respect and responsibility into the study of artists? Biographies of individual artists provide a rich context for continuing discussions about respect (and, in the second semester, about responsibility). As in the Year of the Hero, we read each life story, discuss the virtues inherent in each artist—perseverance, inner strength, peacefulness, courage, determination—and rate each artist on our kindergarten 0–5 Respect rating scale. We also discuss the negative qualities—despair, impatience, anger, desire for intoxicants—that led certain artists to give up and grow despondent. Van Gogh's life, in particular, elicits harsh disapproval, despite admiration for his art (see Color Plate 20), as children spontaneously link self-control with respect and responsibility, writing journal entries such as "HE Painted BOOTIFUL sun FLOwrs BT HE HAD No SLF CANCHRol (control) anD cuT OV His Eer."

Different artists lend themselves to the study of different academic areas. Some, such as Escher, Picasso, and Agam, enrich the math curriculum with their contributions to the study of shapes, patterns, repetition in design, Cubism, lines, and angles. Others, such as Vasarely, Nevelson, Tamayo, and Zuniga, augment our understanding of different cultures, while artists such as Leonardo da Vinci (see Color Plate 21) and Georgia O' Keeffe (see Color Plate 22) promote observational techniques, scientific experimentation, and discovery (What makes things fly? Can microscopes help us to see the insides of flowers like O' Keeffe?). Faith Ringgold, an illustrator of children's books, inspires the children to write and illustrate their own books, leading to the creation of our class library (two shelves of books written and illustrated by our children). As art critics, the children also voice their evaluations of various artists. Picasso, for instance, elicited these comments:

"Picasso's art is good. You never know what he is going to draw next."

"I love his work. He invented a kind of style called Cubism."

"He paints carefully and does not go out of the lines. I like his work."

"His artwork is pretty abstract like Monet's, but in a different style. He makes things look different from what God makes, but it's sort of nice."

"His artwork is nice. It has nice colors in it. It is good."

"His work is one of the most beautiful I ever saw. I like the way he drew a fish and then made it a rooster."

"His art is really good. He uses all different kinds of colors. He drew many people, but he made them look kind of strange" (see Color Plate 23).

"His artwork is a little bit abstract. His paintings are kind of different, because in the picture I copied he drew half a square in the cheek, close to the nose" (see Color Plate 24).

In selecting artists, Mr. D. and I keep gender and diversity in mind. A child's innocent comment—"Are all good artists dead?"—reminds us to include contemporary living artists. Our final ABC list even includes a teacher, a parent, and a babysitter: Agam, Botero, Cassatt, Deis, Escher, Frank, God, Hicks, Indiana, Junia, Kenojuak, Leonardo, Monet, Nevelson, O'Keeffe, Picasso, Quezada, Ringgold, Seurat, Tiffany, Utrillo, Van Gogh, Wyeth, Ximena, Yani, and Zuniga.

Each week is different—a new letter, a new artist, a new country, a new style of art, new books, new videos at naptime. The momentum is exhilarating, as parents, children, and teachers constantly rush off to libraries, delve into the Internet, or call relatives and friends to find out more about Tiffany's stained glass, Seurat's Pointillism, and Zuniga's terra cotta sculpture.

MINING NATURAL RESOURCES

A note sent home each week informs parents about the artist we are studying, the artist we intend to study next, and the progress we have made in reading, math, and respect skills. It also suggests relevant family activities, discussions, and trips to museums and libraries. Parents are invited to help with art projects, to share their own artistic talents, and to provide information about artists whose work they particularly admire.

A mother with family ties to the Pennsylvania-born artist Mary Cassatt introduces the children to Cassatt's "mother and child" portraits, which are particularly relevant because this mom herself is currently expecting a baby. Her presentation conveys the dynamic spirit and strength of Cassatt, who, classified as an Impressionist for a while, broke through boundaries of style, gender, and nationality to become a renowned artist in her own right—a wonderful role model for our aspiring female artists.

Another parent, herself an artist from Colombia, introduces us to her own work as well as that of Fernando Botero. As children view videos of Botero's work and see pictures of Colombian houses and countrysides, the parent's presentation fills our classroom with the sights, language, and tastes of Colombia—fresh papaya, passion fruit, coconut, plantain, and sugar cane.

I enlist the assistance of a Chinese graduate student, Shiuan, to teach children about a young present-day Chinese artist, Yani Wang, who held her first exhibition when she was only ten. We set up three stations. At the first station children are introduced to Chinese paint brushes (bamboo with lamb hair), Chinese black ink (ground by children on a small grinding stone), and rice paper, as they are instructed to paint black monkeys in the style of Yani Wang. At the second station Shiuan explains the Chinese calligraphy on Yani's artwork and shows children how to sign their own name and date their artwork using Chinese letters and numbers. At the third station children make dumplings to be served with a Chinese lunch of rice, stir-fried vegetables, and fortune cookies.

SEASONAL EVENTS

The Artist/Respect/Responsibility theme is woven into various seasonal land-marks. At Halloween, as is customary in our class, children dress up as a real or mythical character from the country of their origin. This year, the requirement is that the character possesses two good qualities that pertain to respect or responsi-bility. The play created around these characters is called "The Master Artist Brings All Things to Life." In each of three scenes Monet brings a different painting and its characters to life. The script provides opportunities for each character to be re-sponsible and respectful.

The parent newsletter at Thanksgiving sums up our activities at this season of grace and reflection:

> Dear Parents,
>
> I can't believe that Thanksgiving is around the corner. It is one of my favorite celebrations—a time to pause, reflect, and offer thanks.
>
> In class we have done a lot of work:
>
> We read several books about the story of Thanksgiving. A particularly good version is *The First Thanksgiving* by Jean Craighead George.
>
> We built our own model of the Mayflower [see Color Plate 25]. Each child made a cardboard cutout of a pilgrim and named him or her after one of the origi-nal pilgrims. We found the original names to be very interesting—Humility, Pa-tience, Truth, Fear, etc.
>
> We read a book about the day in the life of a pilgrim girl (*Sarah Morton's Day*) and discussed the many conveniences we have today—so much to be thankful for.
>
> We made a poetry book about THANKS. The children, inspired by their meeting with author Kay Winters, have begun to create poetry of their own. Illus-trated on our class walls is a lengthy poem about colors, composed by our very own kindergarten class. The poem has remarkable lines such as: *What is red? Red is a pretty, pretty rose, and the color of an embarrassed nose. What is green? Green is the color of my cozy raincoat, and the water under Monet's boat.* We will send home the THANKS book so you can read your child's original poetry at Thanksgiving.
>
> This is a great time to read poems to your child. We are also writing our own joke and riddle books. A trip to the library to find *Easy to Read* riddle books is a good idea.
>
> *Thanksgiving Traditions*
>
> In our class we focus on the two components: *thanks* and *giving*.
>
> In the spirit of giving, we send soup, festive breads, and placemats to a home-less shelter. Kindergartners bake bread, and first graders make soup.
>
> In the spirit of thanks, we have listed the many people, things, and events in our life that we are grateful for and tried to express our gratitude in various ways.
>
> On Tuesday, November 24th, we will join the first graders and have a simple Thanksgiving meal of soup, bread, and cookies. (Please do not send lunch.)
>
> On Wednesday, Nov 25th, please join us for Thanksgiving Chapel at 11:00 A.M. Children will go home at 12 noon.

Artists

We continue our study of letters and artists. The children have been very fascinated by Tiffany's stained glass. After Monet, this has been the artist who most captured their complete attention. The children made their own individual stained glass using markers, paper, and cutout black paper outlines [see Color Plate 26]. Then Mr. D. designed a giant stained glass window with an angel motif, and I assisted by cutting and pasting bits of colored cellophane [see Color Plate 27]. Every now and again we show the children *our* artistic skills—as another means to inspire them. The children watched each stage of the process and were amazed at the end result. Do come in and see for yourself.

For the letter H we studied the work of Edward Hicks (best known for his painting *The Peaceable Kingdom*), and for W we are looking at the works of Andrew Wyeth and N. C. Wyeth. We will try to visit the Brandywine Museum before the winter vacation.

Christmas

Helping others at this season will consist of visiting the Presbyterian home in Bala Cynwyd and collecting mittens and gloves for poor children. We will let you know details in a couple of weeks.

Special

Enclosed is a picture of the young artists in front of their Monet Masterpiece for you to frame or to tuck away as a special kindergarten memory.

Thanksgiving—We give special thanks to moms and dads who have entrusted us with happy, enthusiastic, loving children. We thank you for all your hard work (the hundreds of details you attend to), which enables us to have seven fun-filled hours with your child every weekday. We hope you have a warm, cozy Thanksgiving, full of fun, laughter, and love.

Mr. Deis and Ms. Balamore

At Christmas we, as a community of parents, children, and teachers, choose to decrease the personal giving of gifts and increase our giving to children in need. While delighted with the idea that our class has helped to feed a child in India and one in China for several weeks, the children are a little disappointed that they cannot bring the teachers gaily wrapped gifts for the holiday season. I gather them around to tell them of the gifts they bring me every day—their smiles, their enthusiasm, their happiness, their conversations with me, their honesty, their love. Then I ask them to sit in quiet reflection to think about the question "Why is love the best gift of all?" Their answers, summarized in the following manner, are sent home to parents and still adorn my refrigerator today.

LOVE IS THE BEST GIFT
because
It doesn't cost anything.
You don't have to go and look for it. Its in your heart all the time.
All people like it.
You don't buy it in a store.
It never runs out.
You can carry it anywhere.

It doesn't weigh anything.
It is so easy to carry it in your heart.
It makes everyone happy.

The New Year inspires group reflection about how we, individually and as a classroom community, can make the world a happier place in the coming year. Sitting cross-legged, with eyes closed, for about ten minutes, we think about real actions, what each of us can actually do, not just write or talk about. After thinking about it, children share their thoughts with the group and then proceed to write resolutions on a large paper that has the heading *"I will try to make the world a happier place in the year . . ."* (Figures 4.3 and 4.4). As seen below, many of the actions defined by children pertain to helping parents, taking care of themselves, others, the environment, and "getting gooder."

I WiLL helP MY MOM AND DAD CLeNO UP THE HOWS.
I WL h MY BBsTr (I will help my babysitter).
I Will DOIW A GED FIG For MiE FANS (I will do a good thing for my friends)
I will eat good food this year.

FIGURE 4.3   Making the World a Happier Place

FIGURE 4.4 High Aspirations

I Wl HUG Smun whn da r SAD (I will hug someone when they are sad).
I will Try TO LiSSn.
I will NOt Lie.
I will recycle.
I will Try To Get Ap At A Good TiM.
I WILL HeLP My MOM WATr The AmaRYllis.
I will Smile All THE TIM.
I WiLL PIK UP LITER.

Around Valentine's Day we celebrate the art of Robert Indiana, who created the famous LOVE statue in Philadelphia. With pieces of wood and Sculpey modeling clay, children then design their own love statues as a gift for their parents (Figure 4.5).

FIGURE 4.5   Love Statues

In the weeks leading up to April, in honor of Earth Week, we do a great deal of recycled art. To create artwork like Faith Ringgold, we recycle fabric to make patchwork frames; to make collages like Mr. D., we use straw, leaves, twigs, and recycled wood to produce nature scenes; and to create three-dimensional art like Agam, we use old drawings folded in pleats and pasted onto stiff cardboard from the inside of dry-cleaned shirts.

THE MASTER ARTIST

One day, as visitors to the school peruse our growing "ABC of Artists" chart, a child announces, "I know which artist we are going to study for the letter G." "You do?" I remark. "I haven't yet selected an artist for that letter." "We have to study God, Ms. B. He is the greatest artist. He made everything!"

The provocative questions that conclude every page of *God's Paintbrush*, by Sandy Eisenberg Sasso, provide a great starting point for our discussions about the Master Artist. Later, equipped only with empty picture frames, we walk to a nearby park. Holding frames at arm's length, the children frame a flowering magnolia tree, a bush, a lone flower in the grass, a bug on a leaf, a fallen branch, a cluster of daffodils (Figure 4.6). They lie on the grass, looking upward, and frame the

FIGURE 4.6   **Admiring God's Art**

sky, clouds, and birds. We walk back to school pondering God's art and man's art—houses, bridges, streets, and street signs. On our return, each child settles down to write comments. Never has a topic elicited such focused, eloquent writing. The following are excerpts from longer passages. (Children received help with spelling but not with concept development.)

> God gave people lives so they culde live in pece. He invnted alll the colers in the world. He mand his art work to inspier us with his art. Gods art work is the oldist art work and the newest to.

> He made unaty. He made the pond at jvrne [Giverny]. He mad evrething that I cn ce [see]. He made me so hape.

> He made the oshin with fish and starfish and sharks and octapess and sea wed and fish that aer unown.

Andy's poem, inspired by Sasso's writing, is full of metaphor: "The wind is God's breath, the streams are God's tears." Mr. D., on Andy's request, adds his fine line drawings to the piece (Figure 4.7).

The poems, compiled into a special booklet, are sent home for all parents and grandparents to read and ponder.

God is the Master ARTIST BECAUSE...

....GOd is evrything the wiND is GOds Breath. THe StreeMS ARe GODs Teers. GODS HAir is THe Weeping WiLOS. THe RAinBOW is GODs SMiLe. bODS eves Are tHe SUN AND MOON GODS erBrous Are tHe Clouds God MADe MY FReidS AND Me God MADe tHe Green GRASS AND THe bluSeA AND SKY GOD MADe EVrything I See.

poem by ANDERS Lindgren

FIGURE 4.7   A Poet in the Making

WHAT IF . . . ?

To deepen our imaginative explorations we skew the facts: What if Nevelson never smoked cigarettes in her life? What if Seurat used squares or triangles instead of dots? What if Van Gogh did not lose his temper so easily? What if we had the courage to pursue our beliefs like Cassatt? What if we perceived all people to be short and chubby like Botero? What if we saw beauty in all flowers like Sara Steele? What if Michelangelo and Leonardo da Vinci respected and encouraged each other instead of saying harsh words and criticizing each other? This last question arises when we read about how the two artists fought bitterly over a giant piece of marble.

After pondering this question for a week, Mr. D., attired as Michelangelo (Figure 4.8), and a visiting education student attired as Leonardo surprise the children with an outdoor enactment. In the midst of the school day, we hear a loud commotion outdoors and rush out to find the two Renaissance artists, surrounded by easels, paint, sculpting tools, and other paraphernalia, arguing and criticizing each other's work. After watching them rave and rant for a while, I protest loudly, "Why can't you be respectful toward each other? We have been trying very hard to teach our children about respect and responsibility." The two artists stop dead in their tracks, eye each other suspiciously, and then, noticing the pleading looks of the children, sit down to consider becoming friends. To heighten the suspense,

FIGURE 4.8   What If Leonardo and Michelangelo Were Friends?

they let minutes pass; then slowly they begin to share food, drink, and art supplies. Together, they sing songs, praise each other's art techniques, and even coordinate efforts to outline a new and improved Mona Lisa. The children, eyes shining with delight, clap and cheer. "What if . . ." provides a new vision, a better solution.

RESPECT TRAINING PROGRAM

A Respect Training Program, similar to the Hero Training Program of earlier years, evolves around the end of October. Developed with parent input and implemented for forty days, this home training program consists of specific categories that are evaluated and marked every night:

1. Respect for parents
2. Respect for siblings
3. Speaking politely at all times
4. Cleaning one's own room
5. Manners at mealtimes
6. Helping to clean up as instructed (even if it is not your mess)
7. Cooperation (without procrastination)
8. Bonus points for other special acts of respect

Parents' written comments during the training program provide me with real insights into the child's life. Amy's mother writes:

> Nov. 9th—Amy showed extremely polite behavior when I introduced her to someone today. She extended her hand and introduced herself and was perfectly charming, causing my friend to rave about how well-mannered she was!
>
> Nov. 13th and 14th—Amy learned two songs on the piano using her left hand and her right. She showed great patience and was very proud of herself.
>
> Nov. 18th—Amy has been doing the dishes almost nightly without being asked. She loves doing them and does a fine job.
>
> Nov. 26th—Amy's weakest areas have been cleaning up her room and getting along with her brother. Most days she does well with her brother, but when she is tired at the end of the day, she "loses it!"

The School Training Program emerged from our end-of-day meetings. A wall covered in tall sunflowers, one for each child, is titled "Growing in Respect" (see Color Plate 28). Evaluating their own behavior at the end of each day, children determine whether or not an additional seed should be placed in the center of their growing sunflower. Their candor is abetted by the honest disclosure of their teachers.

Mr. D.: "When I think about all the events of the day, my only regret is that I raised my voice a little too much when I was calling out to Zack as we were walking back from the gym."

James: "That's right, Mr. D., you certainly yelled out loud."

Mr. D.: "I'll try to remember that the next time. I certainly feel better when I don't raise my voice like that."

Rachel: "I was respectful to everyone all day, and I even took care of my lunch and my sneakers. My cubby is organized too."

Mr. B.: "Does everyone agree with Rachel's report?"

Everyone nods. Rachel is given a yellow smiley-face seed sticker to place in the center of her growing sunflower.

Mary: "I don't think I deserve a seed today."

Ms. B.: "Why, Mary? I haven't noticed anything wrong or disrespectful today."

Tom: "I think Mary did just fine. I've been with her a lot today."

Mary, receiving puzzled looks from the children, continues to insist that she doesn't deserve a new seed. Later, she tells us that she wasted a lot of art paper, so she was not respectful to the environment.

Jojo, always the optimist, announces, "I had a great day."

The children shake their heads regretfully. "You got in trouble at gym and at recess, remember?"

I ask Jojo to explain the day's events and to set himself a new goal for the next day.

Jojo: "I got in trouble at gym because I didn't listen to the teacher's instructions, and I got in trouble at recess because I went up the slide the wrong way when children were coming down."

Tom: "What you were doing was dangerous because you could have hurt yourself."

Jojo: "But I was being real careful."

Mary: "We decided a long time ago that no one would do that because it is dangerous, so you shouldn't have done it."

Ms. B.: "Jojo, what is the solution to this problem? Think about a solution that is respectful to you and to others. I would like all of you to think about this for a minute."

Jojo: "I think I shouldn't climb up the slide the wrong way when other children are coming down, but I can do it when there's nobody on the slide."

Rachel: "But that wouldn't be fair!"

Jojo: "Yes, it will!"

Amy: "No, it wouldn't, because we all decided that no one could do it."

The whole class murmurs in agreement.

Ms. B.:   "Jojo, I think the group is telling you that it wouldn't be respectful to the first-grade children, the prekindergarten children, or the teachers, because this was a decision that was reached by everyone who uses the playground, in order to make it a safe place."

Jojo: "Maybe I won't climb the slide here, but I will still do it in the park."

Rachel (the "class mother"):   "Just make sure you're safe and that your mom thinks it's O.K."

John: "Amy helped a child at recess today. She was really good. She stayed with her until the nurse came."

Sarah: "She's never done that before."

"She deserves a standing ovation," Mary declares, and the children stand up to applaud.

The discussion continues in this way until each child has a turn to talk about his or her day, assessing personal behavior in terms of respect and growth. In some mysterious way real community building is taking place within these discussions. A father's end-of-year written comment corroborates my impressions:

> One of the most overwhelming developments in S has been the visible joy he has shown in other children's accomplishments. During the play rehearsals he would come home and tell us how well some of his classmates were doing. It was the same for the art show—he was genuinely excited by what the others were doing, and by how well they were doing. This carried into home where S constantly takes great pride in, and expresses his joy at, the accomplishments of his younger brother.
>
> Another area of growth for S has been his moral development. He has developed a great foundation for knowing what's right and wrong. He still has his conflicts, but will talk through them to get over his frustrations.

RESPECT AWARD CEREMONY

The Respect Training Program concludes with an eagerly awaited award ceremony. The classroom, decorated for the event, fills with parents who sit facing three stairs with the colorful letters R-E-S-P-E-C-T pasted on the risers. The Respect Oath, composed by the children and illustrated on a large poster by Mr. D., hangs on an adjacent wall for all to see (Figure 4.9). On a table close by are laid out individual respect medals (a gold spray-painted teddy bear on a ribbon, in honor of Isaac Bear) and certificates that define both aspects of a child: those she has been good at and those she is still working on. As the ceremony begins, children troop

FIGURE 4.9   The Respect Oath

out in a single file to prerecorded olympiad music. A frequent visitor to the class observing the ceremony writes the following description:

> The ceremony commences, and it is probably unlike any of the ceremonies these children will walk through during their long school career. After three months of kindergarten, most parents have grasped that their child's teacher will weave a higher purpose into everything she does. They know that this is not some cutesy event made up for their benefit. Before their eyes something of real significance is unfolding in their children's lives.
>
> It is not enough for Usha that these children pick up an award and a handful of applause. Usha mines the concept of respect for its riches one more time. As she calls each child by name and they climb down the stairs one by one to stand before her, she asks, "What can you tell us about respect?" As the brief, unrehearsed answers emerge, one can sense and appreciate the hard-earned lessons behind the words. Each child focuses on something slightly different. "Giving." "Not hurting another's feelings." "Being nice to other people." In one way or another most say that respect has a lot to do with listening to other people when they talk and restraining one's impulses to interrupt. It's a big hurdle for them.
>
> Then, standing alone before his peers, assembled guests, and loving family, each child is asked, "Are you willing to take the kindergarten oath of respect?"

After a solemn "yes" is spoken, all place their right hands on their hearts and recite the oath that the class has written collectively:

> I promise to try and be respectful at all times.
> I will be respectful
> to myself,
> to other people,
> and to the environment.
> I will do this because
> I will have a happier life,
> the world will be a cleaner place,
> and everyone will be peaceful.

As the weighty significance of the oath they recite registers in their hearts and then on their mesmerized faces, you can see without exception that these six-year-olds have fully surrendered to their commitment.

RESPONSIBILITY

In January the concept of responsibility is introduced through four short stories from the "Responsibility" video of the *Book of Virtues* series. The stories, with animated characters that hold children's interest, depict the consequences of responsible and irresponsible actions, provoking a great deal of discussion among students. "Re-spon-si-bi-li-ty. You want something done, you can count on me." This video jingle lingers with the group.

The jingle soon becomes our greeting, our start-of-day and end-of-day chant, and our commitment as we begin each new task. When I tinkle the wind chimes in our window to signify the end of free choice and the beginning of cleanup, a spontaneous chorus breaks out: "Re-spon-si-bi-li-ty. You want something done, you can count on me." While painting, children skip away to fetch their smocks chanting, "Re-spon-si-bi-li-ty. You want something done, you can count on me." At lunch a child spills applesauce, and she and her neighbor run toward the sink to get and moisten some paper towels, murmuring, "Re-spon-si-bi-li-ty. You want something done, you can count on me."

RESPONSIBILITY AT SCHOOL

What is personal responsibility? We sit in a circle, shut our eyes, and try to picture each part of the school day, listing personal responsibility actions for each segment. For example, our list for the start of the school day is as follows:

ARRIVAL AT SCHOOL (8:00 A.M. to 8:20 A.M.)
- Make sure you have your book bag and lunch with you when you get out of the car or bus.

- If you have taken your jacket off, remember to put it back on before you get out of the car or bus.
- Make sure you shut the car door properly.
- Thank mom, dad, babysitter, or bus driver for bringing you to school.
- Smile or say something pleasant to others in the bus or car before you leave.
- Greet the teacher at the door.
- Greet other students in the waiting area.
- Put your book bag and other belongings in your cubby.
- Settle down in the waiting area and have fun talking to friends, or introduce yourself to children you do not know. You can bring a book to share with others at this time.

After we list responsibility actions for the entire day, we pose the next question: "Why should one be responsible in this manner?" Children are quick to respond:

"Or else you'll lose all your stuff."

"People will be annoyed with you."

"If you leave all your stuff lying around, other kids could trip on it."

"If you run in the hallways, you could bump into others coming the other way, like Peter did the other day."

"If we're not responsible with the acrylic paint, it could get on our clothes and not come off . . . EVER!"

"If we're not responsible for stuff, we could break it. We would get in trouble, and we wouldn't have stuff to play with."

After a few weeks of discussion we compile this list with its bold caption:

WHY SHOULD A HUMAN BEING BE RESPONSIBLE?
To keep himself safe
To keep others safe
To keep his belongings safe
To keep the environment safe for all
To help others
To enable others to trust him
To make the class, the home, the neighborhood, and the world a safer place for all.

TRUST AND RESPONSIBILITY TO THE GROUP

Since trust and responsibility toward the group (class, family, school, neighborhood) recur frequently in our discussions, we spend some more time on these issues. In silent and guided reflection we ponder how it would feel to live in a class, home, or neighborhood where everyone is responsible. It would be a place where no one says, "It's not my problem, it's theirs," where everyone looks out for one another, and pitches in to help whenever and wherever necessary. Children have no problem envisioning such a place.

"If everyone was responsible in my house, nobody would scream. My house is too noisy right now."

"My house would be peaceful because most of the time I get yelled at for not cleaning up my toys, and my sister gets yelled at for not getting off the phone."

"My house would be really clean if my brother and I were responsible. Actually, maybe not completely, because our kitchen is so often a mess. But it definitely would be better."

"I went to this park, and there were so many soda cans and so much litter. If people were responsible, it would be much cleaner."

"There would be no pollution."

"Yes, and the fish would not be strangled by those soda-can circle thingum-a-jigs."

"Everyone would recycle, and it would be better for the trees."

If one is responsible, one can be trusted—this has been established. But what does this mean in our everyday lives? Role-play enables children to perceive a situation from perspectives other than their own. For example, we enact a scene in which a mom leaves her daughter, Mary, with two friends, Sally and Ben. Because she will be entertaining friends later in the day, Mom instructs Mary to keep the living room tidy and to keep away from the dining room, which is all set up for the party.

The scene is enacted in two ways: In one, Mary decides to give the others a peek at the cake, and the children create a great mess in the dining room; in the other, Mary is trustworthy. Through the process of creating dialogue for the two scenarios, children begin to realize the frustration parents feel when instructions are disregarded and the peace and joy that prevail when trust is maintained.

SITUATION 1

"If I were the mom, I would be really mad. I would say, 'I told you not to go in there. Now look what you've done!' "

"I would be mad too, but I might ask Mary if it was an accident."

"I would tell Mary to go up to her room and stay there."

"I would be so upset, I'd tell Mary that I would take all her piggy bank money to buy a new cake."

SITUATION 2

"If I were the mom, I would be so pleased, I might tell her she can have a special piece of cake—the one with the rose on top."

"If I were the mom, I'd say, 'Oh, Mary, you've been so good, I feel very happy.' "

"I would come in and give Mary a big hug and then give all the children some Popsicles."

"I would say, 'Mary, I knew I could trust you!' "

PRACTICING RESPONSIBILITY AT HOME

A letter to parents informs them about our responsibility curriculum and encourages them to empower their children by entrusting them with specific tasks.

Dear Parents,

While continuing with the concept of respect, we are beginning to study RE-SPONSIBILITY. Our class slogan is "Re-spon-si-bi-li-ty. You want something done, you can count on me."

In class each child is responsible for:

Cleaning up after projects
Cleaning up personal lunch materials
Focusing on individual tasks
Walking, not running, in the hallways
Keeping individual cubbies in order
Bringing hats, gloves, etc. back from drama and gym classes

As we work on the play, more responsibility tasks will be added to the list. This is a good time to assign simple responsibility tasks at home—setting the table, helping with dishes, taking the garbage out, helping with younger siblings. If you find any stories that depict responsibility, please send them in or come in and read them to us.

Cheers!

PRACTICING RESPONSIBILITY IN OUR PLAY

The class play, enacted in February, provides ample opportunities for putting responsible, trustworthy actions into practice. The musical created by the children is an hour and ten minutes long, and there are long wait times during rehearsals. Children who are not on stage are trusted to work on three projects: creating their own ABC book of words from the play, writing a page in their journal, and working on their sketch books illustrating scenes from the play.

Responsibility to the group involves learning one's own lines, paying attention, entering the stage on cue, not laughing or losing control when things go wrong on stage, performing the best one can, using props carefully, being very quiet when one is off-stage, helping to put away the props, and cleaning up the theater. Self-evaluation at the end of the day consists of assessing one's own behavior in terms of trust and responsibility ("I worked on my journal and I did well when I acted. I even remembered to smile at Monet and nod to Paul Bunyan"), setting personal goals ("I will try to cooperate with the others who sit on the log with me in Scene 2"), and coming up with strategies to attain the goals ("I will place my hands on my knees so I don't play with Amy's props") (see Color Plate 29).

"BECOMING" A FAMOUS ARTIST

The play in February is a huge success, and the children, proud, happy, and buzzing with high spirits, continue to be intrigued by the study of various artists. My mind, however, moves ahead to plan a culminating event that will bring together every-thing the children have learned in this magical year. With more than two months to work up to the event, we decide to host an art show opening at the end of May entitled "Artists from A to Z."

Each child will choose one artist to research and portray (complete with cos-tume) at the show. "Becoming" the artist in question, each child will discuss the artist's life (in terms of respect and responsibility if possible), display a painting done in the artist's style, and explain the artist's techniques. Children's artwork from the entire year will also be on display. Each child's exhibit will consist of two important sculptures, one of aluminum foil and papier-mâché (Figure 4.10) and the other of wood. The former sculpture will depict a respectful character, and the latter sculpture will depict a responsible character (see Color Plate 30). Children will write stories that explain their choice of characters.

Children choose artists of differing styles and nationalities: Escher of Holland, Sara Steele of Pennsylvania, Berthe Morisot of Paris, Beatrix Potter of England (Fig-ure 4.11), Leonardo da Vinci of Italy (see Color Plate 31), and the ever-popular Monet of France. With parents' help they write and memorize lengthy speeches about their artist's life and art. Mr. D. and I are amazed at the length of some of the speeches, but no one is willing to shorten their talk. As teachers and parents, we join together to devise mnemonic strategies—action strategies for kinesthetic kids, pictorial aids for visual kids, and taped speeches for auditory kids to listen to over and over again.

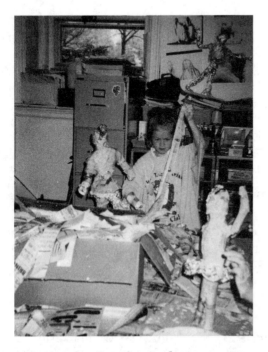

FIGURE 4.10   Creating Sculptures of Aluminum Foil and Papier-Mâché

FIGURE 4.11   Beatrix Potter

On the night of the show, the first presenter, a fairly shy child who has grown tremendously in confidence since the rehearsals began, now inspired by personal communication with the artist of her choice, steps forth to deliver her speech with calm assurance and heart-melting expressiveness (see Color Plate 32):

> Hello! My name is Laurel Burch. I was born in California. I am a self-taught folk artist. At the age of twenty-three I was a single mom with two kids on welfare, but today my jewelry and art are sold all over the world. Through my art I would like to teach children to believe in themselves and in their dreams. My art has different themes like "Fantastic Felines" [points to her huge painted replica of Laurel Burch's geometrical cat face]. I like to write poems with my artwork. My favorite poem is:
>
> > *Look at the world through the eyes of your heart.*
> > *Speak to the world through the voice of your heart.*
> > *Share with the world through the heart of your heart.*[1]
>
> Thank you.

---

[1]From *Fantastic Felines* by Laurel Burch, © 1997. Published by Chronicle Books, San Francisco, LLC. Used by permission.

Amy, our prolific artist, who had been very anxious and reluctant about reading until mid-February, decides to read her speech. She practices for several weeks, often seated by me at lunch, decoding and enunciating words such as *National Wildlife Federation*. Dressed in a soft, flowing dress, her eyes sparkling, she reads without hesitation at the show (see Color Plate 33):

> Hello! My name is Sara Steele. I am a local artist from West Mount Airy, Pennsylvania. I still live in the house that I grew up in. I am a self-taught artist, but I have studied with several teachers.
>
> The first flower I ever painted was an iris. We had irises growing in our garden when I was growing up, and I still collect and grow them. Somebody gave me watercolors and paper when I was little and I was so excited. Now, I am well known for my watercolor paintings of flowers.
>
> I have done several calendars and posters of my flowers. The National Wildlife Federation asked me to do paintings of orchids. I was very happy to do this because I care very much about world peace and about saving the plants, animals, and people.
>
> Here is a picture of me and here is my painting of a rose. Thank you.

MARY CASSATT

Remember the pregnant mom who introduced our children to Mary Cassatt? Well, her son Andy decides that he will portray this Pennsylvanian artist at the show. The children are amazed and amused. A boy wants to portray a female artist—is this for real? But Andy is totally at ease with his decision as he sets about, unperturbed, finding the right dress, hat, shoes, and gloves. A week before the show Andy dresses up in full attire, and everyone is impressed at the transformation (Figure 4.12). However, his "elegant lady" impression lasts only as long as Andy stands still, for his every move reveals the rugged male soccer player that he is. Three girls offer to help him, giving him lessons in grace—how to walk, climb stairs, hold a parasol, and sit with knees pulled together.

The following is Andy's father's account of our art show:

> It is 6:30 P.M. and everyone is here on time. The headmaster, arriving in haste between two other engagements, is astonished at the group's punctuality. "How does she get you all here on time? What's the secret?" A knowing chuckle ripples through the crowd. We have been preparing for this evening for weeks—in a way for the whole year—and we are absolutely serious about Art. For the past week our children have come home with small patches of tape stuck to their shirts with V.I.L. (Very Important Letter) written on them. Two or three pages of detailed instructions have been stuffed into backpacks as we counted down to opening night. Ms. B. has kept a pen next to her bed-table at night so that when a forgotten detail or new idea jolts her awake she can write it on her hand without getting out of bed or turning on the light. Be-

FIGURE 4.12   **Proud to Be Mary Cassatt**

tween dinner and bed students have been trying on costumes, rehearsing lines, and putting last touches on their masterpieces.

The headmaster keeps his remarks brief, but Ms. B. takes her time explaining how we all arrived here tonight. Everyone listens including several of history's most famous artists. They don't fidget or yawn, even though Mary Cassatt's hat is loose and gets in her eyes, Monet's beard is prickly, and Van Gogh has a nasty, hot bandage on the side of his head. Everyone knows how it will go tonight and how to do their jobs. They know it will take a lot of time and care and focus. They radiate confidence as they listen.

Each artist steps up to the microphone to explain her or his art and life. Monet rhapsodizes about Giverny; Van Gogh is obsessed with his art but rues his lack of self-control. My own son, with his long, blond hair, stands up in his wide-brimmed hat, white dress, white gloves clasped around a floral parasol, and says, "My name is Mary Cassatt." Mary explains how she became interested in art, how her father initially discouraged her, how her interests developed . . . and abruptly stops. The audience freezes. "Wait," my son says, "I need to start this over." He brings onto the stage a smock, a pallet and a brush—props that he had forgotten to use in the dramatic transformation from young lady to artist. This takes some time and care to correct while the audience waits. My son is at ease and focused, and so the audience is too. No one jumps out of the wings to help him as he fumbles with the smock. The stage is his.

An hour passes quickly as children stand up and spend five or six minutes talking about their art. There are no chairs in this art gallery, so we stand in attention and listen. When they finish, the doors are opened and we enter the main room in groups. The room is too small to accommodate the fifty or so guests, so it has been arranged that half of the guests will go into the sun porch and enjoy hors d'oeuvres, sweets, and sparkling cider.

Dutifully, for almost an hour, knowing that there are little eclairs, tarts, cookies, petit-fours, pig's ears, and pastries down the hall, each artist stands beside her or his area of the boardroom receiving inquisitive guests. Finally, they are released from their duties, and they turn back into kids. My son inhales a few cookies and then races out the door on winged-boy feet. He scrambles up a tree in his lacy white dress and black Mary Janes. It is almost dark. We came here at 6:00 and now it is 8:30. But we are accustomed to this pace in Ms. B.'s class, where things take as long as they need to take and require focus, discipline, and preparation.

EVALUATING THE ART SHOW

Children's own evaluations of the art show are exuberant. I listen to their excited chatter, delighted that their comments are mostly in praise of others and the group.

"Jojo's painting of the mother and five kids was really awesome. I think the audience loved it when he told them why he had called the painting 'She's All We've Got' " (see Color Plate 34).

"I loved Beatrix Potter's dress. She looked so pretty, and she remembered all her lines and even smiled when she was speaking."

"James looked like a grown-up with his beard, and his Cezanne painting was really, really good."

"I thought everyone did great. For the first time everyone remembered all their parts and didn't have to look at you, Ms. B."

Their writings about the event reveal the same sentiments.

THE ART SHOW

I liked it. wene we frst came to ryan hall and we did not kwoe (know) thir parts and the evning ov the art show was wen everyone new thir parts and wen andrew sat down he gave me space to sit. I had a costoom that made me look like a real man with a beerd. Adieu.

The art was very good becos evrebte noo theyre part. All the people were very hppe. The musk (music) ws grat. They loved the songs. Peter did grat. I liked his costoom.

COLOR PLATE 19 ■ **Young Artists in Front of Their Monet Masterpiece**

COLOR PLATE 20 ■ **Appreciating Van Gogh**

COLOR PLATE 21 ■ **Madonna and Child—Just like Leonardo!**

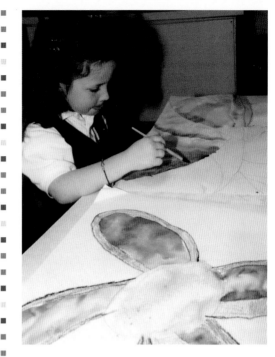

COLOR PLATE 22 ■ **Painting O'Keeffe Style**

COLOR PLATE 23 ■ **Imitating Picasso**

COLOR PLATE 24 ■ **Kindergarten Cubism**

COLOR PLATE 25 ■ **A Model of the Mayflower**

COLOR PLATE 26 ■ **Stained Glass for Sale**

COLOR PLATE 27 ■ **Imitating Tiffany**

COLOR PLATE 28 ■ **Blossoming in Respect**

COLOR PLATE 29 ■ **Characters in the Play**

COLOR PLATE 30 ■ **The Artist with His Two Completed Sculptures**

COLOR PLATE 31 ■ **I Can Be Leonardo da Vinci**

COLOR PLATE 32 ■ **Laurel Burch**

COLOR PLATE 33 ■ **Sara Steele**

COLOR PLATE 34 ■ **"She's All We've Got"**

Trevor was a very fast track runner. He always won all the races that he ran in. He was also the captain of his team.

His most favorite race was the nine hundred meter race, it was also the race in which he had his best time.

COLOR PLATE 35 ■ **Trevor: First Page**

COLOR PLATE 36 ■ **Children's Artistic Rendering of the World Map**

COLOR PLATE 37 ■ **Space Shuttle One**

I am VAry haPPy About the Art Show Because I likeD WAN AvreWon CAM over AND talked to Me And I also Like Wan Avrewon Wat Up ON the stAG AND SAD Tar Part. I thot Avrewon WAS GrAt.

CONCLUDING ACTIVITIES: RESPECT AND RESPONSIBILITY STORIES

For her senior project a high school student, originally from Bangladesh, chose to work with me in our kindergarten. She spent the last two weeks with individual children, typing their dictated Respect and Responsibility stories into a computer. These stories are elaborations on the original stories they created about their sculptures. (We ran out of time before the art show.) The senior's task was to help each child develop his or her story by encouraging them to add adjectives and relevant details. She also interviewed each child to create an "About the Author" page for their soon to be illustrated, published books.

ZACK: THE RESPONSIBLE RUNNER

Zack was a great track runner who ran two miles every day. But he had a problem with pacing himself because he would run too fast in the beginning of the race and run out of breath and energy at the end of the race. One day he went to a track near his house with his friends from his track team. There they met the owner of the track, Mr. Christopher, who asked them if they wanted to run the 400 meter race with each other. The person who would win the race would get an invitation to the Penn relays, the coolest track event in Pennsylvania, and five dollars from Mr. Christopher. The loser of the race would have to make the winner a box where he could keep his toys. Mr. Christopher set up some heats for them. Everyone was really excited, especially Zack. He really wanted to win. He decided to be a responsible runner and pace himself so that he would not run out of breath. For the first two hundred meters of the race he ran slowly, but then, in the last two hundred meters of the race, he sprinted with all the energy he had saved, and won! Zack was really happy that he had become a responsible runner. He won the five dollars, the toy box, and an invitation to the Penn relays. He bought a Power Ranger action figure with his five dollars. The End.

SAMANTHA THE RESPECTFUL FLOWER SELLER

Samantha was a respectful flower seller. She sold her flowers beside the porch of her house. One day a little girl, Krista, asked her for some money and flowers. She was sad because it was Mother's Day and she did not have anything to give her mother. Samantha was respectful of her situation and gave her six dollars and a free bunch of red and white roses. Krista bought a perfume that smelled like lemon, for four dollars. Krista was respectful of Samantha and did not keep the two dollars but gave them back to Samantha and thanked her for her help. Krista's mother was very happy to see the perfume and the roses. Krista told her mother about Samantha and how she had given her free flowers and money. Krista's mother told her to be respectful of Samantha's kindness and give back the four dollars she owed. Krista gave Samantha the four dollars and bought a bunch of sunflowers and daisies from her. Samantha thanked her for buying the sunflowers and daisies. The End. (see Figure 4.13)

TREVOR THE RESPECTFUL TRACK RUNNER

Trevor was a very fast track runner. He always won all the races that he ran in. He was also the captain of his team. His most favorite race was the nine hundred meter race, which was the race in which he had his best time. His coach, William, told him never to be proud of his success and to always respect the others on his team by helping them. On his team was a little boy named Cameron who was very slow and weak. Cameron always came last in all his races and everyone on the team made fun of him. Whenever he would pass by, his team mates would say, "Hey look, there is bald head," or, "Look, here comes Pinocchio." They called him "turtle" because he was very slow. But Trevor respected Cameron and never made fun of him. One day Cameron was

FIGURE 4.13   Creating the Flower Seller

crying because all his team mates, except for Trevor, made fun of him. Trevor felt really sorry for him and told him that he would help him become a better runner. Trevor ran with Cameron after every practice and took him to the gym so that he could build more muscles. He told him to eat less fatty foods like Mc Donald's and Burger King and to eat more vegetables and fruits. After some days Cameron became stronger and faster, and his team mates were surprised and stopped making fun of him. Cameron won the first place in every race he ran. Trevor and Cameron were very happy; they rejoiced. Cameron thanked Trevor for his help and respected him for his kindness. Trevor told Cameron to respect others who are slower than him and help other people who are not as fast as him. The End. (see Figure 4.14 and Color Plate 35)

Other concluding activities included placing all the artists we studied on both a timeline (history) and a world map (geography), taking a trip to the Philadelphia Museum of Art to see the works of artists we have studied, taking a trip to the neighborhood senior citizen's center to show off our artwork, and—a final act of responsibility—preparing the classroom for its next occupants. For three days we become a cleaning crew, with headbands that proclaim "The Responsible Cleaners."

Cameron thanked Trevor for his help and respected him for his kindness. Trevor told Cameron to respect others who are slower than him and help other people who are not as fast as him.

THE END

FIGURE 4.14 **Trevor: Last Page**

Armed with buckets, pails, detergent, sponges, rags, scrubbing brushes, and paper towels, the children set about washing down every shelf, every block of wood, and every plastic toy in the classroom. In three days everything is packed away in containers or covered with plastic or aluminum foil and emblazoned with a sticker that says, "Inspected by. . . ."

Children also write a final statement about responsibility. Given a sheet of paper with the words, *"When I do something responsible I feel _____ because _____ ,"* they write:

> When I do something responsible I feel HAPPY because I FeeL rile grAt to Do SoMetHing responsible.

> When I do something responsible I feel HPPY because I JAS LOVE DOING IT.

> When I do something responsible I feel Grat because I dot Get in Trabl And I do the rit Thing.

> When I do something responsible I feel HAPPY because I HeLP eVeReY one.

> When I do something responsible I feel GRAT because my MOM anD DAD LiKe it.

> When I do something responsible I feel vERy vERy haPPy because I MADE THE WoRLD cLEENEr.

> When I do something responsible I feel GraT because iT iS SaMThiNG ResPoNsIble aND My hrT fels hApe.

> When I do something responsible I feel good because I no IV don Someting rite.

CLOSING LETTERS

It is time to say farewell to Isaac Bear, who leaves us the day before school officially ends. The Kindergarten Etiquette Book is handed to Isaac, and everyone hugs and thanks him for being a part of our kindergarten experience. The next day we find hidden letters from him and his mom:

> Dear [list of every child's name],
> Thank you for having me in your class this year. I had a wonderful time watching and learning. My most favorite things were the play, the art show, the funny poetry book, and the many songs you sang this year. I am also glad that I learned about RESPECT and RESPONSIBILITY. If I practice these when I am young, I will not end up like Van Gogh.
> I will miss you all next year, but I know that you will have fun in first grade. My mom is coming to pick me up tonight, so this is Good Bye. Have a wonderful summer and a great year in first grade. I will be in first grade too, and I will be thinking of you.
> Love, Isaac
> P.S. Don't you think I write really well? I learned a lot this year.

Dear Ms. Balamore and Mr. Deis,

Thank you very much for taking such good care of Isaac for me. Isaac tells me that he has learned so much this year. Please thank all the children for being kind to Isaac. He loved going on the bus ride with the children, he loved watching the play, and he especially loved being at the Art Show. I have bought Isaac an easel, some paints, and some brushes for the summer. He also wants me to get him a palette like Mary Cassatt and a hat like Monet. I guess he wants to be an artist like your kindergarten children.

Ms. Balamore, thank you for teaching Isaac about respect, responsibility, and self-control. He tells me that he has learned so much from watching your children because they have worked hard to accomplish these goals. He tells me that:

S . . . doesn't suck her thumb as much any more.

D . . . does her work much faster and with greater responsibility.

J . . . is trying hard to use a calm, pleasant voice at all times.

A . . . is being more responsible in every way and did not even make a fuss when she was feeling sick at her brother's play.

M . . . no longer wastes paper but is using paper and markers in a responsible way.

S . . . is using words to talk to his younger brother and is not throwing tantrums at home,

J . . . talks about how he is feeling instead of crying when he is upset.

P . . . finally earned his respect award and is trying to have more self-control in the hallways.

A . . . is beginning to accept the idea of having a new brother and is beginning to think of ways he can help his mom and dad with the baby.

[The list goes on to mention every child's development.]

You have such a wonderful group of children, Ms. Balamore. I know that Isaac will miss all of them very much. He asked me to make a special batch of palace-baked cookies for the children. I must tell you that Isaac was very responsible. He remembered to tell me that S . . . was allergic to peanuts and that some children did not like chocolate chip cookies. So I baked some vanilla cookies and some chocolate chip cookies.

Before I end this letter, I do have a request for your class. Please send me the words and music to the *Respect Song* and *The Artists from A to Z* song. Isaac loved learning those songs from Mr. Deis. Thank you again.

Love to all the children,

Emma Bear

The children write fond letters of farewell to Isaac Bear. Some letters are long:

Dear Isaac,

I am really glad that you were in our class. I liked giving you hugs. I liked teaching you about respect and responsibility and the artists. I hope you learned a lot. Have fun in first grade. I hope you will send me lots of e-mail. I will miss you. Love. . . .

And some are short and illustrated (Figure 4.15):

Dear Isaac,

Thank you for coming to our class. Love . . .

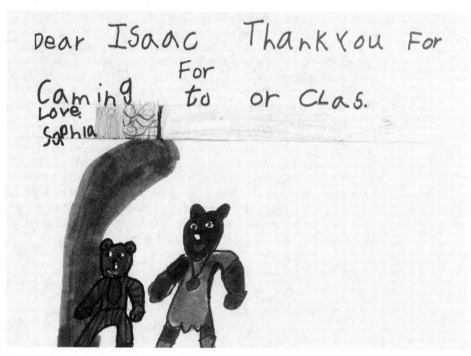

FIGURE 4.15   Thank You, Isaac Bear!

THE LAST DAY

It is difficult to end the adventure, to say goodbye! With children gathered at my feet, Mr. D. strumming his guitar, and parents seated in tiny children's chairs, I read from Dr. Seuss's book *Oh, the Places You'll Go!*:[1]

> *Congratulations!*
> *Today is your day.*
> *You're off to Great Places!*
> *You're off and away!*

The words in the book are very relevant, and I stop often, linking the lines to issues we have discussed in class. The following lines, for example, are straight out of our respect and responsibility talks:

> *You'll look up and down streets. Look 'em over with care.*
> *About some you will say, "I don't choose to go there."*

---

[1]From *Oh, the Places You'll Go!* by Dr. Seuss, TM and copyright © by Dr. Seuss Enterprises L.P. 1990. Used by permission of Random House Children's Books, a division of Random House, Inc.

With your head full of brains and your shoes full of feet,
You're too smart to go down any not-so-good street.

Then we relive the year by singing several of the songs we have composed on our journey. There is a lot of spontaneous clapping, dancing, and hugging. Each child is given a special book, a videotape of the art show, and his or her "published" story. The special book, titled *Artists A to Z,* is an ABC book with two pages devoted to each of the artists we have studied. Each week throughout the year Mr. D. xeroxed photographs of the current artist we were studying, wrote a brief description, and assembled all the material to create a glorious documentation for the children.

Each year while writing end-of-year reports for parents, Mr. D. and I construct special reports for the children—reports that *they* will understand, reports that are consistent with our message of not comparing one child with another, but rather of comparing a child's current work with previous efforts and applauding his or her success. The report usually takes the form of a certificate that commends three specific attributes of the child, recalls a salient incident, and is covered with Mr. D.'s drawings and glittery stickers. This year we include the certificate as the first page of the ABC book. Sarah's first page reads:

> This Special Book is Awarded to
> Sarah Bivens
> on Completion of a Successful Kindergarten Year.
> We hope that you will always appreciate art,
> respect yourself, others and the environment,
> and act with great responsibility.

You have been:

1. A great mathematician, artist, author, and cartographer.
2. A very steadfast, responsible helper.
3. A respectful companion to all the children.

We will never forget your loving smile, your eagerness to learn, and the many, many notes you illustrated for Isaac Bear. Love, Mr. D. and Ms. B.

A final letter to the parents completes our mission for this year and leaves us wondering what the future holds for this particular group of parents and children.

Dear Parents,

Thank you for entrusting your beautiful children to us and for accompanying us on our many kindergarten adventures. Through our study of artists we have traveled to far-off places, through our practice of respect and responsibility we have learned to examine our own actions, and through our acknowledgment of God as the Master Artist we have attained a new awareness.

We hope that the themes of this year pervade our entire life.

> May we always be respectful to
> ourselves, other people
> and the environment.
> May we always be responsible.
> May we always be truly AWARE.

We have loved each and every child of our "funny family." We are so accustomed to their faces, mannerisms, and individual expressions of love that sending them to first grade is both exciting and sad. We will miss them, but we know that they will be cheerfully engaged in first grade projects very soon.

We thank you for your help, support, laughter, and love this year.

Mr. D. and Ms. B.

COMMENTARY

If you asked the children what the year's theme had been, would any have said, "Respect and responsibility"? Amid the riveting study of artists it was everywhere apparent: in the stories read, in the stories written, in the songs and chants composed, in day-to-day reflections and evaluations, in recycled art, in training programs at home, in food cooked for homeless shelters, in the collection of mittens and gloves, in the big events—being an artist, doing a class play—and of course in all of Usha's and Mr. Deis's doings. How does a teacher manage to be so deliberate and insistent yet so subtle? A few observations:

Although there are some leading questions—"If everyone was kind and polite, how would that make you feel?" "Aren't there pretty people who are not respectful?"—for the most part Usha does not do head-on teaching. It is Emma Bear who recalls the kind, gentle children of a former year and Isaac Bear who writes letters to the children commenting on their consideration. It is the children who offer suggestions about the meaning of respect and responsibility. The terms are not explained by the teacher, with questions limited to follow-up instances. Rather, the topics are approached largely as inquiries without any advance assumptions. Terms such as *respect* and *responsibility* are evolving concepts gradually gathering (and changing) their meaning as the children try out, accept, and reject possible definitions and examples. Usha quite genuinely wants to understand the children's thinking. While, as always, she has no doubt about the general picture, how these particular children comprehend and construct the terms is not preordained. Her questions therefore are genuine ("How exactly does one respect another?" "But why should we be polite?" "What is personal responsibility?" "How can you make the world happier?"). It is the children who decide on the specifics, and it is the children who determine whether they have been respectful and deserving of credit. It is the artists who get investigated for their virtues. Usha remains restrained in the telling but tireless in the asking.

If asked what Usha taught them, I suspect the children would say not very much, they just learned by themselves. What they know are their ideas, their discoveries, their queries, their participation, their artist, their writings, and their paintings. Usha understands that children of this age, perhaps uniquely, have a genuine yearning for the good to prevail over the bad, along with a powerful belief in their personal omnipotence. The world is theirs to make. It is their wishes and ambitions, their good will and good deeds that will overcome evil. Anything is possible! Enemies can become friends, the past can be recast, the future is indeterminate. One has only to look at their beloved fairy tales for confirmation: Hansel and Gretel and the Seven Dwarfs overcome wicked witches; Little Red Riding Hood, Peter, and the Three Little Pigs overcome wolves; Jack vanquishes the Giant. Usha taps the romance and idealism of the young, who blur the lines between the real and "what if . . ." worlds. They have expansive moral ambitions and confidence in their own heroic possibilities. She taps, too, their candidness. If they goofed, they goofed. Tomorrow is another day when they can—and surely will—do more, be better.

The themes are made deeply, personally real. Recycling art materials, collecting mittens, practicing respect and responsibility at home, receiving certificates, taking oaths, self-criticism—these are not banal calls to virtue but earnestly felt experiences. They arouse the children's imagination, sympathy, ambition, regret, and pride.

Once again we note that the curriculum is wide-ranging, highly fluid, and recursive. The boundaries are loose; one idea chases another in an ever-deepening pursuit. When it is time to make New Year's resolutions, for example, Usha encourages the children to think of how they could make the world, not just the classroom, a happier place. In their discussions of behavior at the dentist's office and of treatment of waste products, they ask what it means to be respectful. In their pursuit of the theme—respect and responsibility—they move from classroom etiquette to at-home relationships, sweeping up parental input as they tunnel deeper. For Usha this topic, like every topic, is inexhaustible. Respect takes on a richer and more layered meaning as it becomes relevant to the children at a birthday party, in a car, at the supermarket, when cooking, at Thanksgiving, and with various school helpers. These variations on a theme cumulatively have their impact as we see from parental reactions. At the same time the children come to understand that their achievements represent approximations, not mastery. They, and their teachers and parents, can still become "gooder."

The most serendipitous pursuit this year was the study of artists, stimulated by an appealing naptime video of Monet and an observation by the reading specialist. If the children found Monet of interest, then a study of artists would be the vehicle for teaching academic skills and considering further the respect and responsibility theme. However, before one gets carried away by the children's initiative, it is important to note that it was Usha who selected a tape of Monet. It was Mr. D. who put on the music of Debussy (an idea initially of the music teacher). It was Mr. D. and Usha who constructed the alphabet of artists that included Escher, da Vinci, O'Keeffe, Picasso, Tiffany, and Van Gogh as well as less well-known artists from non-Western countries and artists from the local community. She might have made other choices. This is not the world of Disney and TV cartoons. Usha introduces the children to the great riches of our culture while not neglecting those of other cultures. "Introduce" is hardly the right word, for once again the children become those artists. They experience another close encounter.

CHAPTER FIVE

COMMONWEALTH FOUNDATIONS: SETTING THE TONE

The year of the hero, the year of the princess, and the year of the bear—each is a delightful journey with its own unique detours and investigations. Through all the fun and laughter, however, Usha manages to hold on to the deeper purposes of education, relentlessly pursuing goodness and high academic aspirations. What techniques make this work? How can her almost intuitive practices be described? Because Usha uses year-long themes to frame her teaching and because of the momentum that exists in the classroom, we have organized her practices as they emerge at the beginning, middle, and end of the calendar year. Although there is some artifice to this organization—many of the practices are pervasive—it is useful to distinguish ways in which she initially sets the tone (this chapter), then maintains the tone (Chapter 6) and, given the predictable setbacks of children and teachers, restores the tone (Chapter 7). Within these chapters we have grouped the techniques she uses under three core pedagogical principles: *engagement of all children, sensitivity to the commonwealth,* and *reflection on the meaning of action.* It is through engagement, social sensitivity, and reflection that children enlarge their capacities, promote collective well-being, and appreciate loftier purposes. Many of her techniques will be familiar from prior chapters. They are separated here as "techniques" so that the reader can review their applicability. To avoid repetition, our illustrations in these chapters come from activities not previously described.

Usha believes that through spontaneous experiences and robust discussion, children discover for themselves what is required to sustain a harmonious community. Imposing rules of conduct is rarely necessary. But it is not merely a matter of faith. Usha has a bag of pedagogical tools, developed over many years of practice, that are crucial to the implementation of her beliefs.

As we attempt to make these tools more explicitly manifest, it is important for the reader to distinguish *general practices* from specific *exemplifications.* Although the practices are applicable across a wide variety of settings, the examples (italicized headings) are meant only as illustrations. At the level of implementation, teachers will want to select specific subject matter, situations, and techniques congenial to their own school settings, personalities, and comfort levels. For example, Usha believes that child experimentation is a powerful tool for learning. That is the general practice. Rather than renegotiating cleanup and exhorting children to be more appreciative of the custodial staff, she once suggested that the class experiment with not picking up or cleaning for three days. That is the specific example. Although the lesson took hold, some teachers would be appalled at the messiness that was comfortable for Usha.

ENGAGEMENT

The Hook

Children come to school naïve. They may have some vague expectations—a composite of older siblings' reports, parental descriptions, and fantasy—of harder workbooks, bigger rooms, larger puzzles, new friends, and something about "work" and "recess." They may like the prospect of bright new lunch boxes and book bags emblazoned with the latest superhero, but intellectual and moral aspirations? Hardly. When asked, "What will you learn?" the child responds, "I'm going to learn to read and write." Some children welcome school as a ticket to maturity, a sign of growing up; for others it arouses an aura of anxiety, a fear of failure; for most, however, it is just the natural next step. The teacher's first order of business is to replace this matter-of-factness with an anticipatory sense of adventure and mystery, with an edge-of-the-seat excitement about what lies ahead.

Children become anticipatorily excited if *before* the first day they have a bit of information about what to expect—sufficiently rich to entice them and sufficiently incomplete to stimulate a wondering mood. For these purposes some creative teachers have sent home cut-up letters that, when assembled, reveal a secret message about the first day, tickets of admission to a show that children will view, or requests for a stuffed toy to launch a pretend toy store in class. For Usha the best way to achieve both familiarity and wonderment is by sending a letter to each child the week before kindergarten begins. The letter capitalizes on the children's curiosity and allays their anxiety by including four components: the teachers' photographs, some suggestion of the varied activities awaiting the child, a dramatic hook, and a request to bring in something that connects to that hook.

The Letter

Several years ago, in response to a school recommendation that the 500th anniversary of Columbus' voyage be commemorated, we adopted a ship motif for the introductory letter we sent home before school began (Figure 5.1). A boat illustration inviting the children to come aboard on a long and eventful journey with the teachers stirred questions about their shared and mysterious destiny. The children asked:

"Is it for real?"
"Where is it going?"

FIGURE 5.1   Letter to Children

"Who will the passengers be?"

"Will we get lost?"

"Will the boat sink?"

One of the boys showed up the first day with a captain's hat and a suitcase: "I'm reporting at the dock," he said. "I can't wait to take off."

Others followed clutching stuffed animals, travel games, favorite blankets, and snacks.

"Why did you bring your compass?" I asked. "Do you think Columbus carried this on his trip?"

They laughed, "He definitely didn't have a GameBoy in those days."

"I don't think he would take a teddy bear."

"My blanket would be too small for him."

"What might *he* have taken aboard?" I persist.

"Food, clothes, and definitely a compass."

We discuss the letter. I ask them if they know why Mr. D. illustrated the letter with fish and birds. They make their guesses while we keep silent. "Stay tuned," we tell them, "You will soon discover the answer." [Answer: The style of the drawings anticipated our study of Native American culture as part of the Columbus story.]

Referring to the letter, we ask, "What does the Ocean of Friendship mean?"

"We're going to make new friends."

"If we're going to sail on this Ocean of Friendship and our classroom is our boat, what can we do to make sure that we stay friendly?"

"We can help."

"We can share."

"We can be nice."

Mr. D. writes the words "helping," "sharing," and "being nice" on the waves he has already drawn on the blackboard.

When class is disrupted during the following days, we refer to our wave chart and ponder: Did we forget to observe one of the words? Do we need to add a word?

It has been a comfortable beginning. The children have become imaginatively engaged, a momentum has been established. This engagement has put to rest any potential awkwardness, anxiety, or confusion—they can't wait to pursue the class journey further.

A Long Journey: The Growth Motif

Immediate engagement, a good beginning, is insufficient. The children's willingness to participate over time in a long journey with an uncertain destination, a journey that will change them in ways they know not, requires a high level of confidence in the possibilities that lie ahead. This class is not a treadmill, each day like the last; it is not a flat prairie road contoured only by seasons and holidays. This class is moving steadily, though slowly, upward. To make the required effort, the children must be convinced that the climb is moving them toward something that, however vague, is big and worthy. Usha conveys the sense of a long journey and personal transformation by introducing, within the first week, the growth motif.

Kindergarten Sunflowers

When large yellow sunflowers start to lose their luster early in September, Mr. D. and I seize the opportunity to ask local farmers for their giant six-foot tall end-of-season sunflowers. We place them standing tall against the wall.

"Do you know why we call this class kindergarten?" I ask the children.

"Because this is where you go after pre-K."

"Because it's a nice name."

"Because that's what it's always called."

"The word has two parts, *kinder* and *garten*," I tell them, covering each half of the word as I hold it up for them to see. "Does that give you a clue?"

"Garten sounds like garden."

"You're right," I respond, "and if this is a garden, what does *kinder* mean? What will grow here in this garden?"

"Plants?"

"Books?"

"Us?"

"Yes, you and Mr. D. and me too; we're all going to grow here. We will be together for a long time, through Halloween, Thanksgiving, Hanukkah, Christmas, Kwanzaa, the New Year, through spring, and all the way until the summer vacation. We have plenty of time to grow."

We talk about the German educator Froebel (a big word, a foreign word that surprises the children, raising their expectations), who thought of classrooms as gardens where children grow and blossom. We jointly list ways we can grow and get "gooder." The children suggest, "sharing," "helping," "caring," "reading," "writing," "painting," "counting," "making friends," "acting," "drawing," "working on the computer," and "cleaning." At a later time, we will add "patience," "kindness," and "cooperation."

We talk of the faraway lands and people we want to visit as we sail (imaginatively) on our boat. The children blurt out:

"I know someone from Israel. Can we go there? I know a Hebrew word."

"I know how to count up to ten in Spanish. My grandma taught me. I also know how to say hello and goodbye. Let's go to a Spanish country!"

"Do you know any countries where Spanish is spoken?" I ask.

"No."

"Why don't you ask your grandma tonight, and we can talk about it tomorrow," I suggest.

Even though we had planned to talk about gardens, we readily follow the children's detours. Looking at the world map, we locate places we have heard of or visited, and we talk at some length about their differences—time, language, food, clothing, climate; some time later we will get to historical and religious differences. We are creating a sense of distance, travel, and time.

We return to the topic of kindergarten:

"If this is a garden and you are the growing plants, who are Mr. D. and me?"

"The gardeners. That's easy."

"And what will we do as gardeners?"

"Water us."

"Yes, we will shower you with love and hugs and kindness," I respond, laughing.

"You will tell us what to do. That's what teachers do."

"Do you need teachers to tell you what to do?" I counter.

The children, only five and six years old, have definite opinions. Sharing their perspectives, they speak of mean teachers and kind teachers, teachers who listen and teachers who don't, teachers who make too many rules and teachers who let you get away with anything. I ask them what works best in a classroom. The consensus is that some rules are needed some of the time, but they must be fair. I suggest that since we've done okay without any rules so far, how about continuing this way for another week? The children seem surprised. They mumble to each other:

"No rules?"

"Can I do anything I want?"

"Does she really mean it?"

"In my own life," I tell them, "I don't have a lot of rules, but when I can't figure out what is right, I just sit down calmly and think about it. Why don't you try this and see if it works?"

When Mr. D. and I set the tables for snack time, we tell the children that one of our jobs as gardeners is to provide a healthy snack. We ask them, as growing plants, to think about their snack time jobs. They bring in rules they have learned:

"Try everything on your plate."

"Don't take all the food for yourself."

"No crumbs."

"Clean up."

Again I suggest, "Just think about snack time and what would make it best for everyone." I restrain from echoing the familiar dictums about turn taking and cleanliness. These are the sorts of issues children can resolve through reflection because deep down they know what is best.

After snack there is still much to do with the sunflowers. We estimate how many petals and seeds each flower has and decide to verify our hypotheses by counting the seeds in the afternoon before roasting them with butter and salt.

Then the children select sunflower names.

"We can call that huge one Big Daddy."

Everyone agrees. Mr. D. asks the children for help in sounding out the word as he carefully writes the name on a piece of paper before clipping it to a leaf.

"How did Big Daddy grow to be so enormous?" I question.

"It probably got a lot of sunshine."

"It just *decided* to be the biggest one, and it did."

"Does it work if you just *decide* to do something?" I counter.[1]

"Sometimes, like when I decide to finish my breakfast."

"I can clean my room when I make up my mind."

"Not always, it doesn't always work."

"Why is that?" I probe.

"Because sometimes things are too hard."

I ask for an example or volunteer one. I tell them, for example, how I made up my mind when I started teaching kindergarten to play the guitar so we could all sing together. Mr. D. tried to teach me, but after a while, though I tried hard, I realized that I just couldn't do it. So we found another solution: I would play tapes of great songs while everyone sang along.

---

[1]Note how Usha uses the children's own words to help them think more deeply about their own statements—"You will tell us what to do. That's what teachers do." "Do you *need* teachers to tell you what to do? "It just *decided* to be the biggest one, and it did." "Does it work if you just *decide* to do something?"

Back to the naming. A tall sunflower that is small-blossomed and lanky gets named Impatient Izzy (because in its haste to grow, it didn't take time to absorb nutrition). A sunflower that shared its space with a flowering vine is named Sharing Sally. A droopy flower is named Tired Tom, and a perky flower is named Happy Holly.

One year the sunflower discussion generated so much interest that we studied sunflowers for an entire week, dictating stories about them, creating and illustrating number poems ("One sunflower straight and tall growing by the garden wall, two sunflowers sunny and bright turning toward the golden sunlight"), and developing a sunflower pledge ceremony. The children decided that they wanted to grow up like the best of sunflowers—absorbing knowledge patiently, growing straight and tall by trying to do the right thing, and always facing the sun (facing up to the truth). Dressed in yellow, they trooped into the pledge ceremony and stood still as each one solemnly took the oath they had created: "I promise to grow straight and tall like the sunflower. I will be patient and share my space, food, toys, and markers with others." The ceremony concluded with a feast of roasted sunflower seeds, slivers of toast spread with sunflower margarine, and cookies iced with yellow sunflower patterns. A week later, during group problem solving, the children carried the sunflower motif one step further. To correct each other's errors and lapses, they decided to gently whisper a reminder, "Be a sunflower."[2]

COMMONWEALTH

Discovering Who We Are

Children do not come to school as isolates, a collection of five-year-olds distinguishable merely by size, hair, color, and clothing. They arrive thick with family histories, traditions, and values that a class community can tap. The usual "Who Am I" games—my name, how many in my family, my favorite and least favorite activities—are deliberately expanded in Usha's class through projects that delve into family customs, extended familial ties, and remote cultural roots. This gradual self-revelation depends on a growing trust within the community (inclusive of parents); it also establishes that trust.

How I Got My Name

The children's first book, *My Name Is Johari,* is about a young African American girl who cheerfully enters school on the first day, only to have her name ridiculed by others. The teacher in the book asks the children to investigate the meaning of their names. Johari discovers, to her delight, that her name means "jewel." The other children are equally impressed. They stop teasing, and Johari is happy with her name once more.

---

[2]Note the aspirations about *our* growth and growth strategies. It's about *our* growing straight, not *my* straightness; it's *our* pledge, not who wrote the best pledge.

After discussing this story, we ask our parents to write the story of their children's names. Wanting to bring the parents on board with our "getting gooder" motif, we provide them with a sample story from the previous year that illustrates how a name often reflects important values (a relative held dear, an admired virtue). A special Name Day is selected for the stories to be shared with the class. Parents often report that the process itself—revealing to their children how and why they chose their particular name—is a powerfully connecting experience. At school children can't wait for Name Day. When the moment comes, Mr. D. and I replace the bright lights with soft lamps and play gentle music in the background. We let the children lie back on pillows and listen to the special stories that we read and reread.

Dear Jack,
When thinking about what to name you, I told Daddy a family story. As I was growing up with your aunts and uncles, my dad (your Grandpa Jack) used to joke with us and say that all his grandchildren should be named Jack or Jacqueline!!! Now, of course, he was just teasing, but we all loved Grandpa Jack so much that we used to go along with him. So, in honor of Grandpa Jack who had died in 1991 (you were born in 1992) your Daddy and I decided to name you "Jack." We also learned that the name John (and your nickname, Jack) meant "the Lord is Gracious." Gracious means that a person is kind, patient, gentle, and understanding of others. I hope that you will continue to be as nice a person as you are, and that you grow up to be a lot like Grandpa Jack, who was extremely kind, patient, gentle, and understanding of others.
Love you, Mommy

Dear John,
About 100 years ago, a boy was born and he was named John Russell, Junior. He and his family lived in the city of Philadelphia. They took their summer vacations at Cape May, on the New Jersey shore. His two older sisters, Janet and Edith, were school teachers. John did very well in school and was sent to a special school in Philadelphia, called Central High School. He did so well there that he went to college before most of his friends.
While he was growing up, many people must have realized that he had some special gifts. He was a very fair person, and he always made sure he did the right thing. He always loved to read, especially plays and poetry. His favorite plays were by William Shakespeare, who wrote plays in England a long time ago. His favorite poems were by Percy Bysshe Shelley, who wrote poems about the beauty of nature and the deep feelings people have in their hearts.
When he became a young man, he met a young woman named Barbara, and he fell in love with her. But he decided that he should help his country by fighting in World War 1, in France. He was very sad about leaving Barbara because he realized that he might get shot or even killed, and he might never see her again. So he wrote Barbara's mother a letter to tell her how much he loved her daughter, and that if he survived the war he would like to marry Barbara.
In the war, John had to do many things that he was afraid of. One of the things he was most afraid of was horses. In this war, John had to learn to ride a horse. Even though he did not like it, he did it because he had promised his friends

that he would do his job well, and his job included riding a horse in the cavalry. That was very courageous!

He did survive the war and he got to marry Barbara. He also became a lawyer, someone who helps people solve problems in a fair way. Many people respected John because he was so fair, and also because he cared about people's feelings, and because he always wanted to do the right thing.

We gave you the name John because, to us, the name reminds us of a caring, fair, and responsible person, and we hope that in your life you will discover in your own way how to be all those things.

Love,
Mommy and Daddy

We Are the Same

The getting to know one another continues. In pairs we ask children to note their similarities. (To establish a sense of community, it is best to emphasize similarities before delving into differences.) They make giant pictures of themselves using paper, cardboard, and real clothing. We ask them to consider ten ways in which "my partner and I are the same." Mr. D. and I lead off, enumerating thirty similarities from a prepared sheet. Our modeling exposes children to similarities that go beyond the typical five-year-old repertoire of external characteristics ("we both have blue eyes, Nike sneakers, black hair"). We take turns and read aloud:

Mr. D. and I like to walk peacefully on a beach at sunset.

Neither of us have ever been to Mexico.

We like the smell of burning sage.

We both forget and dip our paintbrushes into our drinks in the classroom.

In the last year we read three books that were the same.

We both write endless lists; Mr. D. walks around with wads of torn paper in his pockets, while I write my lists on a notepad.

We both collect bottlecaps to someday make a large kindergarten bottlecap mural.

We laugh a lot at knock-knock jokes, but we both hate, "Why did the chicken cross the road?" jokes.

I grew up in India and Mr. D. grew up in Philadelphia, but we learned the same nursery rhymes.

We hate the feel of glitter in our pockets and thumbtacks in the soles of our shoes.

Now it is the children's turn. In pairs they are given a sheet of paper, some markers, and fifteen minutes to discover their ten similarities. Mr. D. and I move about the room writing down what they tell us. Because they do not yet read, we help them draw pictures or symbols to aid recall: for example, glasses for similarities in grandmas, a television for the same favorite programs, and a pumpkin for their most beloved holiday, Halloween.

The discussions and discoveries are lively. There is talk about families, pre-schools, parties, toys, summer vacations, and neighborhood friends. The children walk around evaluating items in the classroom, determining likes and dislikes:

"I love dress-up—do you?"

"Do you like puzzles? In our old preschool we only had ten puzzles, and I didn't like them at all. They were too easy."

The pair discoveries are shared with the class:

"Guess what? We both had spaghetti for dinner last night."

"We both learned to ride bikes this summer but fell off a lot."

"We both have three lines on our pinky finger."

The lists are then posted (with the children's pictures of themselves) on a large bulletin board in the hallway. For weeks afterward it is a common sight to see children explaining their lists to first graders and other teachers: "Did you know that we're both born in July, and both our grandmas came from California?"

A Teacher's Wedding

We capitalize on naturally occurring events both to increase our stock of shared knowledge and to broaden that knowledge to other people. One year Mr. D. decided to get married. Since we were studying about India, the children and I explored the possibility of having an Indian-style wedding ceremony in our classroom (after the real wedding). To help us plan the event, two children from India brought videotapes of their parents' weddings. Then others brought in videotapes or photo albums of their parents' weddings. So at naptime we watched Jewish, Christian, Muslim, Hindu, and interfaith weddings while we got to know John's Pop-Pop, Mary's Grandma Mindy, Anita's Ammama, and Raphael's crazy uncle Manuel who told the best knock-knock jokes.

Now that I had seen the wedding videos, I began to talk to parents in greater depth of their family traditions and histories, and they began to share other details of their lives with me. Because many wanted to be included in the wedding ceremony, we designated roles for parents as well as children. Two children were priests, two escorted the bride, two escorted the groom, and two were tabla (Indian drum) players. The other children formed a procession as rice, coconut, banana, and incense bearers. The parents were asked to dress up elegantly and be the wedding guests. We prepared invitations, studied Indian customs, learned Indian prayers and songs, and made an illustrated book of blessings for the married couple. The parents prepared the food, my mother helped me make fresh flower garlands, and we were ready—one big community united to perform a teacher's wedding (Figure 5.2).

Trusting Children

Implicit in all of Usha's teaching is the belief that children, even as young as five years of age, can assume substantial responsibility for themselves and can, much of the time, work, play, solve problems, and make choices without adult supervision. But that achievement requires careful, graduated exposure to independence, with frequent opportunities for reflection on strategies that work and strategies

FIGURE 5.2   A Teacher's "Indian" Wedding

that fail. There is risk here. If you're going to trust, you must *really* trust, and that includes giving children the freedom to mess up.

Trust Tables

To encourage independent learning, we set up four or five classroom stations, each consisting of a different activity such as sink-and-float, write-a-letter, fun-with-birds, measure-me. Within the first two weeks two stations become "trust tables" where children work cooperatively on projects without adult assistance; the other two are teacher–child tables for more complex projects. In setting up trust tables, tasks and instructions must be sufficiently simple for children to work independently. At the art table, for example, children are provided with assorted colored paper shapes, drawing paper, scissors, glue, glitter, buttons, markers, and seeds. They are told, "Your task is to make one or more flowers using the materials on the table. Use the large sheets of drawing paper as the background, and make your flowers on them. We will put them together for our mural later on. When you finish your work, put it on the drying table, and organize this table for the next group. I trust you to work on your own at this trust table, helping each other quietly when you need to. This will allow me to work with children on their story project at the next table."

As groups pass through this station, various problems and mishaps occur, but the children, aware that they must not interrupt the teachers, are surprisingly benevolent: To the dreamy child, they may offer ideas for work organization; to the minimally productive child, they may suggest how to enlarge a flower; for those who make messes, they may come up with a plan for containing glitter within a limited space, and rather than complain to the teacher, they may even clean up a messy table. As always, when the groups have been through all the stations, we discuss what did and didn't work. Successful strategies are applauded and tucked away in our mental strategy bag for future use.

As the year progresses, children handle more complex tasks at the trust tables, and trust is expanded into other areas: trust partners who work cooperatively together, trust picnic lunches on the playground, trust theater-goers who can watch middle and high school plays in the theater without constant adult supervision, and trust bakers who make bread for the homeless without sampling the ingredients!

A Theatrical Production

One year we created a complex kindergarten musical that required the characters to enter and exit the stage at different times. We told the children that because Mr. D. and I would be busy with music and lights out front, those who were not on stage had to wait in a tiny room behind the classroom without an adult. We suggested to the children that another teacher or parent be recruited for supervision. The children protested; they wanted to do this on their own. "You can trust us," they insisted, and so we tried. The first rehearsal did not work. Several of the children were distracted by play materials in the back room. "Cover up the shelves, and we will be fine," they promised, and we tried again. The next two rehearsals had their share of problems—children who did not enter on cue, children who forgot to bring their props on stage, and even a few heated arguments backstage. "But we want to do this on our own," they continued to urge, and so we let them devise an elaborate "foolproof" system. To avoid distraction and temptation, we covered the shelves with sheets that we taped to the floor; to prevent forgetfulness, a partner reminded each child of costume accessories and props; to prevent escalation of arguments, two appointed leaders monitored the group; and to facilitate on-time entry, we attached to the wall a detailed entry plan for each of the three scenes. On the final day, despite a couple of disheveled, hasty entrances, the children lived up to their word. Their pride in being trustworthy far exceeded their pride in performing the play.

REFLECTION

Reflection on Collaboration

As we have noted, Usha believes strongly that wanting to grow—ethically and intellectually—is natural to children. Given the right classroom ambience and a few helpful tools, they do so without a lot of coercive rules and direction. This deep faith in, and reliance on, the children's moral core is displayed in a tool pivotal to her pedagogy—reflection. When children disagree, are uncertain, or just stuck, Usha asks them to think it over. When children believe an activity is complete, but Usha knows they can do better, she calls for reflection. When she wants the children's involvement in planning future activities, she brings them together. Much of her teaching and their learning is accomplished through mulling over possibilities. Whatever emerges from these interludes gets her genuine consideration. Showing deep respect for the process, she frequently shares her own experiences and reflections.

But—and here Usha departs from a classical constructivist educational approach—the group discussions are gently constrained. They are constrained by the context she establishes. In the decorations around the room, in the first letter and the theme for the year, the motifs of peace, internationalism, kindness, and unselfishness are manifest.

The reflections are also constrained by Usha's moment-by-moment leadership. Very subtly, through challenging questions ("Does that always work?" "Is that the only thing one can do?"), real-life examples ("I thought I could remember things just like that, but I found I had to write notes on my wrist"), personal views ("Sometimes I think it's okay not to share"), and redirection toward grander goals ("Remember, we set out to talk about how to make this a safer place for everyone"), Usha *leads* the children's reflections so that a worthy and fair resolution emerges. She leads by offering suggestions and recommendations, leaving open territory for them to roam. Thinking, they come to appreciate, helps one become "gooder."

Reflection is introduced early in the school year, for it, rather than a series of rules, becomes Usha's fundamental "management" practice. When problems arise, they are reviewed ("What exactly happened?") and pondered ("How did it go?" "What might we have done instead?" "What might we try next time?"). She creates lots of space for taking account.

Cleanup

Mr. D. and I are realistic. We know that our "no rules" policy will likely result in a giant mess on the first free-choice day, so we allot plenty of time for discussion about the disorder the children create. Sure enough, as children move from one play area to the next, the entire room quickly becomes covered with puzzle and Lego pieces, dress-up clothes, kitchen utensils, Cuisenaire rods, markers, and paper. Soon the children can't find what they need, and the shelves are empty. We ask them to consider the situation together with us.

Ms. B.: "Let's shut our eyes and think about how the classroom looks, now that we have finished free choice."

"It is one big mess."

"We couldn't even walk in the dress-up corner. All the clothes were on the floor."

Ms. B.: "How did it get to be such a mess?"

"Everyone took stuff out."

"Yes, we took stuff out but never put it back."

"I did. I put everything back."

"I wasn't sure where to put some of the things."

Ms. B.: "What can we do to avoid such a mess tomorrow?"

"We can put things back when we are not using them."

"Especially the kitchen stuff and the dress-up clothes."

Ms. B.: "How can we make sure that dress-up clothes stay on hangers?"

"Hang clothes up as soon as you are done with them."

Ms. B.: "Were other areas a mess?"

"The paper money and the pile of pattern blocks."

Ms. B.: "How can we keep the two kinds of paper money from mixing together?"

"Get two money boxes and make them different colors."

Ms. B.: "What would be the easiest way to pick up all the pattern blocks?"

"Sometimes I don't want to put away the pattern blocks if I've built something good."

"And when we make a large puzzle, I want to save it."

Ms. B.: "We could make a decision to save constructions and floor puzzles until the end of free choice, but how about cleaning up all the extra blocks around your constructions. Would that work?"

"Yes."

"It certainly would be better than today."

Ms. B.: "Well let's try it tomorrow. Remind each other to do this, and we'll see what happens."

Sharing

"Sharing," problematic for most young children, is also a topic for reflection rather than a categorical rule. For example, Henry, who has gathered all the yellow octagonal pattern blocks and is constructing an elaborate beehive, is accused of not sharing by Marty, who has decided he also wants just those blocks. The teacher asks Henry to describe the conflict.

"I had an idea to make an awesome beehive that went from one table to the other. So I took out all the yellow blocks, and I was using the black counters for bees, and the plastic flowers for plants. But Marty wanted some of my yellow blocks, and I said, 'No,' because I just had enough to go from one table to the next."

Teacher (addressing the group): "Marty complained that Henry wasn't sharing. What do you think about this?"

"I think Henry needed all his blocks."

"No, I think Marty should have some if he wanted them."

"Marty could have played with the other pattern blocks."

"Henry could have asked Marty to help him finish the beehive."

Teacher: "Do you think it was okay for Henry to say 'no' in this situation?"

"I think so."

"Well, he could have said 'no' in a nice way."

"He could have said, 'Marty, I need all the blocks to finish my beehive.' "

"I think Henry should have shared anyway. In my old school, sharing was a rule."

Ms. B.: "Have you ever started to work on a project, and then someone else comes and messes it up? Sit calmly with your eyes shut and see if you can remember such a situation. How did you feel when it happened?"

Endless stories pour forth about projects destroyed by younger siblings and about feelings of frustration when parents insist that children share even their newly acquired, prized possessions.

Ms. B.: "Maybe this was one of those times when it was all right for Henry to say 'no.' He had a plan and wanted to finish it. I do agree, however, that it would have been best to explain the plan to Marty so that he could have understood why Henry was saying 'no.' But what about Marty? What could he have done?"

"He could have stayed and helped Henry."

Ms. B.: "Henry, did you want someone to help you?"

"I wanted to finish my beehive myself."

Ms. B.: "Marty, do you understand what Henry is saying?"

"Yes!"

Ms. B.: "What could you have done when Henry said 'no'?"

"I could have played with the other blocks."

Ms. B.: "I want all of you to shut your eyes and imagine this different ending. Henry is building his beehive. Marty goes over and asks for some yellow blocks. Henry calmly explains that he needs all the blocks to complete the building he has planned, and Marty moves on to work with other blocks. Can you see this happening?"

"Yes."

Ms. B.: "Henry and Marty, would you like to do an instant replay of the situation using our new ending?"[3]

The concept of sharing is expanded throughout the year as ambiguous situations arise. Sharing food items at lunch, toys brought from home, each other's flavored Chap Sticks, information that one has promised not to tell, a fifth child wanting to join a game created by and for four players—each becomes a topic for group reflection.

Reflection for Improvement

The best schooling prepares children to be their own teacher, directors of the self. What one learns *from* an adult is likely to have a shorter afterlife than what one learns from one's own efforts. By the same token, what one learns *for* an adult will be more rapidly lost than what one learns for oneself.

When children reflect on their work, analyze their strengths and weaknesses, and consider ways to improve, their critical thinking skills are enhanced and their work is authenticated. We are more likely to own (take responsibility

---

[3]Instant replay, described below, is used only when both participants are willing.

for) our self-discovered failures than we are to own the failures attributed to us by others. Self-appraisal is essential for self-knowledge and for self-improvement.

Our Work

Reflection can be a means of self-correction. In learning to write numbers, for example, a child who has written a whole line of 5's is told, "Circle the 5 that you like the best, and underline the one that you like the least." Then, "Why do you like this the most?"

"It's my best five because the two lines are straight and the curved part didn't go under the line like my other ones."

"Why did you like this one the least?"

"Because it looks like an S, not a 5."

"What can you do to write your 5's like the first one?"

"I must write slowly and look at the bottom line."

"I also noticed that you were holding the pencil correctly some of the time. Might that have helped a little?"

Reflection is used for math problems:

- *Estimation* "How many M & M's are in this bag? Which bag has more marbles? Which of these weighs more?"
- *Prediction* "Think about what you have seen each child eat at lunchtime. Now make a prediction about which side of our graph will have more names; those who like corn chips or those who like potato chips?"
- *Word problems* "Shut your eyes, imagine, and solve this problem: Three orange butterflies were dancing around a sunflower. Soon they were joined by two brown ones. Do you see them flying around? After a while one flew away. How many were left?"
- *Planning* "If you are going to solve this problem using beans, what do you need to take to your seat to prevent you from wandering around the classroom later on? Make your plan first."

In geography a mundane book-and-map introduction to continents turns into a week-long investigation when reflection is introduced. I show the children a globe, point out the land and sea masses, and ask, "How did the world get to be this way—shaped like a ball, with land and water all over it?" The answers start slowly and then tumble out as one child is inspired by another:

"I think it had to be like a ball so it could hold together."

"Like when we make snowballs."

"There has to be mud and water together or they will fall off."

"We have to put sand and water together in the sandbox, or we can't make anything."

"I think there was all land and then it rained, like in Noah's ark, and some places became water."

"I think God made it this way."

"I think He planned it all carefully on paper first, then He made it."

We talk about the need for water and land, rain and sunshine, night and day, hot and cold climates; about how climate influences food, clothing, shelter, and everyday habits. We look at books and videos; call up libraries; search the Internet; question parents, relatives, and geologists. We create our own giant map of the world (see Color Plate 36). Each day a few questions are answered, but many more arise and are deliberately left unanswered. "Let's see if you can find the answers. We'll look for answers too," we tell them, and off they go to investigate further.

Self-Evaluation

Self-evaluation by the child can be integrated with teacher appraisal. For example, a child brings her drawing of an Indian scene to the teacher.

Ms. B.: "Tell me about your picture."

Child: "I drew the Himalayan mountains in the back, a temple, two coconut trees, and two Indian people. I drew the trees so the people could take coconuts to the temple for their prayers."

Ms. B.: "How do you think it turned out?"

Child: "Pretty good! I like the temple and the man, but the lady's saree didn't turn out like when you drew it."

Ms. B.: "I agree. Overall, I think you have captured many important details of Indian life. You remembered the carvings on the temple, the red dot on the lady's head, and the coconuts that are used in prayer. I love the criss-cross pattern you used to make the lady's braid. I've never seen you do that before."

Child: "I never knew how to draw braids, so I copied that from a picture I have of Pocahontas."

Ms. B.: "Now let's see what we can do about the saree. Let's look at pictures in the saree book. Notice how this part drapes over the shoulder; you need to make these lines in your drawing flow more smoothly, go all the way up to her shoulder, and then curve down. Do you want to try that?"

Child: "Yes, and I'm going to add some flowers in her hair like in the picture."

Inner Rewards

Children, often accustomed to tangible rewards, may ask, "Will you give us stickers?" They may expect stickers for cleaning up, being quiet at naptime, listening, drawing, writing, and even helping a friend on the playground. Although initially we may give an occasional smiley sticker for special tasks or situations, we are more apt to turn children toward recognizing for themselves what is valuable about their work. Take writing, for example. If a child is not interested in making legible letters, I may suggest that he share his writing with someone at home. When the child discovers that no one can read his illegible writing, he begins to appreciate the need for composing letters and words according to conventional standards:

"I have to write clearly so my grandma can read my letter."

"Even my younger brother, who is only four, recognizes my A's and M's because I write them good."

We then explore the possibilities of effective writing: "You can be a famous author like Tomie dePaola or a poet like Shel Silverstein, you can write to your favorite grandpa in Israel, you can have a secret diary like your older sister, you can create your own mystery map with directions, you can write your own invitations, you can write to people all over the world, especially those without computers." Allowing children time to discover the "WHY" of learning is crucial if they are to be engaged learners. Then they move from outer to inner stickers. Now when a child finishes her writing, I ask, "How does it feel to write three sentences on your own?"

"Great!"

"Your inner sticker must be smiling."

I came to my "inner sticker" convictions only gradually and much abetted by a very significant tutoring experience many years ago. Dave, an intriguing, brilliant child of seven, was struggling to read and write, and I was asked to help. He made it clear from the very start that he thought the learning demands placed on him were pointless: "Why do I need you as a tutor? I can read what I write, so why do I need to spell correctly? When I grow up, I'll have a secretary, and I will never have to write!"

We spent a lot of time with his questions. We explored the origins of languages—how they were the same and different—and hypothetical explanations for why there were so many of them. Now Dave began to pay attention to word patterns in reading and writing, but soon he became frustrated by the irregularities in the English language. "Who made up the English language anyway?" was his constant despairing refrain.

One day he came in radiant. "I figured it out!" he announced. "It took three people to make up the English language because it is so huge. The first guy made up spelling rules for words like *my, by, cry*. But then he died, and another guy took over. This guy wasn't too sure of the rules, so he added different spelling for the same sound like *die, lie*, and *pie*, and then a third guy came in and changed the spelling again for words like *buy and guy*." Dave was animated all morning. English suddenly made sense. He named the three guys Ruley, Bob, and Crazy and started to identify irregular words as Bob words or Crazy words.

After several months of creative debate, winding bypaths, and periods of intense concentration, there was a breakthrough: Dave could read, and read he did—the entirety of two pages. Everything in me wanted to hug him, praise him, say, "We did it!" and offer him a treat. But I watched as he sat hugging the book against his chest and just let him savor the moment. I remained silent until departure time, when I said, "There is a wonderful feeling in my heart." "Mine too," Dave replied, and we never mentioned the incident again, but it had an abiding impact. Fourteen years later, a description of our reading sessions appeared in his application essay for college!

As with the inner stickers and no rules, reflection became key to my teaching only gradually. The importance I now accord it contrasts sharply with earlier practices that were thoroughly rule-based. I used to give children rules for each play area, for sharing, and for cleaning up as well as the consequences for breaking rules by misusing materials, not cleaning up, and fighting. Gradually, I came to realize that although of course conflict will occur, it is distrustful and foolish to suggest the negative probabilities in advance of their occurrence. I also came to dislike rules more generally. Rules produce apathetic compliance; children fall into patterns of not thinking and not questioning, into an excessive concern with consequences, or into scheming—devising endless ways to get around a rule. Children need to think about their behavior, to ask of themselves, "What should I do in this situation?" "What is fair to myself and others?" "How can we get along together?" Although they are too young to formulate moral principles and draw relevant inferences, they are not too young to invent good solutions to the problems of everyday school life, and they are not too young to feel the thrill that comes from linking with others in a commonwealth.

CHAPTER SIX

COMMONWEALTH FOUNDATIONS: MAINTAINING THE TONE

As with any honeymoon, good vibrations will dissipate if not attentively maintained. Every teacher knows a good day won't buy a good week. Usha maintains the tone by going ever broader and deeper: embroidering the thematic content; artfully maintaining suspense through culminating events; connecting more powerfully with children, families, and those far removed; and exploring further the benefits of reflection.

ENGAGEMENT

Theme Elaboration

A major challenge of teaching is to fulfill academic and skill requirements without making them tedious, disjointed exercises. Long-term evolving themes, like any good plot, enthrall children. Once they are captivated by an emerging story, skills and facts can be seamlessly slipped into the day. Initially, the theme can be quite spare, as long as it has the capacity to expand in response to questions, research, and discussions.

An Evolving Project on Space

One year the lower-school principal wanted the kindergarten classes to study space. Because I knew next to nothing about the topic, I borrowed an assortment of books and pored over them, getting stuck on all the detailed facts and numbers. I was not inspired. I created a thematic web as instructed in teaching texts (Figure 6.1), planned activities in all subject areas, and even found a song about planets. And so we began. We painted, sang, and viewed documentaries of the moon landing, but the learning was fragmented. I couldn't for the life of me keep track of the distances between planets or even between the earth and sun. I couldn't remember the names of the constellations, nor could I find them easily in the night sky. Finally, a

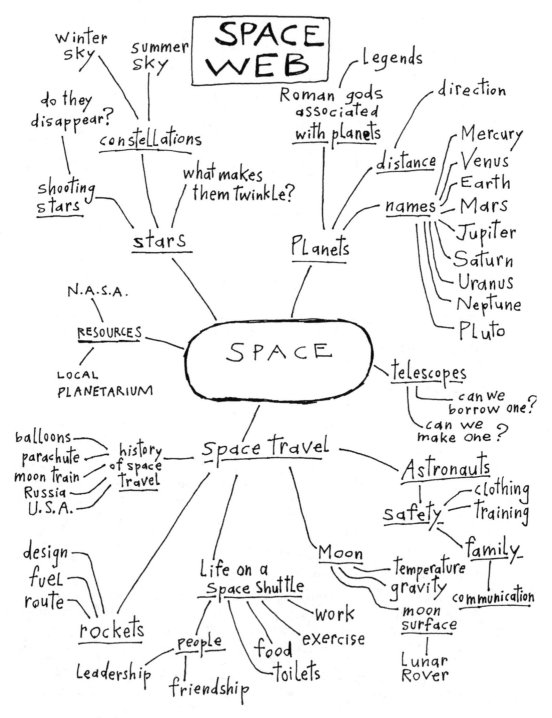

FIGURE 6.1   Thematic Web: Space

child's comment, "Ms. B., I wish you didn't have to look at a book all the time, it's boring," made me stop in my tracks. What was I doing? The children were no more likely to remember distances and measurements than I. There had to be a larger, more cohesive, more personalized purpose to the teaching.

"Why teach young children about space?" I asked myself as I went on a long walk, gazing at the stars. It's to take children beyond their classroom into the mystery of outer space, to imagine future possibilities of travel and life in space, to figure out and to appreciate why the earth is the only known planet to sustain life, to understand how man has benefited from learning about the stars and planets, and to feel awe at the magnificence and vastness of the universe. Suddenly, I am charged. These ideas will generate the children's curiosity. At a meeting with three other teachers we create a more personal hook: We are going to take *them* into space.

We invite the class to sign on for the Space Training Program. We send permission slips home to parents for their signed consent. A few days later children enroll by entering their true name and an alien name into a computer. We measure height, weight, biceps, and calves. We ask the nurse to join us for a check of their hearts and lungs. We review the right foods to eat (nutrition). At the first training camp meeting, questions pour forth:

"How exactly will we travel?"

"Will everyone get to go?"

"Will we fit in one space shuttle?"

"Will you know if it is night or day?"

"How do toilets work on the shuttle?"

"Do you have to live in a spacesuit all the time?"

"Is there a particular place where one can land on the moon?"

"How many days will we be gone?"

"Can our parents come with us?"

"Have you taken other children to space before?"

"Will we stop off at other planets?"

"I'd like to go to the furthest planet, but which one is it?"

"How does one sleep on a shuttle?"

"What do we eat?"

"What will the training program be like?"

"Why can't we go to Mars?"

"What about gravity? I've seen pictures and everyone seems to float."

"Why do they wear spacesuits?"

The children's questions determine our course of investigation. We learn that space shuttles have million-dollar suction toilets (and we experiment with crushed paper and a vacuum cleaner), sleeping bags that are fastened to the sides, food that is not too appetizing, and astronauts who float around in zero-gravity conditions. We convert the floor of an anteroom into the surface of the moon, with astronauts, the American flag, the moon rover, and even a few aliens (Figure 6.2). We study the planets (astronomy) to discover why we can or cannot stop off at each one, and we take a lengthy detour when we discover that the planets are named after Roman gods (history).

FIGURE 6.2   Moon Surface

Mythology comes to life as lunch conversations center on why Mercury was the messenger of the gods. Were the wings on his feet fueled by the closeness to the sun? Why was he also known as the god of eloquence, skill, and thieving? Was the planet Jupiter named after the king of the gods because it was the largest planet? And why didn't the Roman gods wear any shoes? In pairs the children make giant collages of the gods and decorate them garishly with glitter, sequins, and gold paper. We experiment with different textures to create an ethereal backdrop. We fill a child-size tub with water, detergent, and blue paint and blow into it with drinking straws to create a billion bubbles. We then gently press large sheets of paper over the surface and out comes a light blue, bubbly, textured sheet—our "heaven" (Figure 6.3).

Next we decide to build our own spaceships. We draw individual blueprints (art, math) (Figure 6.4), label every part (writing skills), and consolidate the drawings into two master plans (cooperation). Then we build two top-secret shuttles with large cardboard boxes, giant paper cones spray-painted silver and gold, pie plates for radar, an old vacuum hose for refueling, and sleeping bags for the astronauts (Figure 6.5 and see Color Plate 37).

Meanwhile, in our attempts to get strong and fit, we do push-ups, run forward and backward, jump, crawl, slide, and go for long walks on the playground

FIGURE 6.3 Roman Gods

FIGURE 6.4 Drawing Blueprints for a Space Shuttle

FIGURE 6.5   **Inside Space Shuttle Two**

(health). The nurse stops in regularly to check our progress. She gives us a lesson on nutrition. That brings us to another detour. We study the digestive system (biology), make a model using dozens of panty hose to create the length of the small intestines (Figures 6.6 and 6.7), and monitor our lunch every day with a checklist that depicts the four food groups and reads: "For lunch I had . . ." and "For dinner I must have. . . ." The children check their own lunch and report to their parents what food groups they need for dinner. An unanticipated benefit: One parent reported that, miracle of miracles, her child was eating cottage cheese and fruit instead of cookies after school!

Cultivating Patience

The danger of long-term themes is that without immediate rewards, children will lose interest. To stay actively involved, they must find satisfaction in demanding tasks meticulously carried out over an extended time period. At the beginning of the year even a half-hour task seems too long a work period; by the end of the year a whole week might be insufficient to plan and complete a task. That sort of patience, however, takes lots of graduated practice and reinforcement.

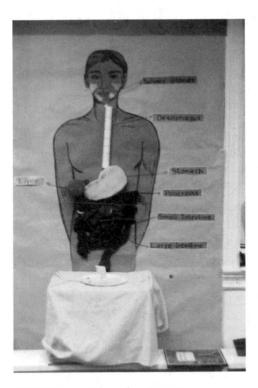

FIGURE 6.6 Digestive System—a Group Effort

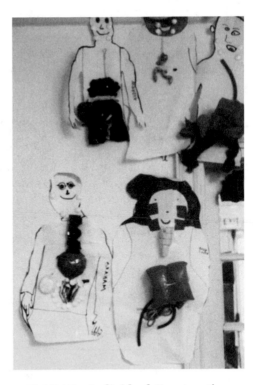

FIGURE 6.7 Individual Constructions of the Digestive System

Coco the Skeleton

At Halloween, when the world around us delights in scary images of ghouls, goblins, witches, and skeletons, we decide to honor the origin of this holiday by celebrating the lives of our relatives who have passed on. Skeletons and death lead us to a long tangent on the human body, the "backbone" of all physical endeavor. We study bone X-rays brought in by a parent and are awed by the many hinges that permit flexibility of the body. Chanting, "I'm all made of hinges and everything bends, from the top of my head to the tips of my ends. I've hinges in front and hinges in back; if I didn't have hinges, I'm afraid I would crack," *we* bend and contort our bodies to maximum capacity. To fully appreciate the function of the elbow hinge, we immobilize the children's arms by taping rulers onto them and then attempt to carry out normal tasks for fifteen minutes. Next we visualize: What if we had no knee hinge? What if our fingers had no hinges? And what if we had no skeleton, just flesh?

Finally, we decide to create our own life-size skeleton with objects from nature such as bark, twigs, and pine cones. Now that we understand the mechanical complexity, symmetry, and proportionality of the human frame, we are determined to make our model as accurate as possible. Mr. D., after enlarging a picture from an encyclopedia, draws an adult-size outline of a skeleton. Children set about measuring different bones and looking for identical fragments in nature. As a group we decide to "go for gold" and accept only the most authentic-looking "bones." The project takes a lot of time, and every moment outdoors becomes a moment of possibility: A clavicle could be hidden in a pile of leaves, or a femur in the woodpile gathered by the maintenance crew. We measure, we collect, we sort, we discard, and we select with care. Some children are more impatient than others: "We're never going to get this done." "What does it matter if one of the ribs is crooked?" But in a few weeks our skeleton, complete with coconut head and christened Coco, is finished (Figure 6.8). Children and adults marvel at the finished product. Its appearance is remarkably authentic. Much has been learned: "Do you like the fibula I found in the park?" "Did you see the patella?" "I found all the phalanges for the left hand!" "I found the tibia in our backyard." Patience and perseverance are the skeletal foundations for serious learning.

Dramatic Enhancements

A problem in traditional classes for the young is the demand for extended periods of sitting still. To keep children engaged, it is crucial to alternate periods of sitting with movement. What more natural way to provide this than by dramatizing a story after it has been read to them? Acting out stories, changing characters and

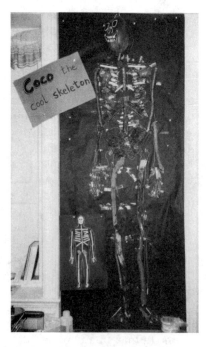

FIGURE 6.8   Coco the Skeleton

plots, is standard procedure in Usha's class. Another benefit is that the children become a part of, rather than apart from, the story. The dramatization, insights, and questions that come from identification with characters and plot are substantial and important to the children.

Warm Fuzzies and Cold Pricklies

It is mid-February. Valentine's Day looms. I use the occasion to stretch the children's appreciation of love. We read *Warm Fuzzies and Cold Pricklies*. There once was a village where everyone gave warm fuzzies to one another whenever they met. Their generosity was limitless, for warm fuzzies never run out. One day, however, an unhappy gnome living alone in a cave, jealous of the villager's happiness, tells a lie: He warns one of the villagers to be more prudent; after expending the 181 fuzzies in his sack, he will have no more. Alarmed, the villager tells his neighbors, and soon everyone is hoarding their warm fuzzies. They become suspicious and distrustful of one another. The gnome then gives the villagers cold pricklies to distribute as a substitute. Everyone develops aches and pains and becomes very depressed.

Mid-story, one of the children (a confederate whom I coached earlier in the day) dashes unexpectedly out of the room and returns alarmed. He informs the children that a neighboring class has broken the artwork we have placed on an exterior table. A dispute ensues as to whether or not the other class, friends of theirs, would have done such a thing. The discussion continues for a while, and then we return to the story. We decide to act out the story, as is customary with many of the stories we read. The children volunteer for parts and easily fall into their chosen roles. As townsfolk they animatedly greet each other, give out warm fuzzies, and then turn sour, hiding their sacks, hoarding the fuzzies, and distributing the cold pricklies.

When the play is completed, the group settles down to a vigorous talk about the book's theme: doubt versus trust. We then apply these concepts to the purported destruction of their artwork. "Are we sure our work was destroyed?" I ask. In single file they go check. It looks fine, untouched. "Maybe one shouldn't always believe the bad things people say without first checking," I muse. "Maybe we should trust that our neighbors will treat our things as we would treat theirs."

Culminating Events

As the reader has noticed, there is drama to Usha's class that sustains interest and suspense. Intrinsic to drama is the anticipation of a climax, the promise of an event down the road when the work will finally come together in a show, a display, or a feast. This gradual ascent to a destination gives children the time and motivation to revise and perfect their work, not to settle for mediocrity; to anticipate an exciting celebration, but not until the rehearsal stage is complete. So they persist, without the usual sense of impatience or drudgery that comes from merely correcting imperfect exercises.

Blastoff

Continuing with our space theme, we prepare for blastoff! Traveling and living together in a space shuttle will require a lot of cooperation. At naptime we practice by sleeping in groups under small tables covered with sheets. We work on a number of cooperative projects to foster team spirit. We also deliberately create scarcity of snacks, art supplies, and work space. We observe who and what falls apart, and we discuss means of apportioning material and space fairly. The need for self-discipline and immediate obedience to commands in emergency situations is stressed. A checklist entitled "I can follow instructions accurately" is created for home and school. The class begins to function like clockwork: Children rush in from the playground as soon as they are called, cleanup happens promptly, everything is put away precisely, no one loiters around the water fountain, and everyone follows the leader, without distraction, to music, gym, and recess, getting there safely in record time.

"When will we be ready for takeoff?"

"When will we be strong enough?

"We are following instructions well, aren't we?"

"We're getting gooder, aren't we, Ms. B.?"

"I can't wait to get to outer space!"

Fantasy overcomes most obstacles when children are five and six years old. Still, the more practical ones voice their doubts:

"How are we going to fit?"

"Will it be hard to breathe?"

"It's only a cardboard box."

I tell them that I will write a letter to NASA describing our training, self-discipline, plans for blastoff, and special space award ceremony. We receive an (invented) "reply" telling us how delighted NASA is about our space training program. Since this is the shuttle's first trial mission, NASA suggests that we send stuffed toys into space to see how that works out. Meanwhile, they will send one of their officials to attend our award ceremony and present special certificates. The class has determined that to receive the certificate, each child must tell the visiting official three interesting space facts, prove that he or she is physically fit, and provide records that indicate personal development in patience, self-discipline, following instructions, cooperation, and problem solving.

The letter from NASA provides a new impetus, and children work extra hard as the award ceremony approaches. On the big day we use the large gymnasium, and children dressed in blue and white march ceremonially as trumpets blare and music plays. A distinguished-looking official (a third grade teacher) displaying several gold medals salutes the children as they march past (Figure 6.9). Next, to demonstrate their fitness, children perform rhythmic exercises: jumping-jacks, sit-ups, and push-ups. The two giant space shuttles, built in the class, are unveiled by the "official." He asks all the right questions and looks suitably impressed. To a rapt audience he delivers a well-prepared speech describing his love for space travel and his various experiences at NASA. Every child then marches forward and states three space facts. In return, each receives a certificate for completing the Space 101 Program, a Milky Way candy bar, and a white space helmet made from a hospital hood with the child's name printed in glittery silver letters (Figure 6.10). A proud

FIGURE 6.9   A Distinguished NASA Official

**FIGURE 6.10   Proud Recipients
of Space Training Awards**

moment! Parents applaud, and the ceremony concludes with a solemn salute to the flag as the national anthem is played.

A few days later in a pretend blastoff, complete with sound effects and lighting (strategically placed lights and table fans directed at strips of red and yellow cellophane paper hanging from the bottom of the space shuttle give the appearance of shooting flames), the joyous and anxious children wave goodbye to their stuffed toys. The first-ever school space shuttle is now in orbit.

COMMONWEALTH

Caring Connections

Just as the imaginary space shuttle requires fueling and refueling, so too do relationships. Children are as apt to fall out of as fall into friendship. The initial getting-to-know-and-appreciate-you must be nourished over the year if increased time with children is to be registered in increased connectedness. Collaboration becomes habitual only if mutual responsibility is ardently cultivated. At the same time the notion of developing individual potential is hollow unless the teacher taps and fosters the talents, tastes, and idiosyncrasies of each child.

Attending to Each Other

It is generally presumed that children are egocentric. They see a box of crayons, and they grab the best and most for themselves; they get stuck on a problem and demand help from the teacher without regard to the other demands on her time. Perhaps—and perhaps not. I have found that it takes just a little guidance for children to take on the needs of others simultaneously with promoting their own. Encouraging mutual helpfulness is not only morally desirable, it becomes a necessity for a teacher attempting to individualize education in a group setting. The idea is to make helpfulness habitual.

The children are gathering the materials they need for an art project. (In this class, rather than each child possessing a set, there are open containers of markers, pencils, crayons, and erasers.) I remind them, "Before you get started, make sure that everyone has his or her fair share of markers."

A child tells me he is finished with putting away his materials. "Is there anyone else you can help?" I ask, "I see Mary is still cleaning up the costume cupboard."

Jesse is having difficulty with his project. "Frances, do you have some ideas for Jesse?" or "Jesse, did you ask Frances?" As likely as not, a third child overhearing me will jump in: "Come over here, Jesse, I think I know what you can do."

I See You

Teacher–student relationships must be caring, genuine, and personalized. How does this get expressed on a daily basis?

- Noticing details of a child's appearance: "You have a new pair of shoes." "You cut your hair over the weekend. It looks lovely." "You went swimming this morning, your hair is still wet." "Does that scowl mean your brother teased you?"
- Knowing children's preferences: "I found a scary book I think you'll love." "I bet you'd like to go play with the boat in the sink." "Ask your parents if they can take you to the zoo. There's a new baboon you'll want to draw."
- Remembering and commenting on various events in the child's life: "What happened at your visit to the dentist?" "Has your Uncle Jacob arrived from Chicago?" "Did you sell a lot of lemonade this weekend?"
- Attention to body language and nonverbal clues: "You look a little tired today. What's wrong?" "You don't do well at recess when it's so hot. Do you want to rest in the shade?"
- Greeting each child separately and differently.

As a visitor to our class noted:

The early morning routine is all about reestablishing a caring connection before the day's adventures begin. One by one as the kids come bustling into the room, each makes his presence known according to his own style. Some take the nonverbal approach, torpedoing straight for Usha's knees, arms wrapping tightly around them with a fierce affection that almost topples her over. Some prefer announcing important events: "Ms. Balamore, guess what happened to my hamster?" When one comes in and uncharacteristically stands apart, coyly grinning, Usha knows that a tooth has fallen out. It's her job to notice and to make a big deal of it. However they want to present themselves, it doesn't matter. Usha celebrates their arrival each morning.

The message is "I see you, and I care."

Weekend Checklist

To remain a motivated learner, the young child must feel that school, like home, is a place where he is acknowledged, safe, and free to pursue his own interests. But how can a teacher impartially attend to all children, given the disproportionate attention always demanded by the naughty, the noisy, the exceptionally slow, and the very bright? The middle group of pleasant, do-all-the-work, polite children can slide through, year after year, relatively unnoticed. In my attempt to be fair, I devised an individualized checklist with four columns: *Personal, Academic, Peers,* and *Other.* Every weekend I take a look at the preceding week and evaluate my knowledge of, and interaction with, every child. I look at each child's name and ask myself, "Have I had a real (personal) conversation with her? Do I know what she has accomplished academically this week? Am I aware of her friendships and social skills? Did I forget to comment on anything of concern or anything to applaud?"

As I mark off each column, I write myself messages on Post-it notes: "Talk to Tom about the book he wanted to bring in. Ask Mr. D. to work individually with Alan on writing projects. Find out why Amira has been playing alone in the sandbox every day." I also list the children with whom I have not had a recent deep dialogue and decide to sit by them at lunchtime the following week.

Mining Parents

As already noted, parents participate in events from the beginning—for example, writing explanations of their children's names and sharing their own wedding stories. As themes grow toward their climax, parents (plus relatives, friends, and neighbors), depending on individual availability and interest, lend more of their skills, talents, and expertise.

Usha is alert to the family behind and within each child. What they do, what they believe, and how they act are all part of class discussions. Within the first three weeks Usha sends home a family questionnaire asking about jobs, interests, origins, languages, travel, and availability (of themselves and extended family). She continues to reach out to families in many ways: by notes and phone calls informing them of class activities or the accomplishments of individual children; by requesting material for class projects; by open invitations to join everyday lunch, nap, and recess activities; by seeking information and assistance with special projects and field trips; and by constantly asking for additional family input. Parents are actively recruited to plan lessons, to make presentations, and to join the class as their schedules permit. Through such outreach Usha has brought into the class an organizer of a world peace conference, a professional baker mom, a clown adept at making balloon figures, and an eighty-year-old brain surgeon grandfather. Others, unable to come in person, contribute through e-mail or taped (video or audio) stories, anecdotes, and responses to children's questions.

A Father's Visit

One year, a father, formerly a submarine operator, came into our class dressed in uniform. He brought along a minimum of props—a large cardboard box open at one end, a periscope, and a sound maker that would make a noise when a child entered or exited the pretend submarine—and gave us a very brief description of living underwater. Then he requested questions. The children were unabashed:

"How does it feel to be underwater?"
"What do you do if your submarine leaks?"
"Where do you pee?"
"Does the pee go into the ocean? (Yuck!)"
"What does that do to the fish?"
"Do you know how long you are going to stay under?"
"What if you come up and there is a ship on top?"
"What if the water ices over?"
"Can you cook, or do you have to take dried food?"
"Will an enemy ship find you? How?"

As quickly as the questions arose, the answers were provided, with vivid details and genuine emotion. The children were intrigued. This man knew (and had done) everything! The lesson lasted an hour and a half, and for days afterward children enacted submarine scenarios in the cardboard box.

Every parent can have a role to play in our classroom if they wish, for everyone is an expert in something. One volunteers to make Irish soda bread, one reads to the children using a Hawaiian puppet, one teaches us Spanish, one teaches us Greek mythology, and everyone has a cultural heritage from which to contribute music, songs, art, and stories about ancestors.

Appreciating Differences

If the sense of the commonwealth was initially structured around the similarities of its members, it is sustained by learning about and valuing differences, not just differences among the children but among peoples of the world, of today and of the past. It is also enlarged through the increasing contributions of each family's cultural wealth.

Children are curious about differences. A teacher of young children must be prepared, at any given moment, to deal with issues of learning differences, physical handicaps, as well as differences in religion, food preferences, ethnicity, and skin color. She must have a carefully planned approach to each of these topics, complete with books, strategies for discussion, and activities. To do this well, however, she must continue to reflect on these issues and determine whether she tilts toward suppressing differences or investigating them.

A Visual Disability

I was informed that a child with very poor eyesight would visit our class in two days. After pondering this opportunity, I rushed off to a five-and-dime store and bought a pair of fake glasses for each child. First, we lightly coated one lens with Vaseline and then, after an hour of looking at the world this way, we coated the other lens. With these glasses on for fifteen minutes children could begin to envision the world our visitor sees. We discussed the blurry images, what activities we could and couldn't do, whether we should or shouldn't help the visitor, and finally, what we could do to make the environment safe and navigable.

Skin Color

Although specific handicaps are dealt with as the situation arises, other basic differences are explored as part of our community-building efforts. To deepen children's understanding of skin color, I have adapted the pigment technique described in a teaching manual. I use this experiment in my class whether or not color is an issue. First we examine the different shades of skin color in our class and try to name these various hues—yellowish-pink, brown, chocolate, peach like the crayon not the fruit, inner-shell color, and so on. Following an explanation about pigment, how varied shades of color are produced by the amount of pigment involved, children divide into three groups to draw large outlines of faces on white paper using black permanent markers. Three clear plastic glasses filled with water are then placed on the table, and children stir a spoonful of brown watercolor paint into one glass, half a spoonful into the next, and a quarter spoonful into the third. Using soft paintbrushes, each group takes one of the three liquids to paint the face drawings. The resulting color differences are quite remarkable. It was just a matter of pigment!

Expanding the Commonwealth

As we saw with the space project, young children are imaginative and have no difficulty visualizing places far away, long ago, or wildly different. Usha capitalizes on this facility by constantly expanding the notion of commonwealth, moving from classroom, to school, to city, to beyond—way beyond. This sensitizes the children to the complexity and interdependence of all lives, illuminating both consciousness and conscience.

The World Wide Web

Several years ago, I developed a technique that vividly illustrates what the experts call *globalization*. The process is simple and suitable for all grade levels. Pick any object in the classroom, identify its components, trace each of the components back to its origin, and map the findings on the blackboard in the form of a giant spider web.

A cupcake brought in for a child's birthday is held up for inspection and then drawn in the center of the blackboard. Children identify the components—sugar, flour, eggs, butter, chocolate—which are drawn in a circle around the cupcake. Then, starting with sugar, each component is traced back to its origin, and we estimate how many people were involved in the process: The baker got the sugar from the supermarket (we draw an arrow outward from the sugar, a car with a stick-figure baker, a square that represents the supermarket, and another stick-figure for the cashier). The supermarket got the sugar from the sugar factory (another arrow, a truck and truck driver, and ten sugar factory workers). The sugar factory got the sugar cane from the farmer (another arrow, another truck and driver, seven men who loaded the truck, and two farmers). We locate places on the map where the sugar cane could have grown—Florida, Hawaii, Brazil—and we choose Brazilian farmers. We count the number of people involved in the production of sugar (Figure 6.11): twenty-four people we may never meet, who have touched our lives through the cup cake. When we finish tracing the origins of flour, butter, eggs, and chocolate (cocoa, milk, sugar), the blackboard has a slew of arrows going in every direction with at least fifty-five people depicted. Children are truly amazed and often roll on the floor saying, "This is awesome!"

Then it is time to unify the pieces. We shut our eyes and imagine the entire process as I tell the story (later in the year children take over the storytelling): "One hot sunny day in Brazil, a farmer named Pedro decided that he would grow the finest sugar-cane on the planet. He worked hard to till his land and planted row after row of sugar cane plants. His young son Manuel helped him on the

FIGURE 6.11 World Wide Web

weekends. A few months later, when the sugar cane had grown big and tall, they rented a harvester, cut down the cane, and sent it away to the sugar factory. . . ."

By now the children are desperate to eat the cupcakes. So we stand up, thank all these unknown people in different parts of the world, and savor the delicacies.

Empathy

The best way for children to truly understand experiences foreign to their own is to get at least a small taste of the actual experience. What if you had very little food and were always hungry? What if you were allowed no choice in what you could do in a school day? What if you were treated differently because of skin color? What if you had to be very still all day like Anne Frank? Usha provides for this through imaginative reconstructions, by role-playing an event.

When the class studied about Michelangelo, for example, Usha instructed one of her graduate students to tape drawing paper underneath all the tables. She then had children lie on their backs, look upward, and draw pictures (pretending that they were painting the ceiling of the Sistine Chapel). Within twenty minutes children were complaining of tired arms and sore backs. Then, with eyes closed, the class imagined what it must have felt like to build your own scaffolding, mix your own paint, and *then* lie high above the ground with paint dripping on your face for many, many, many days to finish a painting. Appreciation of Michelangelo's masterpiece deepened significantly!

The Conquest of Native Americans

Some topics require more expanded role-playing techniques. To have first graders experience the feelings of Native Americans whose land was taken over by Columbus and by later colonizers, we devised an elaborate scheme. For a week, the first grade teacher worked on making her class into a little community, complete with their own flag, president, and vice-president. They listed what they liked about their community—friends, single desks, new games, new books, large windows, beanbag seats—and wrote goals to promote peace and harmony in their land.

On the appointed day, Mr. D. and I arrived at their door with a (pretend) letter from the headmaster to the first grade teacher. The letter stated that because the kindergarten had an unusually large number of children and insufficient supplies, we were permitted to "borrow" material from the first grade classes. The teacher, looking dejected, waved us in as she pretended to read and reread the letter. We wandered through the classroom asking children whether they would trade their books, markers, and even desks for trifles such as colored chalk, pieces of bark, and drinking-straws. At first children traded actively, eager to help the kindergarten children, but as we started to take desks, puzzles, books, and a portable blackboard, the protests began. The children appealed to the teacher, but, pointing to the headmaster's letter (analogous to the letter from the Queen of Spain), she did not intervene. As a final indignity, we insisted that she help us carry a large globe from her class to ours. The protests increased in intensity, a couple of children cried, some tried to shut us out of the classroom, and the class president and vice-president tried to attack our holdings and regain some of the material. Eventually, we sat down with the children, discussed their feelings about the takeover, and related it to their study of Native Americans, Columbus, and later colonizers. The anger, hatred, fear, and helplessness of others was tangibly processed and understood.

REFLECTION

Group Evaluation

In the current educational climate of externally imposed standards, lessons, and tests, it is easy to overlook the generative and self-critical capacities of children. Usha, however, focuses on developing these capacities, and as the year progresses, children engage in higher levels of reflection. Setting personal goals, identifying strategies to accomplish the goals, and monitoring personal growth are incorporated into all areas of the curriculum. Reflection by children is expanded from self-evaluation to evaluation of and by the group, from strategies for individual improvement to group improvement.

Evaluating Our School Play

High expectations and standards for culminating events, together with sufficient time for genuine accomplishment, promote feelings of self-competence—mastery of skills, techniques, materials, and selves. Our projects are shaped first by imaginative innovation and spontaneity; then, as the year progresses, we increasingly critique and fine-tune our preparations. Each rehearsal of a play, for example, is followed by self-evaluation of two kinds: defining current progress and defining areas for improvement.

Ms. B.: "What did you do today that was better than yesterday?"

"I remembered all my lines."

"I smiled when I was dancing."

"I didn't scratch myself when I was sitting on the log."

"I covered my mouth when I had to sneeze on stage."

"I sang much louder than usual. I tried to project my voice like you taught us."

Ms. B.: "Now think about the rehearsal once more. What could you improve, what could you do to make your performance better tomorrow?"

"I forgot some of my actions for the song."

Ms. B.: "What can you do to remember the actions?"

"I could practice in front of the mirror. My mom can help me."

"I was playing with the sequins that fell off Sara's crown and forgot to come on stage when the music stopped."

Ms. B.: "Yes, I noticed that you were late and others had to wait for you. Glitter, feathers, and sequins will fall off various costumes. What can we do to avoid picking them up and playing with them?"

"I can just say, 'No, I won't pick them up.' "
"She could sit with her hands crossed while she is waiting."
"She can look at the stage, not at the floor."
"I sit behind her. I can remind her."
Ms. B.: "Which of these strategies would work for you?"
"I think I'll sit with my hands crossed and look at the stage."

The discussion continues until each child has a goal for the next rehearsal. Letters to parents are also sent home to inform them of the strategies we selected and to seek their thoughts on other ways to improve the play that could be implemented at home.

Silent Workshops

After we have experienced different noise levels—computer games, music, videos, conversation, play—I ask children to consider what sort of classroom atmosphere is most conducive to writing, math, and art. With a little assistance, especially if they come up with poor solutions (for example, when they suggested, "Play Raffi songs all the time," I reminded them of what happened to their work when they last heard Raffi), they conclude that an interruption-free, silent environment works best for these tasks. "It helps us hear our thoughts better, and then our thoughts can drop onto the paper." We evaluate various kinds of music that can be played in the background and select an array of soothing melodies. Every year, a couple of children decide that they work best on their own away from the larger group tables. I have seen a child choose to do all his writing in the privacy of the kitchen corner, another work facing a wall with three chairs around her, fencing her in, and a third who wanted so much solitude that he elected to sit under the computer desk while creating his masterpieces. Individual strategies are respected. Each child is responsible for assembling the materials he needs and finding the place he is comfortable. When this is accomplished, I announce, "It's writing workshop time," and ring a little bell. Mr. D. turns on gentle music in the background, and children begin to work.

Respect for individual ways of working, when it contributes to the greater good of all, continues as the writing task begins. The assignments are usually open-ended (at least partially). Children are aware of several strategies that they can pursue—for example, in spelling a word, they can look at our word list, look at a rhyming book, look at a reading book, look at the letter chart, shut their eyes and see whether they can remember how it appears, or sound it out slowly and write down each letter. When they get stuck, children raise their hands, and Mr. D. or I walk over to them and speak in low whispers, supporting the atmosphere of silence. Children also talk to each other in whispers when they need help or additional material. As task engagement deepens, Mr. D. and I monitor the group and settle down next to those who seem particularly restless or needy. When a child finishes her work, she shares it with one of the teachers and then moves on silently to another activity of her choice. There is no fixed endpoint to silent workshops because everyone understands that variable time is required for individuals to complete their creative projects.

Imaginative Reconstruction: "What If . . . ?"

The world is not always as we might wish. Self-interest, greed, envy, and brute power too often prevail. Although we cannot rewrite the realities, we can imagine different scenarios. By reconstructing historical and classroom events, by playing "what if . . . ?" we can test out our aspirations for a more ideal outcome.

What If the Explorers . . . ?

Although teachers are often assigned controversial curriculum topics that cause them discomfort, their selection of instructional methods can significantly alter the message. When asked to commemorate the 500th anniversary of Columbus's discovery, several teachers at our school discussed their ambivalence about celebrating an event that had so devastated an entire people. Guided by a third grade teacher, Mrs. C., we sought some way to reconsider history from the standpoint of the values we foster today. The events of history must be presented accurately and sympathetically, rendered in terms of the perspectives of the times—on this we were all agreed—but "what if . . . ?" What if Columbus and his sailors came not to claim another's land, but instead to share and to learn from the people of the new world?

Running with the "what if . . . ?" strategy, prekindergarten and kindergarten plunged into Native American culture, second and third graders studied fifteenth century Spain, while a very innovative first grade chose to enact the elements—wind, water, and fire—that made possible Columbus's journey and "discovery." After a month of study and preparation the reenactment took place. A band of Native Americans gathered their harvest, danced, chanted, and carried out their daily chores beside their colorful teepees and wigwams (Figure 6.12). A small child looked across the ocean (a large playing field) and saw a strange sight. Three large white sails, like wings of a bird, approached the shore (cardboard ships with bedsheet sails, held upright and brought forward by children in Spanish costumes). Wind and water whirled around, while the fire of inspiration kept the sailors warm and energized on the long and perilous journey. The meeting of two cultures was cordial, stories were shared, similarities and differences were appreciated, and a true exchange of cultural knowledge and materials took place. With drama, fun, and excitement, our "what if . . . ?" technique moved children from the known to the realm of possibilities.

What If We Designed Our Own Classroom?

The applicability of "what if . . . ?" extends far beyond the teaching of history and can profoundly expand the way one thinks. Nothing is taken for granted; there are

FIGURE 6.12   A Festive Tepee

always alternatives. "What if you were the author? How would you conclude this story?" "What if all classrooms were round rather than rectangular? Would that affect anything?" "What if we all looked alike?" "What if our eyes were on our knees?" "What if we could never be angry?"

"What if we had a week of school that was different from any other?" we asked ourselves one year, and so began a unique adventure. First, we wanted to completely change the look of our classroom, so we removed most of the classroom furniture, piling it up in a back room. We asked parents to send in three unusual furnishings (preferably those with a family or cultural history)—rugs, lamps, pictures, curtains, fabric. Next we thought of five unusual days—story day, backward day, hat day, game day, and opera day. There was a lot to plan: How many things can we do backward? What would be fun to eat backward? Whom could we invite for hat day and opera day? When all the furnishings arrived, our class looked awesome! We had duck lamps and teddy lamps; rugs from India and Africa; an assortment of chairs in every possible color; photographs of fathers, mothers, siblings, and relatives; paintings and wood carvings; fabric from around the world; and even a large princess bed with flowing white drapery. The entire week was open to parents. They trooped in before work, during lunch breaks, and after work to stare and gasp at an unusual classroom. For me the best and longest lasting effect was the children's spontaneous increase in "what if . . . ?" thinking.

CHAPTER SEVEN

COMMONWEALTH FOUNDATIONS: RESTORING THE TONE

Children's preexisting problems do not evaporate once they enter school. The classroom is porous to the wider culture, to the ways of individual families, and to the temperamental variations among children. Even in this benevolent atmosphere children will display the difficulties natural to early social living. Throughout the year various problems arise: A child can be demanding, attention-getting, aggressive, uncooperative, irritable, withdrawn, or sad. Interest and attention can be replaced by restlessness. Jealousy and hurt feelings may threaten friendships. The challenge is how to keep centered on the well-being and forward movement of the entire class while simultaneously lending support to the troubled child. Usha's children are fortunate because the central tenets of her teaching—engagement, commonwealth, and reflection—are sufficiently supple that she can adapt them to individual and situational circumstances. To achieve these ends, not everyone has to be doing the same thing in the same way in the same time frame.

RE-ENGAGEMENT: INDIVIDUALIZING INSTRUCTION

The Bored Child

Some children, some of the time, will lose interest in even the most exciting child-oriented (and often child-generated) thematic unit. While maintaining the general direction, because it is working for most, Usha is always alert to the bored or restless child and willingly sends him or her on a personal detour. Individualizing instruction is more than matching the reading levels of children to the appropriate books; it means matching their captivation as well. Malleable encompassing themes are ideal vehicles for individualizing instruction. As possibilities arise, children can take off in different directions separately or together, for a long or short time, without being "off task."

Personalized Itinerary

In our study of Italy a couple of boys started to pull back as we delved into Renaissance art and architecture. It was too distant, too long ago, too "artsy." I suggested that they look through our books on Italy for a new idea. It came quickly. The daunting feat of climbing the Alpine Slope stirred their fantasies of "guyness" and omnipotence. "How can we get there?" "Do you have to be a certain age?" "How long would it take to get to the top?" It wasn't long before they were into weather conditions, climbing and skiing equipment, grasslands, coniferous forests, rocks, and glaciers.

On another occasion—the theme was China—a child became bored by discussions of silkworms and the silk route. Again, it seemed too remote from her own life and required too much listening. Instead, she determined to write and illustrate her own book of poems about her personal reactions to the strangeness that was China. As poet and book author (her notion of omnipotence) she then was able to revisit silkworms and silk routes—topics that were now actively manipulated rather than passively heard.

The Child with Learning Difficulties

Disengagement is sometimes caused by developmental delays or learning differences. Children feel out of it, left behind. In these instances individualization is the key. Individualization can take the form of one-on-one teaching, peer tutoring, or help from a high school student, reading specialist, or other available adult.

Help across Generations

My mother, at sixty-seven, proved to be the perfect companion for a six-year-old honing his reading skills. One day a week, with immense care and patience, she listened to him read and exulted over his every new accomplishment. She had nothing to prove, no targeted level she was rushing to have him attain, and no dismal predictions based on test scores. She was just there for him, unattached and attentive—a rare occurrence in the hurried pace of today's schooling. The child often chose to stay in from recess to practice his reading before she arrived, and in less than two months he had gained enough confidence to read aloud to his classmates. He may not have caught up to their levels, but he was sufficiently comfortable to join in.

The Insecure Child

A number of children express their insecurity by touting their inferiority or superiority—"I'm a lousy artist" or "I'm the best artist, musician, singer in the class." When all students are required to do exactly the same work at the same pace, these feelings are exacerbated, for there is unavoidable comparison around who has accomplished what. The feelings can be dissipated when, instead of ordinal accomplishments, children are presented with multiple activities that encourage multiple approaches and cannot be ranked.

I Can Draw

The parent of a former student regularly brings to our class a portfolio full of masterpiece paintings representing artists as different as Picasso and Joshua Reynolds. The artwork is placed all over our classroom so that we can analyze the various styles. I distinctly remember a child's sigh of relief when he saw Picasso's work. "Whew, I can draw like that," he said. Another child was entranced by M. C. Escher's designs. "Just like me," he announced, "All I want to do is draw patterns." The individualized approach is followed again when we dramatize a book we have read. Children are allowed to chose their own roles. The quieter ones may initially choose to be trees and grass. They receive as much honor and applause as those who select lead roles.

Based on the children's critique of Leonardo da Vinci's masterpiece ("Why did he paint her in a dirty dress in front of a polluted environment?"), our art show one year was entitled "What If I Had Painted the Mona Lisa?" We gave each child an outline of the painting and invited them to create their own masterpieces by selecting clothing, coloring, and background scenery. Mona Lisa laughed, smirked, and winked; she was attired alternatively in a baseball hat, Hawaiian leis, and a fluorescent pink nightgown as she was whisked away to Paris, Puerto Rico, and a rain forest in Brazil. Everyone is an artist!

COMMONWEALTH

Revealing Our Lives, Our Selves

Children, like adults, often find unfamiliar environments, staffed by unfamiliar people in unfamiliar roles, alienating. The sense of disconnectedness can trigger confusion: "Why am I here?" "I don't belong here." "There is nothing I want to do here." When one feels estranged, the sense of self dwindles and is replaced by feelings ranging from anxiety to worthlessness. By contrast, hospitable environments with strong child–teacher and child–child connections invite engagement. Through engagement the self is furnished; one becomes a person who thinks many wonderful thoughts and does many wonderful things.

Sharing oneself as a teacher is a delicate matter. Too much of it threatens one's personal boundaries. Too little can be a patronizing "I-know-how-you-feel" pat on the back that is not genuinely helpful. Usha is empathic but not at all sentimental. Beyond sharing the impact of the momentary event, she explores how one can address the event—what next?

Sharing Experiences

If you want children to be authentic, to share their feelings, you must do the same; if you want them to take risks, they must see you take risks. Mr. D. and I share our life stories with the children at different times for different purposes. When there are children who appear frustrated with their writing or drawing attempts, scrunching up one artistic effort after another, Mr. D. brings in his artwork (collected by his mother) from when he was four years old. Children laugh at the early efforts of the man they now revere as an artist: "You drew that? You weren't even as good as we are!" He shows them his dozen immature sketches of Mickey Mouse and talks about the importance of patience, practice and perseverance—three "P" words that soon become part of our everyday vocabulary.

When children scorn food that is different, I tell them a slightly embellished story about my first week in America. A gracious hostess served me a large helping of spaghetti in a rich tomato sauce. I recoiled, "It looks like blood and guts," I thought (and I wrinkled my nose). "How can they be relishing it?" Cautiously, I placed just one strand of spaghetti on my tongue, then in a slow, contorted motion closed my mouth. (My hostess must have thought no one ever taught me to eat elegantly.) At first it did taste rather yucky because I was more accustomed to spicy food. But later—a good bit later—I came to feast frequently on all kinds of pasta. It was lucky that I tried that first mouthful.

Occasionally, a needy child will take toys home that belong to the school or other children. When asked about such incidents, they usually tell a self-justifying untruth. Rather than getting into a blame game, we read the book *The Enormous Lie,* in which a child tells a lie for the first time and is followed all day long by this enormous blob (symbolizing a lie). In his attempts to shed the lie, the child climbs a tree, goes down a tall slide, and performs a variety of acts, but the lie does not go away. Finally, the child tells his mother the truth, and the blob vanishes. After reading the story, I share incidents from my childhood when I lied. I describe what I said, how I felt, and why I had lied. Then I ask them whether they have had similar experiences; the floodgates open. One year, as an experiment, I tried the same discussion without any preceding incident or personal disclosure. Children were silent for a long time, sharing was less open, and the discussion was listless.

When children tell me about their shortcomings, I often bring up mine—for instance, my inability to sing. I let them know I can't carry a tune, and persistent effort has not improved matters. However, that doesn't mean I keep silent. A few years ago, for instance, we had a group of children who had risen to every challenge, taken risks, and accomplished far more than I had ever imagined. To honor them in a very special way, I decided to do something I had never done before. With Mr. D.'s help I composed a duet and, in front of parents and other faculty, sang it to the children on the last day of school. For someone like me that was a high-risk endeavor! Everything is a two-way street in our class: If I want the children to take risks, I must do so too.

Sharing a Death

Events best described as traumatic always occur unexpectedly during the school year: Parents separate, a favorite grandparent or pet dies, a brother breaks his leg at a soccer match. By sharing in these events, we support the affected child, strengthen our commonwealth, find ways to cope, and make—or attempt to make—sense of the event.

Parents and children were notified that a much beloved librarian had died unexpectedly. I considered waiting for a child to speak of the event but decided that since I too was grieving over this significant loss to the community, I would bring it up. I told the children that when I heard the news, I felt devastated and took a long walk to think about Ms. T. I asked the children how they had reacted.

"I held my teddy bear real tight all night."

"I was really scared. I can't believe we will never see her again."

"I felt really sad. I will really miss her."

I asked the children to speak of what they would miss about Ms. T. They mentioned the funny stories she read to them, the poems she set to music, and the books they were allowed to take home. I wondered with them what we could do about our sadness. The children suggested writing letters to the family, hanging a photograph of her in the library, and recollecting happy times with her. I asked how we all could help the new librarian who would be taking Ms. T.'s place.

"We'll ask her to read us funny stories."

"We'll bring her here and show her our work."

"We'll show her around the school."

One of the children inquired a bit petulantly why Ms. T. had to die instead of getting well. I saw behind this question the children's unvocalized fears and confusions over death. It was an opportune moment for us to delve more deeply by reading a story about *The Fall of Freddie the Leaf.* Freddie, the last leaf on the tree, contemplates the cycle of life and realizes that he has to fall. He must fall so that new leaves can grow and continue the cycle. "But what," I asked, "if leaves didn't fall, flowers never faded, and animals and people never died?" I drew ten butterflies on the board. The children shut their eyes and imagined what would happen if these ten butterflies never died and the reproductive cycle went on and on. The children volunteered:

"Butterflies would fly into our mouth."

"We could not see each other."

"We couldn't do any work."

"Now imagine," I suggested, "a world in which no insects, birds, animals, or people ever died."

The children didn't want to think of death as a good or necessary event. They argued that the old ones could stay and just not have any babies. I pushed deeper, "No babies? No children? No classes like this? Everyone old?" The children relented. Dying as part of life was beginning to make moral sense to them. Then each child was asked to draw a picture to represent something they learned from the story or the discussion. They drew pictures of a world with infant, young, and old creatures; of Ms. T. smiling down at growing children; of angels welcoming old people in a kingdom of clouds. Mr. D. and I moved from one child to the next asking about the drawings, eliciting and discussing personal feelings, making sure that each was heard.

Becoming the Other

There are moments when the usual mild-mannered approaches fail and something stronger, more dramatic is called for. Children locked in conflict, for example, cannot drain their emotions or resolve their problems through discussion; children frustrated by the demands of collaboration will challenge the teacher's procedures. In such moments Usha's goal is for children to (psychologically) sit in the seat of their antagonist. She uses two variants of role-playing—*instant replay* and *role reversal*—in such instances.

Instant replay proceeds by first asking the antagonistic participants to enact, not merely describe, the conflict exactly as it occurred. Next, small groups of children branch out into various corners of the room to brainstorm peaceable conclusions. Assembling after five minutes, each group *reenacts* the scene in a different manner to produce a better ending. The advantages and disadvantages of each solution are discussed, and teachers address issues of body language, eye contact, sincerity, and tone of voice.

In role reversal the children can experiment with being anyone of their choice (including authority figures) and act as they choose. For example, Usha will reverse roles with the students and let them take over. After experiencing life at the top of the authority pyramid, they are likely to be much more accepting (even demanding) of reasonable restrictions.

Instant Replay: Resolving a Conflict

While playing in the sandbox, Carla and Denise simultaneously find a shiny, turquoise-tinted feather. Both claim it. Meanwhile, a third child, Sarah, sees the feather and insists that it is her lost possession. Carla and Denise accuse Sarah of lying. She starts crying.

During instant replay, children come up with various solutions: Each child should keep the feather for a week; Sarah must prove ownership by providing a witness who saw her with it earlier in the day; it's only a feather and not worth arguing about; place it on our nature display table so that everyone can enjoy it. All agree that Carla and Denise should not accuse Sarah of lying. The three girls are then allowed to retreat into a quiet corner, select a final strategy, and enact their decision for the group.

Role Reversal: A Presidential Election

One year the children, vigorously echoing the partisan politics of their parents, became unusually animated over a presidential election. So to help them understand the election process and to give them a chance to be in charge, we elected our own "President for a day." In three supervised groups the children selected party leaders, determined party policy, and created party slogans. Standing on classroom tables and holding pretend microphones, the three candidates made their campaign speeches. Candidate One promised an extra hour of recess. Candidate Two promised all-day free choice. Candidate Three promised that all rules would be determined by the citizens. Candidate One prevailed by a large margin and was sworn in as president for a day. Mr. D. and I immediately abdicated all our authority.

The new president (Ms. P.) decided instantly, with a defiant glance in our direction, that she would undo classroom procedures. Starting with free choice and then lunch, she proposed that no one need clean up—and no one did. With a giant mess behind them, the children cheerfully trooped off for their "one-hour recess."

Next Ms. P. suggested that a special videotape of her choice be shown during an extended nap period. When everyone had settled down with their sheets and pillows in the movie room, she stood up and announced, "You can do whatever you want. You can move as much as you like."

I signaled Mr. D. with a wink. Holding a large sheet in outstretched arms, he moved slowly across the room, obstructing the children's view of the television, while I engaged two children in a loud discussion about the movie. Some restless children rolled around, chatted, and wandered in and out of the room, while others shouted, "Stop! We can't hear the movie!"

Within ten minutes, Ms. P. was standing on a desk shouting, "Okay, everyone, the rule has changed. NO MORE MOVING, AND NO TALKING, AND NO GOING TO THE WATER FOUNTAIN EITHER!"

The rest of the afternoon was a disaster. Children reentering the classroom were dismayed by their own mess. Ms. P. tried to persuade them that using our special markers and multicolored crayons would be fun, but it was not pleasant to draw on tables littered with open lunch boxes, half-eaten sandwiches, spilled milk, applesauce, and yogurt. Mr. D. and I directed every question, complaint, and demand to Ms. P., who looked exhausted. Grabbing my arm and glancing frequently at my watch, she asked, "Is it two o'clock yet?"

At 2:00 P.M. we sat our citizens down amid all the mess and evaluated the day's happenings. Several citizens were disgruntled.

"Some of it was fun, but most of it didn't work," was the general consensus.

Ms. P. volunteered, "I didn't like it when Mr. D. walked around at naptime. Tom and Maya spoke too much, and Dennis kept leaving the room and slamming the door."

"I wonder if it would have been easier if you had not changed our usual ways of doing things?" I mused, leaving the question open.

We went on to discuss the importance of personal responsibility within a group, the need to respect an individual's space, the role of leadership, and the function of established procedures within a classroom community. One-hour recess, the only heartily endorsed venture, was incorporated into our weekly schedule.

Humor

The complexity of teaching is sometimes daunting. All day long teachers have to make decisions that affect children's hearts and lives: Is Jane pretending to be sick? Is intervention necessary in the water-play area? Should recess be curtailed if children continue to push each other off the slide? But sometimes when tensions build, when there is trouble between children, or an embarrassing incident occurs, the simplest course is to cut through it with humor.

A Bit of Laughter

Without humor I would not survive teaching; neither would my students. Humor is the best way to deescalate a crisis. For example, four children set off diligently to wash paintbrushes, turn on the faucet too rapidly, and get drenched in colored water, with streaks of paint dripping down their faces. They turn around to whine and complain, see me laughing outrageously, and join in.

John, who has been standing against a tree for most of recess, is being teased by others for not joining a game. I notice a wet patch on one side of his trousers and realize that a "little accident" may be the cause. So I laugh and tell the children that I can figure out what John is doing: He is probably trying to stand still like the yogis in the Himalayan mountains. John agrees, and I decide to stand still beside him, like a yogi, until all the children go into the classroom.

On his birthday, a child, eager to distribute popcorn to his friends, rips open the large bag, sending kernels of popcorn all over our new rug. "Laughter first and cleanup after" is our motto on all such occasions.

REFLECTION

Taking Time Out

Reflection is as essential for recharging the batteries as for igniting them. Because reflection is used extensively in planning work and solving problems, the children find it a natural technique for collecting themselves when distressed. Children come to understand that moving away from the group, even when requested by the teacher, is an opportunity to think, not necessarily a punishment.

Reflection Spaces

Spaces for personal reflection are created in the classroom and are often self-selected by teachers and students for quiet reading, planning a project, or simply to "meditate." Over the years children have given them different labels: "thinking chairs," "reflection corners," "peaceful place," and, one particular year, "meditation hut." Our study of India that year unearthed a wonderfully illustrated book, *Painted Prayers*. The photographs, depicting an Indian village whose huts were brilliantly painted with symbols of prayer, led children to build a meditation hut out of a giant refrigerator carton. During the day a child often would head toward the hut saying, "I can't think of what to write next. I'm going to meditate for a while." "I worked so hard on that new puzzle, I'm going to take a break and decide what to do next." "Our group is making such a noise, I need to be quiet for a minute."

On a spring-break trip to Washington with his parents, a flustered child from our class paused to "meditate" under a tree to calm himself down as the group rushed from one monument to another. The astounded father watched as his son sat calmly amid crowds of hurrying tourists, regained his equilibrium, and emerged happily, ready to comply with the itinerary.

Procedures for effective use of reflection spaces are established in consultation with the children. During classroom discussions, for example, when a child is disruptive (e.g., poking another with a plastic witch hat), a raised eyebrow is understood to be the first signal. A neighboring child will then, if necessary, softly remind the child to stop. If the child continues, the teacher, without disrupting the discussion, quietly motions him toward one of the reflection spaces. Her stance calmly indicates, "You know what this is about. Think it over." The child can choose to stay close to the discussion and sit on a reflection chair nearby or move farther away to a cozier reflection space that has a rug and cushions. The child is trusted to reflect on his behavior and return as soon as he thinks he can participate in the ongoing discussion.

Teacher's Reflections

Reflection is a two-way street. Together with the children, Usha reflects on the relative success of projects. She also reflects on her own trustworthiness and invites children's comments on whether she has kept her end of the bargain.

How Did We Do?

At the end of each thematic unit I reflect on what was learned academically, what was accomplished socially, and what could be improved, discarded, or expanded. For example, on completing our study of space, my reflections were as follows: We had done well academically—writing journals, poems, and stories about space; measuring jumps, pulse beats, blood pressure, temperature, and rainfall; learning space facts; drawing blueprints; and constructing spaceships. We had done well socially—learned to work in groups, shared resources, established and followed "space training" procedures, and cooperated with children in the neighboring kindergarten class. What could be improved on? Start the unit with a captivating hook, get more information and material directly from NASA, seek more assistance from parents on such large projects, and never underestimate the power or persuasiveness of childhood fantasy. (One disappointed child thought he was really going to outer space, despite the cardboard space shuttle, plastic food, and the first grade class located right above our launch pad.)

I share my reflections with the children, ask them what they liked and disliked about the space project, and then ask for their help. "If I were to teach the same topic next year, what should I do differently?" They sit with their eyes closed, as is our practice, ruminate on the events of the last two months, and offer these insights:

"You could plan a trip to NASA instead of space. That's a trip you could really go on."

"When we found out that astronauts sleep upright, you should have let us try it out by hanging a sleeping bag on the wall and taking turns at naptime."

"Never use spray paint indoors. Some children are allergic to paint fumes."

"You should learn a little more about space before you try to teach us."

"Make sure kids like Tommy understand that we are not *really* going to space."

Finally, I send home a questionnaire for parent feedback. Parents offered the following suggestions: Give us a weekly update on space activities; provide us with materials we can read so that we can converse intelligently with our child about gravity, constellations, and Roman legends; tell us in advance about culminating events so we can plan to be there; give us suggestions about how to deal with our child's extreme enthusiasm about the trip to outer space.

How Did I Do?

If children are to feel safe in my classroom, they must be able to trust me. From the very first day, therefore, my personal goal is integrity: My words and actions must be as one. Constant self-evaluation is essential but not always sufficient. Did I seem impatient while encouraging them to be patient? Did my tone of voice convey something different from what I was saying? Did I unintentionally reward tattling? With hundreds of teacher–child interactions each day, it is not always possible to keep track of everything one has said, done, and inadvertently promised. At the end of each unit and especially a week before the end of the year, I ask the children, "Have I followed up on everything I promised?" "Is there anything I haven't done or have done wrong?" They reply:

"Sometimes your cleanup area was not very organized."

"Sometimes you broke your promises."

"You told us you were going to try not to be angry this year but you did forget—jtwo times."

"You told us we could have popcorn and watch a movie with you when it rained a lot. That never happened."

"You said that maybe we could walk down to the park and make bark rubbings of different trees."

"You said we could make our own fancy name tags for our next field trip."

"You said my grandma could come in and spend an afternoon with us."

And so in the last week we fulfill all promises as we design the name tags we don't really need, walk to the park that has the same trees as our playground, invite Grandma who has visited us several times but "never for a whole afternoon," and settle down for movies and popcorn. Trust has to be maintained at all costs, and a promise is a promise!

CHAPTER EIGHT

QUESTIONS AND ANSWERS

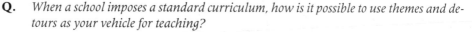

Q. *When a school imposes a standard curriculum, how is it possible to use themes and detours as your vehicle for teaching?*

A. Moral themes (such as respect, responsibility, honesty, and peace) form a canopy under which almost all prescribed curricular content can be studied and discussed. These themes arise whenever two or more people come together; they are pervasive and fluid and can be worked into any subject area. Thus units on the family and neighbors, storybooks and poetry, historical events and legends, even such mundane topics as birds, buildings, seasons, or holidays, all lend themselves to moral instruction. Math and science, too, can be morally relevant, for they deal with questions of how we know and what we know. Particularly at the elementary level, where science is oriented to the environment, one can talk about the awesomeness of nature and our responsibility to preserve and protect it. Sensitivity to nature can be an abiding year-long concern, rather than a one- or two-day event devoted to earth celebrations. If moral education is central to your teaching, the large, encompassing moral theme you choose can provide the necessary moral twist to any topic of study, sparking meaningful, life-relevant discussions. The theme of caring, for example, can be applied to topics as varied as boats (caring for boats, caring for travel companions, first-aid kits), plants (experiments about taking care of plants, poisonous and medicinal plants), families (career choices, caring for the elderly, chores at home), division (sharing materials fairly among different groups and individuals), and seasons (providing for differing needs of people, plants, and animals in each season).

When one is confronted with a prescribed curriculum and strict time limits, a more daunting problem is how to incorporate detours. If a child asks an intriguing question but time does not permit pursuing it in class, one can suggest exploring the topic over the weekend. If the teacher can just jump-start the child—"I saw three books on that topic at the library" "Could you and your parents check it out on the Internet?" "We can look it up together at recess"—much can be accomplished. However, it is true that this work must be squeezed into the spaces of the day, embarked on as an extra with the teacher supporting the student for the fun of it, not for grading or credit.

Q.   *What if parents are less available?*

A.   Parents have a very important role at school. They help the teacher, they provide resources that enrich the class, and their involvement closes the home–school gap, making instruction more meaningful for the child. Although there is no completely adequate substitute for parent participation, there are some alternatives. For help in the class, older students are usually only too glad to work with kindergarten children. For resources, lean on others in the school community. Ask the music teacher (and other specialists) if some of her work with songs and instruments could be related to your theme. There are retired people in the community (Usha has used members of the Retired Senior Volunteer Program), as well as neighbors, friends, and even strangers who may have more time than parents. Once Usha needed an expert on Indian dance but knew no one who could fill the bill. So one day she decided to introduce herself to a salesperson from India whom she had spotted at a local store, asking if she, or anyone she knew, could assist with the students. As it happened, the salesperson had both knowledge and interest. She came to class and was a big success. People like to contribute their expertise. Often it is a question of helping them to identify their potential contribution and then just asking.

Q.   *Is it possible to teach this way when the class is large and there is no assistant?*

A.   Without doubt it is more difficult; everything takes longer. It is therefore crucial that teachers and administrators who value meaningful learning continue to campaign for smaller classes. Meanwhile, shortcuts have to be established (working in groups, children helping each other), and every possible resource should be tapped to get additional help for big classroom projects. A large class also underscores the need for developing trusting relationships (recall the discussion of trust tables) so that the teacher can work with a small group, knowing that the rest of the class is spending their time productively.

Q.   *What happens to these practices when one has children with special problems, either academic or behavioral?*

A.   Inevitably, there will be children who have difficulty with the academic material. When there is such a child, one needs to work with the specialists in the school, but the problem should not be "turned over" to the specialist. The teacher, specialist, and parents must work together. With a reading problem, for example, the specialist can suggest remediations to be carried out by the teacher in the classroom, work that can be done at home, and help that needs one-on-one sessions outside the class with the professional. In making such a three-pronged effort, it is important to stay in good communication with one another and evaluate progress frequently.

     The same principles apply to a child with a behavioral problem. The difficulty should be identified early, a referral made to a school counselor or psychologist, and the remediation carried out in the classroom, in the home, and with the specialist. Being watchful, anticipating difficulties, supporting strengths, and giving assignments through which the child in question can shine all help to buffer the child's competence and alleviate the distressing behavior. In each of the three years described in the book, Usha had children with academic or behavioral problems. Each child's problem was dealt with individually, with parent and specialist support. On occasion, when a significant learning disability was identified through extensive teaching, testing, and retesting, a child was referred to special schools that catered to the disability.

Q.   *In a private school there is no problem expressing religious feelings (though not sectarian ones), but what if you teach in a public school?*

A.   Every teacher must be careful not to advocate a particular religious creed while being respectful of the children's individual beliefs, including their disbelief. That does not mean, however, that the spiritual life is off-limits. Children do a lot of God-talk. The spiritual for them is closely linked to fantasy. God, like fairies and princesses, is often more present to them than to adults. Recall that it was a child who, in the alphabet of artists, suggested God for the letter "g." If you are comfortable with incorporating a spiritual dimension into your themes, go for it! But it is entirely possible to create a moral curriculum without reference to anything religious. For example, instead of referring to God as the creator of nature, refer to the miracle of nature and our dependence on it. Goodness—"getting gooder"—is a goal that can be supported entirely through secular content.

Q.   *What if you need to teach particular skills—long division, spelling words—that do not fit naturally into the theme?*

A.   Just teach them! There is no point in artificially forcing skills into a theme and thereby compromising the integrity of your subject. There is always some need for drill, accuracy, and memorization. Not every moment has to be theme-related.

Q.   *What if you, as a teacher, are not artistically or musically inclined?*

A.   First, every teacher of young children should own a book on blackboard drawing for teachers (available at all major book stores). Basic shapes—triangles, circles, rectangles, squares, and diamonds—can be used to draw every variety of plant, animal, habitat, and building, and straight lines (used as stick figures) can be used to represent all human actions—running, walking, jumping, throwing a javelin. A teacher who is not musical can inspire a love for music by playing tapes and CDs as background music for various activities and by using biographical videotapes of famous musicians. She can teach children the words of a song and use taped music to help children learn the melody. Usha, who sings in a monotone, did this effectively for many years.

Furthermore, until you are in your own classroom, you may not really know your own capacities, and until you have a project up and going, you also may not be aware of the assistance modern technology offers. When there is a will, there is a device. It is not necessary, for instance, to draw at all. If you want an animal, an instrument, or a habitat, all you have to do is download its image from the Internet and magnify it for your classroom. What's important, however, is to select those expressive modalities that you enjoy. Perhaps you want to do more out of doors or more with dance or sports or literature. Another solution is to invite the help of those whose expertise and interests complement your own. Once again, there are people with talents within and outside of the school who will be pleased to assist if asked.

Q. *What if you, a teacher, do not have a knowledge reservoir that extends from castles to crystals to cubism to clavicles?*

A. A good teacher is an eternal student. Just go to the library and get an assortment of children's books that you can dip into as needed. Don't be shy to tell children, "I don't know the answer to your question. Let's look it up."